BIG
PODCAST

How To Grow Your Podcast Audience,
Build Listener Loyalty, and
Get Everybody Talking About Your Show

DAVID HOOPER

Big Podcast
PO Box 121135
Nashville, TN 37212-1135

Visit BigPodcast.com for more information on podcast marketing.

Audiobook edition available at Audible.com.

Some names and identifying details have been changed to protect the privacy of individuals.

Although the author and publisher have made every effort to ensure that the information in this book was correct at press time, the author and publisher do not assume and hereby disclaim any liability to any party for any loss, damage, or disruption caused by errors or omissions, whether such errors or omissions result from negligence, accident, or any other cause.

Ordering Information:
Quantity sales. Special discounts are available on quantity purchases by corporations, associations, and others. For details, contact the publisher at the address above.

Orders by U.S. trade bookstores and wholesalers. Please contact Lightning Source: Tel: (615) 213-5815; Fax: (615) 213-4725 or visit lightningsource.com

Printed in the United States of America
ISBN 978-1-60842-888-5

Thanks to you. I hope this book helps you spread an important message and bring people together, because it's time to speak up and let others know they're not alone.

Thanks for reading Big Podcast!
GET YOUR FREE
Audience-Builder
TOOLKIT

To help you get the most from this book, I've put together a companion toolkit to help you <u>easily create great podcast episodes</u>. It includes:

- Episode notes templates
- Episode idea generator
- Podcast intro scripts

- Episode title swipe file
- Storytelling cheat sheet
- ...and more!

Go to **BigPodcast.com/toolkit** to download it now

Contents

READ THIS FIRST

In September of 1982, a young clothing designer started a new company.

He needed to move quickly, so he named the company after himself to avoid possible trademark conflicts that might delay him. Then, like now, most new companies don't survive. And this is especially true in the temperamental fashion industry.

Because of the downturn in the American economy and restricted financing opportunities, he decided to manufacture his product in Italy. This gave him a better shot at getting credit, since he could get financing directly through the Italian factories he was working with.

He had his name. He had his product. Now he just had to sell it.

At the time, there were two ways to sell clothing:

1. Showcase your product line to buyers during Market Week via a room at the Hilton New York Hotel.
2. Rent a fancy showroom within a couple of blocks of the Hilton New York Hotel.

Most companies went with a room at the Hilton because that's where the buyers were. But it was easy to get lost among the 1100 other clothing manufacturers spread out in guest rooms across 30 floors. Beyond the sheer number of competitors, every company looked basically the same, showcasing similar product in every room.

No matter how good you are or how much money you have, it's very hard to distinguish yourself in circumstances like this.

The "fancy showroom" option wasn't much better. The buyers were in the hotel, and even something just a couple of blocks away might be too far to get their attention.

On a whim, he called a friend in the trucking business.

"If I could figure out how to park a 40-foot trailer on the corner of 6th Avenue and 56th Street during Market Week, would you lend one to me?"

His friend replied, "This is New York. You can't park a bicycle for 15 minutes, let alone a truck, on the corner of 6th Avenue and 56th Street. But if you can figure it out, not only will I lend you a trailer, I'll help you decorate it."

So he called the mayor's office and asked, "How does one get permission to park a 40-foot trailer on the corner of 6th Avenue and 56th Street?"

They answered, "This is New York. We only give permission under two circumstances. One, if you're a utility company servicing our streets, or two, if you're a production company working on a movie."

That afternoon, Kenneth Cole went to a stationery store and changed his letterhead from "Kenneth Cole, Inc." to "Kenneth Cole Productions, Inc." The following morning, he filed a permit to shoot a full-length motion picture called *The Birth Of A Shoe Company*.

His models became actresses. He hired a director — sometimes there was film in his camera, sometimes there wasn't. Two New York City policemen, compliments of the mayor, acted as doormen.

When people came to the trailer, in the spirit of building anticipation and curiosity, he kept them behind a velvet rope and made them wait to enter.

When the show ended three days later, he'd sold 40,000 pairs of shoes.

Within three years, Kenneth Cole opened his first store on Columbus Avenue in Manhattan. Today, Kenneth Cole stores can be found in countries around the world.

To honor its unusual beginning, his company is still known as Kenneth Cole Productions, Inc.

Step Right Up

Like Kenneth Cole, you have a "production company." Like Kenneth Cole, it can take you from being relatively unknown to a recognized brand within your industry and beyond.

This book will help you do that. If you have any questions, let me know. You can reach me via my website at BigPodcast.com.

Best wishes!
David Hooper
Big Podcast

INTRODUCTION

The Two Places Podcasts Go To Die

There's a term known within the podcast community that describes what happens to *most* podcasts. I want to make sure it doesn't happen to you.

Podfade.

Urban Dictionary defines "podfade" as:

When a podcast begins putting out episodes more and more sporadically and at greater intervals. Typically begins with only one episode missed, but if a podcaster isn't careful, it can compound. Podfade often leads to podcast death.

This can happen surprisingly quickly. The majority of podcasters release fewer than seven episodes of their podcast before "podfading" into oblivion.

What happens to podcasts that *do* make it over the seven-episode hump?

The majority will suffer from something far worse – being ignored. This is more painful than being invisible, because people know about your podcast, but don't care whether it exists or not.

If your podcast is invisible or being disregarded on purpose, it might as well not exist.

This book is about making a podcast that's the opposite of "invisible" – a podcast that's so on-point it can't be ignored.

This Is A Book For Professionals

You've got a message to spread, and your podcast is the perfect way to do that. It's your flag in the ground, which lets the world know, "This is what I believe."

I'm planting a similar flag with this book.

This book is for pros. This means your podcast is either already up and running, or you're in the process of making that happen.

Either way, you're looking to go from where you are now and create something great – something that matters.

Will your podcast ever be perfect? No. But if we'd waited until things were perfect, none of us would have launched.

That doesn't mean we release junk; we're professionals, not hobbyists.

That's the difference between people like us and podcasting dabblers. We move forward, learning (and getting better) as we go, while they get caught up in theory, technology, and worrying about the perfect microphone.

The perfect microphone is the one in front of us. And we use it to create great content that helps people, not just to hear ourselves talk.

This means taking risks, some of which won't work.

We take podcasting seriously, but precious it's not. Podcasting is a way to distribute a message, not a Fabergé egg or priceless heirloom.

Our podcasts are anti-fragile. The technical problems we face, the interviews that don't go well, and mistakes we make are what makes future episodes stronger, because these things make us better.

This doesn't mean we're careless. When it's time to record a new episode, we show up prepared. We have an outline of what we want to talk about. If there's a guest, he's been vetted and researched ahead of time.

We respect the people who listen to us. We stay focused on the selected topic and deliver on what we promise. We don't release "noise."

The Lie People Tell About The Internet

A lot of people will argue that the Internet is a great thing because it "levels the playing field."

And what does a "level playing field" look like? A massive room where everybody is shouting.

Who will hear *you* in all that noise?

Nobody.

The solution to this problem is to create your own playing field — stop playing everybody else's game.

Podcasting isn't a one-to-many media, reaching millions via satellite and broadcast. You don't have to "keep most of the people happy, most of the time." Podcasting is more similar to a one-on-one conversation, where the content is tailored for a specific person — it's an opportunity to go deep and be specific.

You can't win at podcasting by playing with old rules designed for "one-size-fits-all" mass media. To be successful at podcasting, you have to know who your audience is and give them *exactly* what they want.

And what they want is to hear *you.*

Why not go balls-out spreading your message? Why not own the fact that you want that message to reach as many people as possible? There's no shame in that.

You're a podcaster. This isn't the time to be meek. Wanting to reach as many people as you can — and change their lives in a positive way — is a good thing.

If you have something to say that will help people, you owe it to them to do everything you can to reach them with that message.

The reason so many podcasts are ignored and never gain traction is because they have hosts that pull punches; they back off because they're too scared of offending people, scared of coming off as too bold, or otherwise being rejected. Resist the urge to play small like these podcasters do.

Softening your message is disrespectful to your audience because it doesn't allow them to hear who you really are. People want a powerful and authentic host, not an actor pretending to be somebody else.

If you're Christian, praise Jesus. If you're gay, don't act like your same-sex partner doesn't exist. If you're passionate about gardening, or mental health, or photography, let people know.

The people who listen to you can make their own decisions about whether to continue listening. If they don't like what you have to say, they can disregard it, turn you off, and never listen again.

You want to play to win instead of "playing not to lose."

Podcasting in an authentic way means you might lose some subscribers (or never get them in the first place). It means that some people will go to Apple Podcasts, Google Podcasts, and social media to leave negative reviews and complain.

This hurts. People rejecting you and your message hurts.

But that's not what takes most podcasters out. Most podcasters die the slow death of being either ignored or forgettable.

Some reaction, even if it's negative, is better than being part of the cesspool of podcasts that aren't even bad, frustrating, or agitating enough to be memorable. That's the worst place to be, because *nobody* likes what's there.

How To Win At Podcasting

There are two sides to *every* topic you could possibly discuss on your podcast. Most of the time, there are more.

Pick one.

Even if the topic of your podcast is "safe" and could be discussed by the entire family over Thanksgiving dinner without things getting weird.

Even if you're a squeaky-clean host who doesn't have any skeletons in his closet.

Even if the thought of this makes you uncomfortable because you "don't want anybody to be angry."

Stand for something. Give people opinions – something they can accept or reject for themselves.

People who want to listen to something "safe" already have that option – it's called broadcast radio.

Those who want sanitized, air-brushed, and flawless content don't need you. They can get that delivered any time, day or night, by a golden-voiced host that sounds amazing, is always happy, and always has traffic updates five minutes after the hour.

You've scanned your local radio dial and heard *that* guy.

But you can't name him. And neither can the majority of his listeners.

Fortunately, you don't have to play by these rules. And because of that, you can give people content that has the power to change their lives, not just keep them listening long enough to hear more advertising.

Memorable (and relatable) is the Christian podcaster having a crisis of faith, the weight-loss podcaster who shares about a recent food binge, and the host of a parenting podcast who admits that sometimes her kids are little shits, too.

This is the kind of content that changes lives, and every podcaster, regardless of the subject of his podcast, has the opportunity to do just that if he's willing to take risks, state opinions, and make mistakes.

This is the kind of opportunity available to *you*. And this book will help you make it happen.

My Podcast Philosophy

In this book, I've summarized how to develop a podcast that will expand your authority and reputation, showcase your specialized knowledge, and spread your message.

Why aren't more podcasters able to do these things? Why do most podcasts fail?

The reason is that the majority of podcasters either underestimate the work it will take to create a podcast people want to listen to (and will share with their friends), or they believe, consciously or subconsciously, that a high level of podcasting success isn't even possible.

"That works for other people, but it won't work for me."

As you read this book, you may feel like this. And you may be right — not everything in this book will work for you. Still, I encourage you to try what I suggest. The strategies within this book have helped thousands of people, many of whom were also skeptical when first learning about them, and you may be pleasantly surprised when you find they work for you.

On the other side of the coin will be people who think, "I can skip this part." And again, you might be right. If you already have an established podcast, some of the things I'm suggesting might be too basic for where you are now. Or, if you don't have a podcast, and think "podcasting is easy," these things might not feel important.

I encourage you to reassess your thoughts and assumptions about podcasting and where you are with your podcast. Resist the urge to simply ignore my recommendations without first trying them for yourself.

Everything within this book is important. This book isn't a series of techniques; it's a philosophy. Once you understand this philosophy, you'll finally "get" podcasting and how to be successful with it.

The reason most podcasts aren't successful isn't lack of proper marketing techniques, hosting skills, or professional equipment. What kills most podcasts is lack of awareness (and therefore lack of understanding) about what makes people listen to podcasts in the first place.

I can fix your "lack of audience" problem, but I'm not going to do it by patching the holes of your current podcast. Instead, I'm going to help you tear down your existing podcast and build a new (and better) podcast.

Don't worry, your effort will be worth it. A successful podcast won't just improve *your* life, business, and finances; a successful podcast can do these things for the people who listen to you as well.

Podcasting Success Is Possible

Podcasting success is possible. The scary part of this is that *you* are 100 percent responsible for whether your podcast is successful or not.

Nobody is going to come save you. Nobody is going to make you famous. Nobody is going to show up with a ton of listeners who are interested in what you're doing.

That's on you.

So how are *you* going to going to get those listeners? How are you going to make them care about your podcast?

That's what this book is about.

It's possible to attract a big audience, change lives, and make money with your podcast — if you know what to do.

You're in the right place at the right time. Podcasting is no longer the "amateur hour" declared by Steve Jobs in 2010. Its growing pains are over, and it's now a legitimate media platform you can use to spread your message, increase your reputation as an expert and authority in your industry, and make money.

Let's get going.

MODULE 1

A COMPELLING MESSAGE, A HUNGRY AUDIENCE

CHAPTER 001

YOUR MESSAGE

First of all, let's get clear on something. *Somebody* is listening to your podcast. Maybe not a lot of people, and maybe not even the people you want to reach, but the world is big enough that you can pretty much throw anything up online and somebody will check it out.

You don't want just "somebody" listening though – you want as many listeners as possible and listeners who do more than use your podcast for background noise. To do this, you need the foundation of a compelling message.

What's Your Message?

Everybody's an evangelist for *something*. Each of us has our own "secular religion" of beliefs we feel are the best way to live.

What message do you want to spread? This is the foundation on which everything else about your podcast will be built.

A general message won't be motivating to you or interesting enough to keep listeners engaged. You need to be specific.

To help craft a compelling message for your podcast, I suggest answering the following questions.

1. What are you excited about?

What topic can get you out of bed in the morning? What topic are all of your friends sick of hearing you talk about? What's the one thing that, even when you're exhausted, you still have the energy to discuss and participate in?

Don't worry about the size of the potential audience. Your podcast won't be of interest to *everybody*, regardless of how general it is. Instead, focus on a message designed for a very specific audience that's as enthusiastic about the topic as you are.

2. Where can you add the greatest value, and how can you do it in a unique way?

The world needs podcast hosts who are enthusiastic and show up fully.

The world needs podcast hosts who have a deep understanding of the subjects they're talking about. And perhaps most important, the world needs podcast hosts who aren't afraid to express opinions.

In short, know what you're talking about and pick a side. Your goal as a podcast host should be to add something that hasn't already been said to the conversation people are already having.

Want to interview entrepreneurs? Want to talk about making money online? Want to do a "true crime" podcast? Great – do the podcast you want to do. But bring something unique to the table.

3. What outcome do you want for people who listen to you?

Think of this as your "why." This is important because, as Friedrich Nietzsche said, "He who has a why can endure any how."

For long-term success in podcasting, you need more than an exciting subject to cover, you need more than a lot of downloads, and you need more than a big audience. You need a *connection* with your audience.

Podcasting is lonely. Most of your time will be spent in a room, completely alone, with just a mic and recording equipment.

You'll likely get feedback from the people you reach with your message, but that's just talk. The outcome you help listeners achieve is where rubber meets the road.

What do you want that outcome to be?

Your Message Starts With You (But It's Not About You)

People often look at life like a teenager in high school. You've met him – the one who thinks his problems are unique to him and that no one else could possibly understand what he's going through.

We've all met that kid. We've *been* that kid.

But that kid is wrong. None of us is unique in that way.

The world is a big place, filled with people who are very similar to each other. We're isolated from one another, though. Because of this, it's easy to feel alone and without connection.

This is where podcasting can help.

A quick story ...

In 2011, during a routine physical, Lee Silverstein's doctor told him, "You're 50, go get a colonoscopy."

He did. The results came back positive.

The cancer was caught early enough that the recommended treatment was surgery. Chemo wouldn't be necessary. A second doctor agreed.

The surgery was a success and Lee moved on with his life, but continued to monitor his situation. He got married. And just 17 days afterward, he found the cancer had spread to his liver.

Once again, doctors recommended surgery, this time with six months of chemo.

He successfully completed both. Then his life really changed.

While working at a career college, he got a call from a friend who needed meeting space and wanted to use an empty classroom. Being a good host, and being curious about the meeting, he sat in on it.

That's how Lee Silverstein learned about podcasting.

"It was like a lightning bolt hit me," he says. "I had to start a podcast. I needed to help people who had heard the three words that I'd heard, 'You've got cancer,' to give them hope and let them know that this isn't an immediate death sentence."

Today, *We Have Cancer* has dozens of episodes, interviewing cancer survivors, caregivers, and medical professionals. It educates, inspires, and shares stories of hope.

To deliver this kind of message via your podcast, you must:

Know Who You Are. Podcasts that have impact have hosts who embrace who they are and are comfortable with themselves. Then they make everything bigger, bolder, and louder. It's not an act — it's simply an extension of their original selves.

Take Action First. Don't wait to be recognized, don't ask for permission, and don't follow trends.

Take Risks. Like gambling, the biggest payoffs in podcasting go to those who take the biggest risks. If you play it too safe, you'll never win.

Set the Pace. Most people are lazy and sluggish. If you wait for others to set the pace, you'll never get anywhere.

Keep People Guessing. Giving your audience the same thing every time is comfortable, but it's not stimulating. Change up what you're doing on a regular basis to be more interesting and keep people's attention.

For maximum impact, your message needs to be delivered in a unique way. There's no point in doing something other podcasters have done when other podcasts are a click away.

Maximum impact means bringing something new and different to the table. This is a tough sell, which is why so few do it.

People aren't always open to "new." We want what we're used to, because it's comfortable. If you're doing something different, something that asks people to be open to a new experience, or something that makes people uncomfortable, expect some resistance.

But don't let resistance keep you from delivering the message you need to deliver.

CHAPTER 002

YOUR FOCUS

Even if you've already decided on a "niche" for your podcast, most podcasts will benefit by a narrower focus. Not only does it enable you to give a certain segment of the population *exactly* what they want and feel passionate about, it also gives you clear boundaries about who to target when marketing your podcast.

Ironically, the first step in narrowing your focus is to "go big." This can be done using the 5W method.

Who? - *Who* specifically is the audience you're going to work with?

What? - *What* problem do you want to help the people in this audience solve?

When? - *When* would these people need your help? Would your skills best be utilized by beginners, or should you focus on people who are more experienced?

Where? - *Where* are these people? How are you going to reach them?

Why? - *Why* are you here? What are you bringing to the table that nobody else can?

One way to really dig in to these questions and narrow the focus of your podcast is to use a process I call SCRAPE – segment, combination, related, antithesis, problem, experience.

S = Segment

You have an audience for your podcast in mind. How can you segment this audience so that the group you choose to focus on feels like you have something especially for them?

This element of determining the focus of your podcast may be the most difficult. We, as creators, like to be inclusive. We want what we create to reach as many people as possible, and that means being accessible to many different people with different interests.

But this isn't broadcasting; this is podcasting. You don't have a big-ass tower where you can blast your signal to everybody within a certain geographic radius. You have to take a different approach.

People who are listening to your podcast have a choice. They can just as easily get somebody else's podcast as they can yours, so make sure you give them something helpful, memorable, and personal.

What one person loves, another isn't interested in. Once you've chosen the people you want to focus on attracting, focus on making something they'll *love* and don't worry about those people for whom it isn't a match.

Here are seven ways you can segment your audience:

1. Via Product or Activity

Take a broad focus, then segment that focus into sections.

As an example, if the broad focus is computers, you could segment that into specific brands or types of computer. For example, a sole focus on

Mac computers. Or focus on different brands of computer, but only laptops.

This works great with any topic. Start big and work your way down.

How many levels down can you segment your initial idea and still have a viable audience? For example, let's say you want to do a podcast about dancing.

LEVEL 1 = dancing
LEVEL 2 = partner dancing
LEVEL 3 = ballroom style
LEVEL 4 = Smooth (not Rhythm)
LEVEL 5 = Foxtrot

Can you take segmentation too far? Yes. But most people don't take it far enough.

People sometimes settle for general, "something for everybody" content, but nobody is completely pleased with it. It's far better to really please just *some* people than have most people only tolerate you.

In the event you go too far with segmentation, you can always expand your focus later. This is an easy fix. For this example, perhaps adding additional "smooth" dances (Waltz, Tango, etc.) would help. And if that's not enough, adding select "rhythm" dances (Cha-cha, Rumba, etc.) to broaden things a bit more.

But keep in mind that every dance mentioned here takes place in a ballroom. We're not talking modern, ballet, tap, jazz, pole, or street dancing. The people who do these styles of dance usually aren't the same people who do ballroom.

This is why you want to really know your audience. To do this, you need to get the people you're trying to connect with on the phone (or meet with them in person) and really listen to them talk about what they love (and want more of) and also what they need help with.

2. Via Lifestyle

Let's say you want to do a podcast about parenting. That's a great segment of the population itself, but how can you segment it even more?

- Single parents
- Single mothers
- Single fathers
- Same-sex parents
- Single gay parents
- Single lesbian parents
- Parents over 40 years old
- Parents of newborns
- Parents of multiple-birth children
- Adoptive parents
- Adoptive parents of special-needs children
- Adoptive parents of international children

Segmenting by lifestyle will help you to go deep with your content. Almost all parents deal with very basic issues of parenting, such as being patient with their children, discipline, and toilet training. Segments of the parenting population mentioned above, though, also deal with specialized issues, which aren't always as easy to find solutions for.

When you can provide solutions to specific problems, you'll attract people to your podcast.

By focusing on specialized content, your podcast becomes the solution for a specific segment of the population whose needs aren't being met elsewhere. You won't attract everybody, because what you do isn't for everybody. But you'll attract the people who need you the most, and because of this, they will be extremely loyal to you.

3. Via Geography

Imagine I have a new business connection TO introduce to you. He's somebody who could help you take your podcast to a completely new level.

I'd probably say something like, "Hello, I'd like you to meet John Smith. He's based in Chunky, Mississippi, and he's increased ad revenue for every podcast he's worked with."

Increasing revenue is exciting. But if you'd grown up in Chunky, Mississippi, that would be the first thing you'd mention.

You'd be thinking, "I'm from Chunky, Mississippi! I wonder if he knows anybody that I know? I wonder if we've been to any of the same places?"

This is how powerful a geographic connection between people is.

Neighbors is a storytelling podcast hosted by Jakob Lewis that focuses on the lives of ordinary people. It's a show about human connection.

Lots of podcasts tell personal stories. But *Neighbors*, as the name implies, focuses on *local* stories. It's produced in Nashville and features the stories of people from Nashville.

And if you're from Nashville, *Neighbors* just got a whole lot more interesting to you.

Geography isn't the only way to segment your audience, but if there's a way to incorporate it into what you do, it's one of the most powerful.

Examples of how you can use geography in this way…

- New York City on $100/day
- Weekend entertainment options in Las Vegas
- Miami restaurant reviews
- Toronto for new immigrants
- Real estate investing in Los Angeles

C = Combination

Is there a way to take what you do and run it through a different, not-so-common filter? My marketing podcast for experts, *RED Podcast*, does that.

"Marketing" is a general topic. There are thousands of marketing podcasts, so the topic alone isn't enough to make *RED Podcast* stand out.

My *specialty* (and the filter I run everything through) comes from my background in marketing for the entertainment business. I use my entertainment marketing skills to market non-entertainers. That's the unique combination.

The quick and dirty of how it works:

RED Podcast is designed for people who create something based around an idea or message. I then help them share what they've created using great marketing.

This is the *exact same thing* I did when working with musicians. The only difference is the vehicle used to spread the message – instead of a music album, the message is spread via blogs, books, podcasts, radio shows, television shows, online videos, and other media.

Everybody, musicians and non-musicians alike, wants the same things for their personal brands — increased exposure, more authority, and greater leverage. They also want the results that come from having these things, including more product sales, a bigger audience, and more money from what they create.

I could talk about all of these things via a general "marketing" podcast, but it's much more interesting to listen to lessons and examples involving sex, drugs, and rock and roll.

Combination, borrowing an idea from one industry and implementing it in another, is how innovation happens. This is how Henry Ford "invented" the assembly line — he took a concept used in a pork processing plant and applied it to his automobile factories. FedEx's system of delivering packages was based on an almost 200-year-old process banks used to clear checks. Apple's colorful iMac computers were created using a tinting process Apple engineers learned from the candy industry.

What elements from aspects of your life can you combine with what you're talking about on your podcast to give listeners a completely unique experience?

R = Related

This is a great option if you already have an established podcast and want to do an additional podcast or episodes for your current podcast that will be attractive to a similar audience. It allows you to use the momentum of your established podcast audience and expand on it to attract new people to your established content.

Rob Cesternino of *Rob Has A Podcast* has done this extremely well. When he started his podcast, he focused on a single reality television show – *Survivor*. Since people who like *Survivor* are likely to enjoy similar shows, he's expanded to producing dedicated episodes about other competition-based reality television shows including:

- Big Brother
- The Amazing Race
- RuPaul's Drag Race
- Dancing With The Stars
- Jersey Shore

In addition to expanding what he talks about in dedicated episodes of *Rob Has A Podcast*, Cesternino has also produced additional stand-alone podcasts for his audience including shows about *Big Brother, The Bachelorette,* and *The Challenge,* among others. He is constantly and consistently changing the podcasts he does based on current television programming.

If you don't want to commit to doing an additional, ongoing podcast, consider a one-time, limited-episode evergreen option.

I've had great success doing this for spinoffs of my podcast for podcasters, *Build A Big Podcast.* These spinoffs, including *28-Day Podcast Jumpstart* and *Podcast Interviewing School,* are just 30 episodes each and focus on helping listeners of *Build A Big Podcast* solve specific podcasting issues.

Doing a limited-episode podcast allows you to create and release something once, but continue to receive its promotional benefits. They have a very long lifespan and, as long as the content is evergreen, will act as lead generators for your primary podcast with minimal promotion.

Not interested in creating multiple podcasts? Look into starting (or joining) a podcast network with related podcasts produced by others.

A = Antithesis

Most people aren't successful. Because of this, Earl Nightingale's advice on how to achieve success was, "Whatever the great majority are doing, do the opposite."

"Do the opposite" is also a great way to focus your podcast.

Tim Ferriss has practically made a career out of this. Whatever people are doing — working long hours, spending years learning important skills, or eating a specific diet — Tim Ferriss almost always advises doing the opposite.

They zig. You zag.

This doesn't have to be combative. Nick Loper used a noncombative but opposite approach with his podcast *The Side Hustle Show.*

Most podcasts on entrepreneurship are about building and running full-time businesses. *The Side Hustle Show* is for people who have a job and are building a business in addition to doing their regular work.

Here are some ideas how antithesis could be used in podcasting:

- Improving Your Marriage Through Non-Monogamy
- iAmish - Technology Reviews By An Amish Guy
- How To Live Off Credit Cards — A Personal Finance Podcast
- Eat More Food, Lose More Weight
- Jews For Jesus

The concept of antithesis can also apply to individual episodes. *Freakonomics Radio* often uses this technique to develop tension within their stories and keep listeners on edge.

Tension sells.

P = Problem

I have a good friend who lives in Las Vegas and is raising a little girl. She once told me, "There are a lot of bad things for kids to get into out here. My main goal is to keep her off the pole."

As in stripper pole.

There *are* a lot of "bad things" that can happen to a kid, in Las Vegas or anywhere, but the one she was focusing on was her city's extensive (and lucrative) sex industry. Not keeping her kid away from gambling. Not keeping her kid off drugs. Not keeping her kid from getting pregnant.

Parents have different objectives for their children and are in different situations.

But a goal to "keep her off the pole" narrows things down considerably. Combined with a geographic approach for parents in Las Vegas, looking at city-specific issues due to its massive gaming and entertainment industry, things are narrowed down even more.

Based on her statement and what little we know about her (location, basic situation), here's the profile you can now build upon:

- Mother raising a young, female child
- In an urban area
- Surrounded by a culture of "bad influence"
- Lots of temptation around, including quick money and peer pressure
- Wants positive opportunities and a good life for her child

Knowing these things, you could put together a podcast focusing on one or more of these elements of child rearing:

- Self-esteem
- Personal boundaries
- Resisting peer pressure
- Parenting in an urban environment
- How to provide positive opportunities for children

All of these things would focus on solving the original problem.

What are the big problems your listeners are facing?

E = Experience

When establishing a focus for your podcast, it's important to consider what you have to offer as a host and leader. Specifically, what unique experiences do you bring to the table?

The experiences you've had in business and life have affected what you're doing now (or want to do), even if the two seem unrelated. They've helped you create a unique combination that nobody else has and, because of this, you've created something that will be difficult for others to copy.

Don't ignore what's brought you this far. Instead, embrace your unique combination of skills and talents.

This can be difficult, especially if you're trying to move away from your past and want to recreate yourself in a new way. Like a nerdy teenager transferring schools in hope of reinventing himself, you probably don't want to talk about the past. But like a nerdy teenager, you can't just walk away from your reputation, even if you change locations.

There is no such thing is a clean break. Like Buckaroo Banzai said, "No matter where you go, there you are."

Don't hold back. Your experience is important. The work you've done in the past can help people, even if it seems insignificant to what you're currently doing.

CHAPTER 003

YOUR AUDIENCE

When selecting the direction for your podcast, you should consider potential audience size. However, having a massive audience isn't nearly as important as most people think, which is why you shouldn't be afraid of going deep within a niche.

Kevin Kelly is the founding executive editor of *Wired* magazine and a former editor/publisher of the *Whole Earth Review*. His "1000 True Fans" theory says a solo creator can be successful with 1000 fans who will:

1. Buy "anything and everything" you produce.
2. Tell their friends and turn them into fans.

These "true fans" will drive 200 miles to see you speak, fly across the country to attend your seminar, buy your books, read your email newsletter every time it's published, listen to interviews you've done with others, and tell their friends about you.

Is it possible to cultivate 1000 people like this? Yes. But 1000 is an arbitrary number.

Forget how many fans you need and focus on the right fans. You can have massive success with only 100 people if you have the right 100 people. In fact, you could do it with 10.

ɪ𝗇ot all fans are created equal. Some can assist you (and your podcast) in tremendous ways that go way beyond simply listening and enjoying it.

Most industries are controlled by *very* few people, and it's absolutely possible to have a successful podcast without a large number of listeners. To do this, though, you have to focus on having the *right* listeners.

Who are the people who would make a big difference to your podcast (and the business behind it) if they were fans of yours?

Us vs. Them

People listening to your podcast want to feel like they're part of something. When you succeed in making them feel this way, you give them a reason to listen that goes beyond your hosting talent, your guests, or your production quality.

People are tribal. Even the most introverted, isolated, and passive of us associate with specific sports teams, religions, political parties, and lifestyle choices. And even though we don't like to admit it, these associations influence our outlook and let us know where we stand in the world.

The communities built around successful podcasts are no different. Thinking of your podcast as a "voice" for a certain tribe will help you connect with a specific and dedicated audience.

The most successful podcasts have a clear separation between listeners and non-listeners. Like a primitive tribe, a listener is "in" or "out" — there is no middle ground.

Your podcast should imply that listeners who are "in" are superior to those who don't listen. "We" see the truth. "We" know what's going on.

People who listen to Dave Ramsey pay in cash and *never* buy on credit. They feel superior to those who do.

People who listen to Rush Limbaugh think they're better informed on government issues than the "low-information voters" who don't listen to Rush Limbaugh.

People who listen to Alex Jones feel they see a "truth" that others don't, such as the U.S. government's involvement in the Oklahoma City bombing, or the filming of fake moon landings to hide NASA's secret technology.

For the most dedicated fans, there is no middle ground.

All Podcasts Are Interactive

Every successful creation has two elements: how it's presented and how it's received. Without both, it might as well not exist.

Writing this book would be pointless if nobody read it. On the same note, recording your voice and releasing it as a podcast is pointless if nobody listens.

Because of this, you must treat those who listen to your podcast as equals in its creation process. Without them, you have no podcast.

Acknowledge your audience. What does that look like?

I was at the Podcast Awards in Las Vegas. The event was at the Las Vegas Convention Center, in a massive ballroom that was about 30 percent full. About 20 awards were presented, and only a handful of the winning podcasts had representatives there. In short, few people, even those winning awards, cared enough to attend.

The exception was Rob Cesternino. He took full advantage of the Podcast Awards opportunity by making his podcast listeners part of the ceremony. When he accepted the two awards *Rob Has A Podcast* won that night, he played to *his* audience via a selfie stick-mounted mobile phone which transmitted the entire experience via Facebook Live.

natter that the ballroom was 70 percent empty. It didn't matter that he was one of the few winning podcasters who cared enough to show up in person. It didn't matter that he was the only one doing this.

The only thing that mattered was that he let his audience, those who had put him in this position, be part of the experience.

You and your audience are a team.

Your podcast isn't about you. Even if you're like Rob and have named it after yourself, it's not about you.

Yes, as somebody trying to build a personal connection with listeners, it's good to include personal stories and other elements to share your human side, but less is more when it comes to these things and personal elements should *never* compromise the purpose of your podcast, which is to be helpful to the people who listen.

Every episode of your podcast should be done in service of your audience. Great podcasts are created for their listeners; they're not therapy sessions for their hosts.

Can listeners learn from your shared experiences? Yes. But don't dump your problems on people. Those who listen to you aren't professional counselors being paid for that service, nor are they close friends with whom you have personal relationships.

The Power Of Making People Feel Good

You don't have to be a great host to be successful in podcasting; you just have to make the people who listen to you feel appreciated.

Musician Jimmy Buffett follows this philosophy. When you go to a Jimmy Buffett show, you don't see him on the JumboTron, you see the audience. He builds community by making his fans part of the show.

You can do the same thing with your podcast. Read their emails, acknowledge positive reviews you receive, and thank them when appropriate.

Lewis Howes does a good job of acknowledging fans on his *School Of Greatness* podcast. In his "Fan Of The Week" segment, he reads a positive review, mentions the reviewer by name, and encourages listeners to leave their own reviews so they can have an opportunity to be mentioned themselves.

Jake Brennan of *Disgraceland* does something similar, giving away branded merchandise to fans and acknowledging them by name at the end of every episode. In addition, he always acknowledges the people who have worked with him to create that episode, including writers, musicians, mixers, engineers, and editors.

People want to feel understood and appreciated. Do this and you'll attract listeners for your podcast.

Jen Briney is a great example of how far you can take this. Not only has her podcast, *Congressional Dish*, attracted a substantial audience, it's 100 percent fan-funded. This allows her to be accountable only to listeners instead of advertisers.

How did she do it? She built upon the foundation of a clear and focused message, then backed it up by thanking every single person who donates at the end of her episodes.

An Instant (But Not Necessarily Dedicated) Audience

Every musician knows the best way to get a quick audience is to play the already-known songs of other people. This is the ultimate example of choosing "ease" as a career approach.

This happens in the movie business, too — it's why movie studios produce so many sequels. *Fast And Furious 8* may be forgettable as far as great filmmaking, but because the name is recognizable and the formula has been proven, it's able to take advantage of the existing audiences of the seven related movies that came before it, and it's more likely to be profitable.

Like musicians and movie studios, podcasters also have an option to acquire a quick audience: Interviews.

Just as a movie studio can adapt an already successful television series or hire a well-known actor for its new film, you can leverage the already-popular content and existing audiences of "celebrities" within your niche via interviews. When you interview already-popular people, even if they're not household names, you're able to take advantage of an audience that already exists.

With this route, you don't need to build an audience from scratch. That work has already been done by the people you're interviewing. And because of this, the path is a lot smoother, since it has already been blazed.

But where does the path take you?

You'll get listeners quickly. Nothing wrong with that.

And because you'll have listeners, you'll get sponsors more easily. Nothing wrong with that.

You may even make money… *Nothing* wrong with that.

So what's the problem?

It's easy to have quick success when you're building on the back of something that already has momentum. But understand the downside, which is that it's very likely the success you have will peak quickly and then disappear if you don't bring your own personality and content to the table.

Know Your Audience

Copywriting legend Robert Collier advised those selling via direct mail, "Always enter the conversation already taking place in the customer's mind."

I advise you to do the same when creating a podcast — "Always enter the conversation already taking place in the listener's mind."

Why are radio hosts like Howard Stern, Rush Limbaugh, and Glenn Beck so popular? It's because they have their fingers on the pulse of what their audiences are thinking and feeling, and, like a mirror, they communicate these thoughts and feelings back to them.

If you want to have a podcast people listen to, you need to do the same thing. But how?

The best way is to *be* your audience.

Would you listen to a podcast about drinking craft beer from somebody who doesn't drink beer or, if he does, prefers Budweiser? Probably not.

When you're a member of a group — whether it be a formal organization, such as a church, or something more loosely knit, such as people who enjoy running — you'll have a much easier time connecting to people within that group than somebody who's trying to connect from the outside.

A great example of a type of connection is the one you share with other podcasters. As a podcaster, you have certain things in common with others who podcast, so when you meet each other, there's likely instant rapport.

When you meet other podcasters, you probably talk about things like:

- Microphones
- Your mixer setup
- Software you use to record your podcast
- Media hosting
- Getting more listeners

This "ritual" is the way you see if somebody's "in the club." There's a very specific communication style (and language) used. You don't have to explain it because insiders already know.

Every group, whether it's formal or informal, has its own version of this. And if you're tapped into how the group thinks and feels, you'll be successful with them.

How To Build True Connection With Your Audience (And The Individuals Within It)

Even if you're part of the group your podcast is for, you should always strive to improve your ability to effectively communicate with listeners and consistently create content they'll be enthusiastic about. Trends and habits within any group are always changing, and both you and your content need to change with these things.

If you're a fan of comedy, you know that stand-up comedy is always evolving. While there are certainly "evergreen" jokes and concepts, they must be delivered in a certain way for an audience to connect with them.

For example, the concept of love and relationships is timeless, but what an audience in the 1950s thought was funny won't be the same thing today's audience laughs at. People still fall in love and have relationships, but our modern approach to these things is very different from how things were done in the past.

Your content is similar. While the big concepts that you're talking about today will likely still be relevant in the future, the related examples you share and how you talk about these topics will need to be different for your listeners to connect with them.

A phone is still a phone, but only *some* people understand how to use a rotary dial. Or a pay phone. Or know what a "busy signal" sounds like.

Every podcaster (and audience) has a version of this.

Are you still connected to your audience? You may not be as connected as you think.

There is a tendency for content creators, whether they be comics, podcasters, authors, bloggers, or musicians, as we get more successful, to stop doing what got us our success in the first place. And the biggest thing most of us stop doing is directly connecting with the people who enjoy our content.

Keep connected with the people who listen to you. If you don't keep an "ear to the street" and stay in touch with what they're going through, they'll leave you for somebody who will.

How To Deepen Connection With Your Audience (Or Destroy It Completely)

A successful media personality built his business by helping people with their finances. When he started, he was hands-on and in-the-trenches, leading his own workshops and selling his own self-published books.

Just a few years before, he'd been overextended and lost everything. Because of this, he was totally connected to the message he was spreading. He'd lived the experience of his listeners and was the perfect person to provide both advice and hope.

He was his audience.

Today, several years later, he lives in a multi-million dollar mansion. His garage, at just under 1500 square feet, is bigger than most homes.

He flies in a private jet. When he goes to a speaking event, he's picked up on the tarmac by a limousine, which takes him straight to his hotel.

He does his speech. He gets back in a limousine. He returns home via his private jet.

This isn't meant to criticize him; I only mention these things to point out that he's living a *completely* different lifestyle from the people who are listening to him.

This is how you get disconnected from your audience. You lose touch because the relationship you have with them is that of the mogul — somebody they're trying to impress and win the approval of — rather than somebody who can relate to them and assist them because of this.

The world has no shortage of advice. If that's all people needed to better themselves, whether it's losing weight, getting out of debt, or creating a better marriage, change would be as simple as going to YouTube and watching one of *millions* of generic how-to videos.

Real impact happens when you connect with people through their hearts. And to connect with listeners on that level, you must understand them. Empathy, your capacity to recognize feelings that are being experienced by others, is your number-one podcast marketing skill.

If you can master empathy, you can master the art (and business) of podcasting. When you understand what people *really* mean when they speak, why they listen to your episodes, and why they take (or don't take) action, you can write your own ticket and get anything you want via podcasting.

If you take away one thing from this book, take away this:

Let your audience be the star.

You may be the one behind the microphone, but your podcast is never about you. Never. It's always about the audience. More specifically, how it makes the audience feel.

What's the best way to really understand your listeners, so you can make them feel good?

Talk to them.

I'm not talking about short conversations with people who call you on the air to ask questions — that doesn't count. Same for short messages via Twitter or other social media.

If you really want to know what your audience is going through and be able to talk *with* them rather than at them, you're going to have to invest some time getting to know them on a one-on-one basis.

Every week, I have one-on-one conversations with people who read my blogs, listen to my podcasts, or are otherwise being exposed to the messages I share. I want to hear what each person is experiencing in his own words, not via an automated, multiple-choice survey or focus group that would lump multiple people together.

Get to know your audience as individuals, not as a faceless group. Behind every "download" is a person, and the more you understand them in this way, the better you'll be able to assist them as a whole.

I approach marketing this way for *everything* I do, not just podcasts. I did it for this book.

Is it more work? Yes. But if you've thought, "This guy is speaking directly to me," as you've been reading this book, you can see how valuable this extra work is.

This attention to detail is what separates the podcasts that people love from those they simply tolerate. You can still have *some* success, even a lot of success, without reaching out and communicating with listeners individually, but you'll never have the same level of connection as a podcaster who takes the time to have these conversations.

True connection, like the one you want with the listeners of your podcast, can best be summed up with this quote by Ernest Hemingway:

"When people talk, listen completely. Most people never listen."

That's the secret to podcasting. It's not about microphones or slick marketing or publicity as much as it is making people feel like they're understood. This is done by giving the people in your audience a voice, saying the things they can't, and saying the things they feel ... and that starts by listening to their needs.

CHAPTER 004

YOUR FORMAT

There are over 170,000 ways you can order a drink at Starbucks. Go to Moe's Southwest Grill and you can create 17,030,314,057,236,500,000 different meals.

How is this possible? Take basic, foundational ingredients, and add some flair. Serve things up in a different way.

You can do something similar with your podcast. And because you're the one adding the flair, I'm focusing on the basics, which you can then add upon.

All podcasts will fall into one of three formats — solo, interview, or co-hosted.

Interview Format

The "interview format" podcast is, by far, the most popular hosting format for podcasts.

Interview Format - The Pros

You Will Meet People

If you're like most people, your favorite topic of conversation is yourself. On average, people spend 60 percent of conversations talking about themselves. When communicating via social media, this number jumps to 80 percent.

Talking about yourself activates the neural regions of your brain associated with pleasure, motivation, and reward. In other words, it feels good.

Interview-format podcasts will help you in two ways:

1. When you let others talk about themselves, they associate you with giving them a pleasurable experience. This builds a connection that can be beneficial to your business.
2. If you're skilled at interviewing, you'll get great content for your podcast.

You'll Keep Things Fresh

One of the major problems that solo and co-hosted podcasts face is a tendency for the delivery, ideas, and topics discussed to become repetitive and stale. Bringing in a new person to interview every episode helps to make sure this won't happen.

But only if it's done right.

As humans we have a tendency to associate with people who are just like us. If you look at where you live, for example, you'll likely see people who are very similar to who you are — the same color, same basic religion, similar economic status, similar political beliefs, and similar culture.

The same happens in podcasts. Because of our tendency to associate with people with whom we're most comfortable, we reach out and respond to those with similar beliefs about the topics we focus on.

An interview isn't a debate, but it *is* something that can bring a new perspective to your show and stimulate discussion. There's no need to bring in somebody who thinks just like you do or somebody who's been interviewed dozens of times already — those thoughts have already been heard.

The Zambians are right: "If two wise men always agree, then there is no need for one of them." When doing an interview for your podcast, focus on discussion, not agreement.

You'll Get Traffic (Maybe)

One of the big reasons people do an interview-format podcast is to ride on the coattails of something that is already established. It's the same reason the band at your local bar plays cover songs — people already know the material, and there is a demand for it.

If the only reason you're interviewing people is because you hope it's going to bring in some traffic, while that might actually help you to generate interest in what you're doing early on in the life of your podcast, in the end, like a band playing cover songs at your local bar, it's not likely to get you where you really want to go.

Yes, it's nice to have established people as guests. They already have established audiences who are looking for their content, they likely have communication skills which will make your job asking questions (and getting good answers) easier, and should they pass along what you're doing via social media or a mailing list, more people will likely pay some attention to you. But you can't count on any of these things.

People who have big audiences get them by putting out lots of content, doing lots of promotion around this content, and otherwise spreading their messages in whatever ways they can. Your interview with one of these people is likely to be one of many, part of a continuous marketing and promotion plan designed to leverage *your* audience for them, not the other way around.

Sure, if you're *Good Morning America* or another national outlet, you've got a good shot at somebody mentioning his interview with you. That's because *Good Morning America* brings credibility with it. It's an honor to be chosen as a guest on *Good Morning America*.

Does your podcast offer this kind of credibility and reputation? Not if you're interviewing anybody and everybody you can get.

In the end, the only way to really take advantage of easy traffic from big guests in an interview-format podcast is by doing things the hard way — building your credibility yourself, not through the people whom you talk with.

You Don't Have To Prepare As Much (Or Bring All The Content)

One of the great things about sharing the podcast stage with somebody else is that she's going to bring a lot of knowledge to the table. You can fill twice as much time, maybe more, with the same level of preparation it would take for you to prepare and deliver half as much content on your own.

But you *do* have to prepare. You can't just show up to an interview and expect things to go well if you don't have some idea of who you're talking to and what you want the conversation to focus on.

You Don't Have To Be An Expert

It's possible to have a very successful podcast on a subject in which you're not an expert. In fact, sometimes podcasts with hosts who aren't experts on the subject being discussed are even *more* successful than podcasts with hosts who are experts because hosts who aren't experts are able to approach things more similarly to how their listeners do.

The "curse of knowledge" is real: It's a cognitive bias that leads experts to find it extremely difficult to think about problems from the perspective of people who are less-informed – people such as listeners.

A Better Type Of "Interview"

All of the things I've written here are true. You don't have to be an expert to do an interview-format podcast. And you don't have to prepare as much for an interview podcast (as opposed to a solo-format podcast) because you're not the solely responsible for the content being delivered.

But just because you can get away with creating a podcast where you're not an expert on the subject or are able to shortcut your preparation time doesn't mean you should.

Which of these would you rather hear?

1. A general-interest interview done by a local news reporter with no specialized knowledge of the guest or subject;
2. A deep conversation on a subject, guided by an expert who has shared knowledge and similar experience as the person he's talking with.

The answer is choice number two — a deep conversation. This is especially true for podcast listeners, who, unlike listeners to broadcast radio, have made a conscious decision about what they want to hear by searching it out ahead of time. Podcast listeners don't listen to you because your podcast is what's on in the background, because they have limited choices, or they don't have better options — if they're listening to you, it's because they want to.

Most interview-format podcasts are the equivalent of a local "City This Morning" television show, produced by the local television station and aired before network programing begins for the day. Every city has one (or more) and they're full of segments such as:

- A local chef cooking a "healthy snack"
- A local personal trainer showing exercises for a "flatter tummy"
- A local hairstylist showcasing "hot new hairstyles"

These segments almost always involve one of the "City This Morning" hosts asking basic questions read off notecards and pointing out the obvious…

"Wow! This sure is tasty! And it's healthy too!"

"Could you do these exercises at home or at the gym?"

"It looks amazing!"

None of the content is particularly memorable. The host simply echoes what has already been said (or shown) and doesn't know enough about any of the subjects covered to go any deeper.

The result is a show that few people seek out these shows and even fewer (if any) would miss one if it disappeared completely.

You want something better for your podcast. It's for this reason that I suggest you format your interviews more like conversations between two experts, one of whom is you. Not only is it more interesting to listeners, it will also better serve them.

Do what it takes to make yourself an expert and create the con[v]
people listening want to hear.

Interview Format - The Cons

Scheduling And Editing Time Suck

You want a podcast that has high standards. Unfortunately, the more you rely on other people to provide content for your podcast, the more you'll have to defend those standards.

If your podcast is even somewhat successful, people will come out of the woodwork to pitch guests. Sometimes these pitches will be from the individuals who want to be on your podcast themselves. Sometimes you'll hear from their representatives — publicists, book publishers, spouses, assistants, and virtual assistants.

Many will contact you more than once.

If you have a popular podcast that's easy to find, and you're easy to connect with, handling this in the correct way will be a lot of work for you (or somebody). And if you're not good at being selective about who you let on your podcast, you'll soon find yourself doing interview-related things all the time — scheduling, preparing, actually doing the interview, editing the interview, and answering follow-up questions.

You can cut down on this work by learning how to say no and properly vetting potential guests before you schedule an interview. Some of this vetting can be automated by having potential guests fill out a pitch form with exactly the information you need to make your booking decision, including:

Transition? Over time [handwritten annotation]

- Background information
- "Why do you think you'd be a good guest for {PODCAST NAME}?"

- 3 topic pitches
- Bio
- Website
- Examples of previous interviews
- Examples of other online media, including articles, books, and videos

You can cut down on the noise of potential interviewees by having a policy to make the first move. In other words, you go to them, not the other way around.

You can make scheduling easier on yourself by using an automated scheduling tool (see BigPodcast.com/resources for options), which will give potential guests pre-approved dates and times that you are available for to record and allow them to automatically add appointments to your calendar without the back-and-forth of finding times that work for both of you.

But you're not going to get away from editing interviews, many with people who can't um ... speak ... errr ... without ... using... ummm ... filler words. Editing takes time, even with the most skilled hosts and guests.

Technical Issues

It's nice to be able to walk into a studio, hit record, and go for it. Recording everything in the same room as your guest doesn't mean you'll never have technical issues, but the chance of something going wrong with a local recording setup that you control is far less likely than when you record people over the Internet, which for the great majority of podcasters is done via Skype.

There are a million things that can go wrong when talking to somebody via Skype, and this is greatly magnified when trying to get a quality recording of that conversation. Internet connectivity comes and goes, dogs bark, and kids interrupt. There are power outages, microphone problems, and sirens bleeding through from the street outside.

None of the things that go wrong are issues you can't work around. However, know that, like building a house, it always takes twice as long and twice as much money to build a great podcast as you think it will.

In other words, plan for problems.

This isn't to say that you shouldn't do remote interviews for your podcast. Plenty of people, including me, successfully do this all the time. When it comes to technical issues, though, know this is part of it, regardless of how good your equipment is or how experienced you are with using it.

You Are Secondary

When you have guests on your show, it's no longer *your* show. Yes, you're ultimately in charge, but you're stepping aside to bring in other people and focus on their expertise, rather than your own.

Your goal as a podcaster may be to be a conduit for others. If that's the case, having the primary focus of your show be interviews with other people is a great match for you. However, if you want to be known as an expert yourself, know that having too many episodes where you're interviewing others, compared to episodes you record on your own, may jeopardize that.

It's Been Done

The biggest con when it comes to interview-format podcasts is there are a ton of them. On one hand, that shows there's a market for interviews. But on the other, how will you stand out in such a big crowd?

Are you podcasting about one of the following subjects?

- Making money online
- Entrepreneurship
- Time management
- Leadership
- Marriage and relationships
- Weight loss and dieting
- Fitness
- Real estate
- Social media
- Sales

If so, you've got a lot of competition. If you're going to have any success, you're going to have to bring something different to the table than what's already there.

As a host, you should have a different interviewing style than the next guy, as well be able to share unique perspectives yourself. Regardless of how different you are, though, if you're interviewing the same people as other top podcasts, a lot of your content and feel is going to be similar to what already exists. Because of this, it may be forgettable.

If you're hell-bent on covering any of the topics listed above with an interview format, "niching down" will help your podcast to stand out and attract listeners who will be dedicated to you and your message.

You Give Up Control

When you're a solo operation, you control everything — the overall topic, content within, the recording quality, and all the tiny little details.

Don't like how something sounds? You can easily record it again.

Not feeling like recording today? You can record later with little problem.

And you'll never stand yourself up.

When you bring somebody else into the mix, you lose *a lot* when it comes to control of your podcast. This isn't always a bad thing, but it can be.

Nobody else is going to care about your podcast as much as you do. Even with the best vetting, guests will show up unprepared, without the proper equipment, or without a quiet place in which to record.

Your entire release schedule can easily be thrown off because of technical issues or poor content.

Then what? You're on your own. Unless you've got an extra episode in the can, if you want to keep your release schedule on track, you're going to have to find somebody else to interview or go solo for an episode.

Finding somebody else at the last minute creates its own set of problems. When you're in a pinch for time, you often have to settle for who you can get, not who you want. Beyond that, your pre-episode prep will be rushed and you probably won't be as prepared as you like.

If you're a control freak who wants everything about your podcast to be perfect, an interview format is not for you.

Solo Format
Solo Format - The Pros

Total Control

The best thing about a solo podcast is you can record, edit, and release episodes whenever you want. You're in total control of these elements.

You can decide *what* you want to talk about. You can decide *when* you want to talk about it.

If you want to do a couple of episodes in a single day, you can. You could record a dozen episodes in a single day.

Don't like the thought of approaching people to be interviewed on your podcast or trying to find a mutually-suitable time to record with a co-host? Neither of these things will be an issue for you when you do a solo podcast.

Regretting the name you chose for your podcast? Change it.

If you want absolute freedom when it comes to podcasting, a solo format is for you.

You Are The Authority

There's a rumor in the podcasting community that you'll get credibility by interviewing people who are already established. Then, by asking these experts questions, you'll also be seen as an expert.

Neither is true — especially when the interviewee in question has absolutely no discrimination when it comes to being on podcasts (and other media outlets) and has more or less told the same story he's going to tell you hundreds of other places.

You may be able to reroute the established audience of somebody else to listen to your podcast, but those people are coming for person you've interviewed, not you — you're just a vehicle.

Still, like so many fantasies, the rumors about this shortcut to credibility and expertise persist because we want to believe them. I thought the same thing when I started my broadcast radio show, *Music Business Radio*.

Interviewing people *has* helped me in that I've been able to meet some amazing people I might not have gotten to meet otherwise. But has it made me appear to be more of an expert? Not really.

Many people who listen to me on the radio think I'm a journalist. They have no idea I'm actually a marketing guy and that my purpose for being on the radio, at least initially, was to market myself.

That plan backfired.

Certainly, being on a podcast (or on the radio) is helpful when establishing authority. But if your show is based on you asking questions of other people and yielding your authority to them, that's not going to help you in the same way a solo-format show would.

This is the reason there were *zero* interviews on the first 112 episodes of my marketing podcast, *RED Podcast.* As an expert myself, I didn't need anybody else to "give me credibility."

If you have the knowledge, stories, and a point-of-view to share, and you want to be considered an authority, you'll likely have the most opportunity with a solo-format podcast.

Solo Format - The Cons

Stale Content

When your podcast is just you, it's easy for things to get stale. You can burn through content, personal experiences, and your overall knowledge of a subject quickly. And it's easy to get into repetitive patterns in the way you deliver information, which can become boring to listeners.

If you find yourself running into these situations, which can and will happen eventually, you have options. One of the best is to bring in the experiences of people other than you. Not only will this allow you to get additional content to put on your show, you also get something from which you can create additional commentary.

Here are three ways to do this, without switching to an interview format:

1. Listener Mailbag - Encourage people to write you with content you can use on your podcast.

HOW TO DO IT: The easiest way to do this is to ask for feedback on a specific episode. For example, "What did you think about my comments on this episode? Am I right about this topic? Reach out to me at email@email.com and let me know."

WHY TO DO IT: Beyond getting listeners involved with your content creation and keeping things from getting stale by adding the experiences of different people, a Listener Mailbag is a great way to callback to previous episodes and encourage listeners to review your older content.

2. Listener Voice Mails - Have listeners call in and leave commentary on previously released episodes and share stories via voice mail.

Like the mailbag, a voicemail box is a great place to get listener feedback. Recordings you can play on your podcast get listeners emotionally connected with each other and help to showcase the community around your podcast.

If you don't want to set up a voice mailbox, have listeners record voice memos on their phones and email them to you.

One of my favorite ways to use voicemail is within ongoing segments. Dave Jackson has one on his show, *School Of Podcasting*, called "Because Of My Podcast" in which listeners tell stories of what they've been able to accomplish because they started podcasting. For example, meeting celebrities to interview, getting more business, or getting all-access media passes to events they wouldn't have been able to attend otherwise.

3. Question Of The Day (Or Week) - Listeners answer a specific question via voice mail or email.

HOW TO DO IT: You're looking for stories. This isn't trivia and you're not trying to stump people.

Create questions that the majority of your audience will be able to answer. For example, experiential questions.

If you host a podcast on marriage, something like, "How did you propose to your wife?" Or if you're on the other end of this, with a podcast focusing on divorce recovery, "How did you know it was time to end your marriage?"

Set up a voice mailbox or an email address that can accept audio files. Then let listeners submit their stories.

WHY DO TO IT: This segment is especially powerful because it takes listeners from passive to active participants in your podcast. It puts the focus on them, letting them share their personal stories.

Segments like these build community. Listeners learn about other listeners and hear what they're doing in similar situations. And because listeners are connecting with other listeners, they'll feel even more connected to your podcast, since it's your podcast bringing them together.

Need more episode ideas? I've got dozens of free podcast episode templates available via my site at BigPodcast.com.

You Need A Less-Common Type Of Skill

Interview format episodes aren't necessarily less work than solo episodes, when you consider that you have to find somebody to interview, vet him, do pre-episode prep work, schedule a mutually agreed upon time to record, and work with a variety of technical issues you won't face when doing a solo episode.

So why are so many podcasts 100 percent interview format?

It's because, for *most* people, the skillset needed for solo podcasting is underdeveloped.

From the time we were little, we've interviewed people. We talk a little, we hand things over to somebody else, we listen, and the process repeats itself.

We "interview" people daily — talking on the phone, checking out at the grocery, and interacting with co-workers. Yet how many people routinely get front a group and take over *all* the speaking duties?

Not many. And because of this, we haven't developed the necessary skills to do it well.

What are those skills?

Broadcasting by yourself, like public speaking, requires you to get the mechanics of speech down, such as correct pronunciation, have a delivery style that gets the attention of people (and keeps it), and perform the physical aspects of speech, including proper breath control. You also have to have an organized thought process that takes a listener from Point A to Point B in a linear way that she'll be able to understand.

Beyond this, solo podcasts don't provide the psychological and emotional buffer that podcasts shared with a co-host or interviewees will. It's more pressure to have 100 percent of the attention focused on you and be 100 percent responsible for whether your podcast succeeds or fails.

It Takes More Planning

Imagine this …

It's just you. You walk up to the microphone and hit the record button.

Then what? Where do you start?

There's no, *"John Smith is my guest today"* or *"Welcome to the podcast, John."*

But you've got to say something. What will it be?

This is the pressure of having to deliver a solo podcast. You've got 20 minutes to fill, maybe more, and every bit of it is 100 percent you.

Because of this, you've got to plan.

An outline is fine, if you're somewhat good on your feet. You can also write everything out, word-for-word, but if you're not good at delivering content like this, it's going to sound like you're reading.

And you *don't* want to sound like you're reading.

In addition to needing a higher level of skill to deliver a solo podcast, you also have to do more planning. Even when you factor in the work you have to do when interviewing somebody — discovery, vetting, approach, booking, research, recording, and editing — a solo podcast, for most people, is still going to be a lot more work.

How To Get Good At Solo Podcasting

Practice. Outline episodes, record episodes, and make mistakes. You don't have to release everything, but you'll have to go through the motions of making complete solo episodes if you want to get better at solo podcasting.

Don't wait to get started until you have "more experience." Don't psych yourself out and get in your own head, making the necessary work worse than it actually is.

I know about this personally. I did hundreds of interviews on broadcast radio, for more than 10 years, and had released 150 co-hosted and interview episodes of *RED Podcast* before I did my first solo episode.

Nobody talks about failing on their first attempts. And you certainly don't hear these first attempts when it comes to radio and podcasting. So trust me on this — *everybody* sucks for a while, but if you keep at it, you'll get better and have something you can be proud to release to the public.

Co-Host Format

A co-hosted podcast is a good medium between an interview-format podcast and a solo podcast. It allows you to keep your credibility as an expert intact while having another person to share in the other responsibilities that go into creating a podcast.

Co-Host Format - The Pros

Skill-Level = Moderate

It takes a moderate level of skill to co-host a podcast. The content you create can basically be delivered in a "conversation" format, which is *a lot* easier than a solo podcast, but adding a co-host, because conversations can easily become unfocused, requires you to pay close attention to staying on topic.

Solid Level Of Control

You have a good level of control with a co-hosted podcast. It's fairly easy to schedule time to record when there are just two people involved and you're both on the same page. And unless you or your co-host are uptight and want to approve edits before episodes are released, both editing and episode release dates are flexible.

Like a solo podcast, a co-hosted podcast allows you to have solid control over the content you create. You don't have to worry about a guest randomly hijacking the discussion, changing the subject you want to cover, or turning an episode into a sales pitch.

You can tape multiple episodes in a single setting. If you end up with an episode you're not happy with, you can ditch it and start all over again. You can do basically whatever you want, as long as your co-host agrees with you.

Some Schedule Flexibility

Any time a project involves more than just you, things can get complicated, and a podcast is no exception. The good news is, the fewer the number of people who are involved, the less likely you're going to run into issues around foundational elements of producing your podcast, such as finding a time to record. Scheduling and producing a non-interview, co-hosted podcast is certainly easier than scheduling and producing a podcast with a guest who isn't used to your routine and doesn't care about your schedule as much as his own.

Co-Host Format - The Cons

Stale Content

Like a solo-format podcast, it's easy for a co-hosted podcast to get stale. Everything you're likely to burn through on a solo-format podcast — personal experiences and stories, knowledge of the subject you're talking about, and the way the content is delivered — can easily become repetitive. Plus, your interaction with a co-host can get stale.

Imagine the interaction between two television characters who are dating (or potentially dating). The first season, it might be interesting…

- Will he ask her out?
- He was so close to asking her out!
- Yeah!! He did it and they're going on a date.
- Now they're in a committed relationship.

Then what? They move in together, he gets fat, she gets a prescription to Prozac, they rarely interact with each other anymore, and they both watch the clock, counting down the minutes until they die.

That would be a boring television show. Which is why television writers add new characters and suspense to keep *tension* within the relationship and keep viewers interested.

Things like:

- An old boyfriend from high school drops by.
- Oops! She's pregnant!
- How did this happen? Was it sabotage?
- Could a one-night-stand be the father?
- Let's go on a talk show and get a paternity test.

Obviously, you're not going to have this specific situation or interaction with a podcast co-host, but similar *tension* is something you should strive for.

A co-host is not a "yes man." The job of co-hosts is to bring things to the conversation that aren't already being said.

Easy To Get Sidetracked

Just because you're involved doesn't make it interesting. And just because you have a co-host whom you love talking with doesn't mean all your conversations are interesting, either.

When creating content with a co-host, it's very important that you constantly ask yourself, *"Do the people who are listening to this care?"*

It's important to bring personality to your podcast. It's important to show listeners that there's a person connected to the voice they hear. But never forget that people don't listen to your podcast because of you, they listen to your podcast because of how it makes them feel. If they could just as easily get those feelings somewhere else, something without *you*, they would.

This rule applies to all hosting formats, by the way. I'm mentioning it here because the problem is most common on co-hosted podcasts.

I had a guy reach out to me for help on his co-hosted podcast. He was trying to break into comedy and knew of my work in the entertainment business.

Every week, he'd get together with a couple of friends to do a weekly "pop culture" podcast, talking about current events and the latest video games, movies, and television shows. When I asked him who he was trying to reach, he told me, "I am my demographic."

This is good! The best way to know your listener is to be your listener.

But nobody wants to listen to a dude get together with a couple of friends, smoke some weed, and play videos games while having random conversations like which flavor of Doritos is best, whether porn star Lisa Ann really looks like Sarah Palin, and the legitimacy of various conspiracy theories.

It's too random, even for a pop culture podcast made for people "just like you."

Keep your niche tight and your conversation focused. If you get off-track, get back on. If something doesn't add to the conversation, edit it out of the final episode.

Easy To Get Derailed

If you have a co-host simply because you're afraid of hosting a podcast on your own, know that you're betting a lot on her and her participation in creating your podcast.

What will you do if your co-host gets sick and can't record a new episode with you? What will you do if your co-host quits or otherwise moves on from working with you? These are questions you need to ask yourself (and have answers for).

Partnership, whether marriage, business, or podcasting, can be difficult at times. It requires both good communication and compromise. And no matter how good you are at good communication and compromise, there will be times when you and your partner won't come to a consensus.

What "not coming to a consensus" looks like:

- Breakup
- Uncomfortable tension within episodes
- Apathy toward episodes
- Lower frequency of episodes
- Increased planning time for episodes

Then what? Are you going to let something like this stop you from podcasting?

Plenty of people have. Obviously, you can find a new co-host, but if you don't bring in the right one, the situation might repeat itself.

Other options to get your podcast back on track:

1. Guest Co-Hosts - You can bring in temporary co-hosts to either try them out before bringing one person in for good. You can make guest co-hosts a permanent thing.

Rotating co-hosts is not a bad format, as it allows you to be the consistent element of a podcast, giving you authority normally reserved for solo hosts. But like an interview-format podcast, bringing in a new co-host for every episode means you're going to spend a lot of time scheduling and bringing people up to speed.

2. Interviews - If you were doing interviews with your co-host, resist the urge to bring in a co-host for more interviews. An interview-based format is a good place for you to step out on your own.

3. Solo - If you're used to doing episodes with a co-host, doing them by yourself probably won't be pretty at first. If you want to go solo though, this is part of the process. You'll never become a great solo podcaster without doing solo podcasts. As a bonus, you'll benefit from the major upside of having the freedom to do whatever you want, whenever you want.

Tips For A Successful Co-Hosted Podcast

Plan Ahead

You and your co-host both need to be prepared before taping an episode. There is no point in having two hosts if only one knows what he's talking about.

What's the topic? What are the main points you want to cover? Who is doing the intro?

Good Communication And Rapport Between Hosts

This should be obvious, but co-hosts need rapport with each other. You don't always have to agree with your co-host, and you shouldn't *always* agree with your co-host, but if you don't genuinely like (or at least respect) each other, listeners are going to know it.

Disconnection between co-hosts will do one of two things. It will immediately turn people off. Or, if people do stick around, it will focus their attention on the discord between you, leaving the valuable content you're creating to be ignored.

Recording Advice

Regardless of whether you record in the same room or from different locations, each host needs to record to an individual track to properly edit and work around various post-production issues, such as inadequate recording level, background noise, and more than one person talking at the same time.

Text Chat

If you're broadcasting live or taking calls during your recording, it's a good idea to have an instant messenger program where you can send and receive messages via text. If you record to tape and edit before releasing, this isn't as necessary, because unneeded communication can be edited out of the final release, but it can still be helpful if you're on a tight production schedule.

Lead And Follow

Like ballroom dancing, there can't be more than one leader on a podcast. Both leaders and followers are equally important in making a co-hosted podcast work.

A leader takes charge of the segment, telling the stories and setting the pace. A follower adds reaction, insight, and details. A follower helps the leader tell his story and moves the segment forward through follow-up questions.

This is a common style on morning broadcast radio. Often, one or two male hosts will take the lead, with backup by a third, female host. For some segments, such as news, the female host will take the lead.

- Establish Roles

The Dick, The Doll, And The Dork

Podcast talent coach Erik K. Johnson describes a common, male-male-female morning show format as, "The Dick, The Doll, and The Dork." It's a three-person show, and each person has a specific role.

The Dork is typically the leader of the show. He's the affable one who is a little bit quirky, the guy everybody loves — the "aw shucks" guy.

The Dick is the jackass who says things he shouldn't be saying. He rubs people a little bit the wrong way. You want to like him, but he's just a little irritating.

The Dork puts the Dick in his place, saying things like, "Oh, don't say that." The two roles bounce off each other. They're the opposites.

The Doll is the brains of the organization. She's the smart one who puts *everybody* in their place. And she's the voice of reason.

As an example of how everybody works together, let's say the show got a letter from a listener named Kim. Kim found another woman's number in her man's mobile phone and she wants to know what she should do about it.

The Dick is going to go, "What's the big deal? You know, it's just another chick."

The Dork will say, "Hold on a second. You don't know what's happening here ..." He's going to be kind of in the middle.

The Doll will say something like, "Kick that guy to the curb. There's plenty more fish out there!"

Whether you use "The Dick, The Doll, and The Dork" organization for your co-hosted podcast or you use something else, remember that you must know your role and you have to stay in your role because that's what people expect of you. If you change your role in a co-hosted show, it messes with the chemistry. For example, if the Dork starts saying everything the Dick does, then someone is not needed.

Be a co-host, not a parrot.

Boundaries

Have you ever been in a conversation with a couple when one drops a bombshell about the other? For example, a wife says something like, "When Nick and I first started dating, he got arrested trying to solicit a prostitute who happened to be an undercover cop ..."

Nick is uncomfortable. You're uncomfortable. Even the hooker, if she was listening, would be blushing.

It's a bad situation for everybody.

Boundaries about what's considered appropriate to discuss are variable. You'd think it would be obvious that a person wouldn't want to talk publicly about something like paying for sex, or drug use, or [insert thing you'd never talk about here], but some people think nothing of it.

Which is exactly why you need to be clear with any co-hosts about topics and personal information you don't feel comfortable talking about.

Topics you may want to set boundaries on:

- Children
- Your marriage, significant relationship, or lack of either
- Personal finances
- Details about your life such as where you work, where you live, or where somebody could find you
- Things you've experienced that you'd rather not share publicly — DUI charges, domestic abuse, drug use

- Your association with specific groups — Alcoholics Anonymous, Freemasons, Communist Party

Boundaries often are within the middle ground, instead of a simple "yes or no" rule as to whether something is allowed. For example, if you talk about your kids, perhaps you have restrictions not to mention their names. Or, if you want to talk about your work, not giving specific details which would allow somebody to identify where you work.

Coming up with boundaries is up to you. The one boundary I recommend to everybody with a co-hosted show, though, is "Never make your co-host look bad."

Don't Be An Asshole

"Never make your co-host look bad" goes beyond saying insulting things about your co-host. It also includes anything you wouldn't want to be on the receiving end of such as being one-upped, being ignored, or always being disagreed with.

Remember, the focus of both you and your co-host is to keep episodes moving forward. You're on the same team. A podcast isn't the place to work out personal issues between people.

Is This Thing On?

Hell yes it's on! By the time you hit record, you need to know what you're going to talk about. The only thing worse than listening to a podcast host wonder out loud what the topic of the episode he's recording should be is when two or more people do it together.

Systems

Don't reinvent the wheel every time you do a new episode. Have a system in place where you either handle everything or episode preparation is split between you and your co-host(s).

Here's a template for you to use:

1. Get together with your co-host(s) and brainstorm ideas for possible episodes based on your individual experiences related to your podcast's topic as well as feedback and requests you've received from listeners. The idea is to come up with as many ideas as possible, so there should be little to no filter on what you write down. For this part of the process, you want quantity over quality.

2. Go through the raw list of episode ideas you created in Step 1 with a filter, dropping the bad ideas (or modifying them so they're good) and adding potential episodes you didn't think of the first time around.

3. Take your now even bigger list of episode ideas, come up with a "hook" you can build everything around, and create outlines with core ideas that support each topic. The majority of the time, this will be the part of the episode creation process in which you discover if you have enough content to create a compelling episode, if you simply have a "segment" that should be included within another episode, or if the idea is junk and should be canned.

If an episode idea makes it this far, put it on your calendar to record it.

4. Before recording, take the rough outline of the basic episode and once again consult with your co-host(s). Does everything make sense? What needs to be added? What needs to be removed? Come up with a basic roadmap of where the show should go and what your overall positions are about each topic.

In addition to coming up with the "meat" of each episode, come up with the soft content you're going to cover. This includes personal intros and stories to connect with listeners emotionally and get them ready to receive your main content, any specific promotions or announcements you need to make, and also anybody you need to recognize within the episode.

To hear examples of soft/intro content, listen to any episode of my podcast, *RED Podcast.*

NOTE: On occasion, topic ideas that work on paper don't work as well in the studio. When this happens, ditch the idea as soon as you realize what's going on. If something isn't working at any point during the episode creation process, don't force it.

1. The episode audio is edited and the file people will download is created.
2. Episode notes are written.
3. An episode-specific graphic is created.
4. The downloadable file and episode-specific graphic is uploaded to a media host.
5. The episode is published.

That's it. Every co-hosted episode is created this way. And like the episode itself, you should know ahead of time who is responsible for what.

Which Hosting Format Is Right For You?

All podcast formats have their pros and cons. And just because somebody is having success with a certain format doesn't mean that you'll have that same level of success.

There are as many ways to work within a specific hosting format as there are podcasts. To get a better understanding of options available to you for your podcast, listen to at least a dozen other podcasts and see which show format and style personally resonates with you.

Then think about producing episodes in the format you like best.

Will you be able to easily fit recording into your schedule and be flexible about your schedule when working with others on an interview or co-host format podcast?

Do you have the time, stamina, and interest to pre-qualify guests, interview them, and edit their mistakes?

Are you ready to take 100% responsibility for a solo format podcast?

In the end, the only way to truly know which hosting format is best for you is to jump in and experiment. And keep experimenting! If the hosting format of your podcast (or anything else about it) isn't working, you can always change it.

A Bonus Hosting Format – Putting Your Listeners To Work

Ryan Gray is a former Flight Surgeon in the United States Air Force. He's host of several podcasts designed for medical doctors and students, including *The Premed Years* and *The MCAT Podcast.*

One of biggest issues both medical doctors and students face is isolation. The practice of medicine is a stressful one and "community" among those who do this kind of work is often lacking.

All podcasts, if done right, provide some sense of community for listeners. Ryan's podcast *MedDiaries* takes this to a new level by having listeners provide the majority of the content.

Here's how it works:

Listeners call a phone number attached to a robust voicemail system and are greeted by an auto-attendant with the following message:

"Thank you for calling MedDiaries. We're glad you found us and that you're willing to share your story. Our lawyers are making us say this next part: By recording your diary entry or feedback, you understand that we will use it for the podcast and any other means we think will help others. We will retain the rights to your message forever."

Before recording starts, callers hear additional reminders that:

1. Recordings will be made public and released to the world.
2. Callers shouldn't say anything that could easily identify them.

Recordings are then put together to create new episodes. "Diary" episodes are released at the beginning of the week. Feedback on those episodes, also taken via the voicemail line, is received and released at the end of the week.

While this is similar to "listener feedback" segment options mentioned earlier, it also differs considerably, as messages can be up to 30 minutes in length and are the basis for the entire show.

All Hosting Formats Are Flexible

All hosting formats can be mixed up, changed up, and otherwise delivered in the way that best works for you. One option is to use differently hosted segments within a podcast episode.

Mark Maron's *WTF Podcast* does this every episode. Each starts with an extended solo segment that's followed by a one-on-one interview.

Crooked Media's *Pod Save America* rotates between several hosting formats:

1. A co-hosted discussion.
2. A co-hosted discussion, followed by a co-hosted guest interview.
3. A co-hosted discussion, followed by a one-on-one guest interview.

4. A panel discussion (usually done in front of a live audience) followed by a guest interview.
5. A panel discussion (in front of a live audience) followed by audience questions and interaction.

CHAPTER 005

YOUR PODCAST NAME (AND IDENTITY)

Keep it short. That's the first rule of naming for a couple of reasons. One is that iPhone podcast apps, podcast listings in Apple Podcasts, and other ways your podcast will be consumed have limited room to work with. The shorter the name of your podcast, the better chance the full name will be listed.

Beyond the limitations of podcast directories and software, the shorter the name of your podcast, the more memorable it will be, the easier it is for people to type, and the easier it is for you to put the name in the limited space you'll have within show and episode graphics.

Your podcast title should be specific and to the point. It's far better to call your podcast *How To Make Money Online* than *Makin' Bank* or *Cha-Ching, Bitches!*

The best option for your podcast name is something that stands on its own, without help from a description or subtitle.

A podcast name that promises a solution to an existing problem will get more attention than a name that focuses on prevention of something.

People want help with their current situations, not advice on future issues may never happen.

How To Lose 100 Pounds is a solution to a problem. *Obesity Prevention Podcast*, as the name suggests, focuses on prevention.

Unless your podcast is about puns, avoid puns. And even then, a podcast name like *So Much Pun* or *That's Punny* might take people hearing it a few times before they'd get the joke and actually look up *So Much Pun* or *That's Punny* instead of *So Much Fun* or *That's Funny*.

The same thing happens when you mix numbers and letters or misspell common words trying to be cool. Titles like *GR8 Marriage* or *3133+ Hackers* confuse people.

What was the name of that Prince song?

"I Would Die 4 U"

"I Would Die 4 You"

"I Would Die For U"

You get the idea. For your podcast, it's YOU, not U. It's AND, not N.

If you don't take my advice on this, at the very least, get a .com domain name for each possible spelling. For example, GR8marriage.com *and* greatmarriage.com.

Along these lines, beware of clever. A podcast about hair called *Curl Up And Dye* is confusing for the reasons above, plus it's a name that has been used way too much for salons already. Every city in the U.S. has a hair salon called Curl Up And Dye.

Don't Name It After Yourself

Unless you're a household name, don't name your podcast after yourself. Even most people who are household names would be better off not doing this for a couple of reasons.

1. Naming a podcast after yourself can hurt its growth.

The reason you know *The Oprah Winfrey Show* on television or *The Glenn Beck Program* on radio is because these shows, and others like them, were launched to captive audiences using already established networks. When either one aired, listeners had few other content options, all of which were similar.

Podcasting doesn't work like this. There are hundreds of thousands of options for people to choose from. There is no "network" that forces these options upon people. If somebody is listening to you, it's because she wants to.

Podcasting doesn't force content on listeners via an established network and distribution system — listeners have to find us. They do that by searching for the subjects that they're interested in.

2. You want options.

You want the option to leave your show without damaging it. That's hard to do when the show has your name in the title.

The Adam Carolla Show is dependent on Adam Carolla. Without him, it doesn't exist. That's one reason why his network's spinoff podcasts are hosted by other people.

Did you see *Home Alone 3?*

Of course you didn't see it. I did casting for *Home Alone 3* and I didn't even see it. The movie wasn't bad (according to reviews), but few saw it because the actor everybody associates with *Home Alone,* Macaulay Culkin, wasn't even in it.

Don't let something similar happen to what you create. Being dependent on a "key man" will kill your podcast.

3. You are not your show.

The flipside of a show being dependent on you is that you can become dependent on your show. Anybody who has ever had success with his own radio or television show will tell you that, when things are going well, you have *a lot* of friends.

What happens when your ratings drop or your show gets canceled? Many of those "friends" disappear.

But *you* didn't get canceled, your show did. And while your celebrity might have lost a little heat, even with a canceled show, you're far from over.

When the show goes away, *the show* goes away. You, as a talent, celebrity, or influencer, *do not* go away.

You are bigger than your show. Your name is worth something. Don't simply throw it on the podcast you host for ego reasons or, if you're already established, a cheap hit of promotion.

An Old-School (And Sneaky) Trick

Before the Internet, if you wanted to get connected with a needed service provider, the first place you'd go was the phone book. Specifically, the "yellow pages."

Let me explain the concept, as many people have never used yellow pages.

All businesses with phones were listed in a big book with thousands of pages and tens of thousands of other businesses. To make it easier to find the correct business, everything was organized alphabetically by category. For example, "book stores" would be listed before "plumbing services."

If you needed a plumber, you'd look up "plumbing services" and the alphabetized listings would start all over again, this time based on the name of the company. "Abbot's Plumbing" would be before "Zach's Plumbing."

If you didn't know what you were looking for, you'd start at the beginning of the category and go down the list until you found a name that resonated with you or, if location mattered, a business based upon that. Many people would call the first number listed.

Which is why plumbing companies (and others) started to pick company names that would appear earlier within the alphabetical list. "AAA Plumbing" instead of "Abbot's Plumbing," for example.

And if a company wanted to be really sneaky, they'd call themselves something like "A AAA Plumbing." The extra A? That stood for "Asshole."

Many podcast directories are organized using a similar system. In Apple Podcasts, for example, categories are listed in alphabetical order. Within the category, users are given the option to sort podcasts by "featured" (popularity) or "name" (alphabetically).

In the Apple Podcasts directory, the majority of users sort podcasts by popularity. With hundreds of thousands of podcasts included, this is the most effective way for users to find quality content. If a user chooses the "name" (alphabetical) option though, those with podcast names that start closer to the front of the alphabet will have an advantage over those that come later.

If you can make the name of your podcast something like "A [Podcast Name]" or, if you don't mind the criticism you'll get from a name like

"A AAA [Podcast Name]," you'll be displayed higher on lists that are alphabetically sorted. Over a long period of time, the extra exposure you get by doing this can be substantial.

YourPodcast.com

When it comes to domain names for your podcast, the best-case scenario is that you'll be able to get a .com domain name that's the exact name of your podcast. Alternative suffixes such as .co, .net, or .us aren't nearly as valuable because the majority of people automatically type .com when entering a web address and you'll lose not only people typing in your domain, but also traffic from social media, forums, and blogs, because links from those places are more likely to be wrong.

If the .com domain that's just the name of your podcast isn't available, you have a few options:

1. You can buy it from whomever owns it.
2. You can also add "podcast" to the end, such as REDpodcast.com.
3. You can use an abbreviated name, such as EOFire instead of *Entrepreneurs On Fire.*

You can create a domain name from a catchphrase or a common saying used in your podcast.

Phoebe Judge opens every episode of her podcast, *Criminal,* with, "I'm Phoebe Judge and this is *Criminal.*" Her domain is ThisIsCriminal.com.

You have similar alternative domain options:

ListenTo_____.com

_____Now.com

Go_____.com

_____Online.com

WeAre_____.com (for a co-hosted podcast)

Play_____.com

_____Stories.com

Your Podcast's Subtitle

A great title is important to your podcast. A great subtitle "backs up" the main title and makes it even more powerful.

What a subtitle does:

- Identifies the podcast's target audience
- Brings people in (or excludes them) via differentiation
- Lists benefits of taking action by listening and subscribing
- Shows movement — how listeners will benefit by listening

Example ... *The Side Hustle Show*

This is a podcast hosted by Nick Loper. "Side hustle" is a common phase among entrepreneurs which, more or less, means something you do for money other than your main job or business.

But let's say you don't know what "side hustle" means. Or you're looking to do something full-time.

How do you know if *The Side Hustle Show* is for you? The subtitle — *Business Ideas for Part-Time Entrepreneurs.*

The subtitle shows *exactly* who this podcast is for and, by doing that, excludes the people it isn't for. Sure, a full-time entrepreneur could probably get some great ideas from *The Side Hustle Show*, but it's not made for full-time entrepreneurs. And because of that, the part-timers, who are often neglected and have to settle for "full-time entrepreneur" content, love *The Side Hustle Show* even more.

When thinking of a subtitle for your podcast, consider "movement" – the destination people will find themselves if they listen to your podcast. Using *The Side Hustle Show* as an example, consider where "part-time entrepreneurs" who listen to it will be if they take action on what they learn.

Perhaps, *The Side Hustle Show — Make A Full-Time Income With Your Part-Time Business.*

Or, *The Side Hustle Show — Turn Your Part-Time Hobby Into A Full-Time Business.*

Be specific, don't repeat yourself, and use keywords that potential listeners will be searching for. Also keep in mind that the best subtitle in the world won't fix a bad title.

Your Podcast's Description

A listener should know what your podcast is about from the title and subtitle alone, but the "description" field in Apple Podcasts and other podcast directories is what will likely make a potential listener commit to taking a chance on you.

A properly-worded description will cause a listener to say, "This podcast was made just for me."

To do this, your description should let people know:

- Who the podcast is for
- The topics your podcast covers
- What the results of listening are

The title of my podcast, *RED Podcast*, is brandable, but not very specific if you don't know the meaning behind *RED*. To clarify what it's about, I use the sub-title, "The Marketing Podcast For Experts."

But what does "experts" mean?

That's where the description comes into play:

"Build your authority, turn customers into evangelists, and unleash the hidden money in your business. How to take your idea and make a name for yourself, within your industry and beyond. This is the podcast for bloggers, podcasters, speakers, marketers, nonfiction authors, and other creative entrepreneurs who want more impact, influence, and income."

It's both keyword-rich and very specific as to who the podcast is for and what people can expect when listening.

Another popular business podcast, *The Fizzle Show*, is in the same situation. What does "fizzle" mean?

Like *RED*, "Fizzle" is easy to remember. It's a short, easily-brandable name that is easy for current listeners to pass along. These word-of-mouth recommendations can help get somebody to pull up a few episodes via search, but few people are likely to commit via listening (or subscribing) from the short, non-descriptive titles alone.

For *The Fizzle Show*, it's the description that sells it:

"A podcast for online business builders who want to earn a living doing something they care about. If you're interested in self-employment, work/life balance, making stuff that grows an audience, and all the modern online business stuff, you're in the right place."

Every Word Matters

People are busy, and you're competing with *thousands* of other podcasts. The quicker you can get to the point and get buy-in from somebody reading your description, the better.

Just because you have the ability to use an unlimited number of words in your description doesn't mean you should. Many people skip over a description entirely if it looks like too much to read.

Avoid a description like this:

"The Jimmy Johnson Show is all about you! On this podcast, Jimmy shares essential information to help you and your business grow. Listening to this podcast will increase your leadership ability and add value to your life. Every single episode is packed with value. You'll learn strategies that will make you look at leadership and life in a new way and learn to focus on what really matters. Jimmy will teach you practical, easy-to-use strategies that will help you improve your leadership and grow your business. The format of each episode is simple — one hour of incredible interviews with successful business people, followed by action steps you can immediately implement to help you grow your business. Here's what you'll learn — leadership, sales skills, team building, communication, life planning, communication styles, goal setting, business automation, outsourcing, crowdfunding, search engine optimization (SEO), social media, Facebook, Twitter, YouTube, podcasting, blogging, ebooks, affiliate marketing, how to get more done, and everything else you need to make money online (and offline)."

Reading a description that is too long is like listening to friend who never seems to get to the point.

Cool story, bro.

Don't be *that* guy. Instead, think like a comic with a limited amount of stage time. Cut out excess words that don't add to what you're trying to accomplish.

How I'd write Jimmy's podcast description: "Actionable strategies and real-world advice from successful entrepreneurs to help you to grow your business. Make more money by improving your leadership, communication, and sales skills. Get more done in less time. Enjoy a better work-life balance."

Done.

Imagine you had a weight-loss podcast. Don't wear them out with the specifics of how you're going to do this, like, "Eating less, exercising more, low-calorie meals that don't taste very good, dealing with cravings, skipping dessert, sweating your ass off, and handling backhanded compliments." These things are what's in the way of what people want, which is to "lose weight, look better, and feel better."

Focus on the results people are going to get, not the work it takes to get there.

The Double-Edge Sword Of Keyword Stuffing

Keyword stuffing is the practice of inserting a large number of keywords into descriptions, titles, and other content in the attempt to artificially increase credibility, notoriety, and search numbers by attaching to somebody with a lot more credibility, notoriety, and search numbers. In podcasting, it's common to see this done within a show's title, description, or author field.

For example, it's not uncommon to see an author labeled something like "Jimmy Johnson | Marketing expert similar to Seth Godin, Guy Kawasaki, Eben Pagan, Frank Kern, and Marie Forleo." Or, "Jimmy Johnson | A comic alternative to Marc Maron, Aisha Tyler, Adam Carolla, Joe Rogan, and Grace Helbig."

This happens within titles of podcasts all the time. For example, "Jimmy Johnson Podcast: Internet Business | Entrepreneurship | Make Money Online." Or "Jimmy Johnson Podcast | Interviews With Celebrities Like Kim Kardashian."

Does it work to get more search traffic? It can. It can also piss people off, make you look like an amateur, and get you banned from certain podcast directories.

Podcast Cover Art – The Foundation

What looks great when it's viewed full-size on a desktop computer isn't nearly as easy to see (or read) when it's compressed to fit on small screens such as mobile phones. Because of this, your podcast cover art should be bold and simple.

This means:

1. Less is more. Don't clutter the space you have with unneeded imagery or text.
2. No more than five words on your podcast cover. Anything more and the font size you'll have to use to fit everything in will be too small to easily read on a mobile device.
3. No "fancy" fonts. Avoid fonts that make people work to figure out what you're trying to say, including handwritten and "cursive" style fonts.
4. Use contrasting colors. No dark text on a dark background or light text on a light background.
5. No text on top of a photograph or complicated background as this will make it difficult to read.

Podcast Cover Art – The Big Picture

Before people hear your podcast, they'll see a visual representation of your podcast. Because of this, all graphics for your podcast should visually communicate what people will get when they listen.

Imagine walking into a bookstore. You expect the romance books to look a certain way, the business books to look a certain way, and the religious texts to look a certain way.

People expect the same thing when looking at podcast cover art. If you have a business podcast, it needs to look like a business podcast. If you have a comedy podcast, it needs to look like a comedy podcast.

This isn't to say you can't be creative, or should use generic imagery that everybody else seems to be using, but you shouldn't have to explain what's on the "inside" of your podcast when somebody sees your cover art for the first time – it should be (at least somewhat) obvious.

You know what's not obvious? A smiling person next to a microphone.

Unless you're a celebrity with a face that's recognizable when placed inside a very small square, I suggest leaving off any photos of yourself and focusing on artwork with text (the title) that explains what your podcast is about.

There are two reasons for this:

1. **You have limited space.** You need as much room as possible to convey important things about your podcast and photos often take up 50% or more of that space.
2. **Not having a photo leaves some mystery.** Mystery is interesting.

People are listening to you, not watching you. Let them find out who you are via your voice.

Think about the popular radio hosts. Do you know what Terry Gross looks like? Ira Glass? Delilah?

It doesn't matter. You know them and feel connected to them because of their voices.

A quick story ...

Jack Johnson was a music manager in Nashville. In 1965, he signed a young artist to a contract with the RCA Victor record label, where the artist caught the ear of producer Chet Atkins.

The artist, Charley Pride, was black. His style of music, country, was primarily white.

For the first two years of his career, Johnson made sure *none* of Pride's photos were on his album artwork. This wasn't to insult Pride — it was to force potentially biased listeners to connect with his voice.

Once that happened, success followed.

By the early- to mid-1970s, Pride had become the best-selling performer for RCA Records since Elvis Presley. He's had 39 No. 1 hits on the Billboard Hot Country Songs charts.

This is the power of "mystery" and getting people to connect *only* with your voice.

Society is much more open-minded today, but photos are a double-edged sword. If you're extremely good-looking, people will have judgement about that. If you wear religious headwear, people will have judgement about that. If you're older (or younger), people will have judgement about that.

And some people just won't like you.

In 2011, radio host Dave Ramsey started a spinoff podcast of his syndicated radio show, *The Dave Ramsey Show*. The title was *EntreLeadership*.

Dave Ramsey has *never* been the host of *EntreLeadership*. Still, as a podcast produced by his company, it was decided to put his photo on the cover art.

Was it an ego play? Maybe. Regardless, Dave Ramsey arguably has enough recognition among listeners that his photo on a podcast's cover art could help that podcast get more listens.

However, if you can't stand Dave Ramsey and don't want to listen to him, you're going to skip *EntreLeadership* and listen to a podcast that he's not involved with.

The double-edged sword strikes again. For every person you gain by using a photo of yourself, another will skip over you.

Today, the artwork for *EntreLeadership* is all text, with no photos of Dave Ramsey or any of the three hosts he's used.

Will The Real Podcast Host Please Stand Up?

Grammar Girl is a podcast on grammar hosted by Mignon Fogarty. Each episode provides short, friendly tips to improve your writing.

"Short and friendly" isn't what most people think of when they think of learning grammar. To deliver content in this way, *Grammar Girl* is big on personality.

Yet her name, Mignon Fogarty, doesn't appear in the title of the podcast or the byline. The image of "Grammar Girl" used in the artwork looks like clipart.

Why?

Because *Grammar Girl* was designed to be bigger than the host. Should Mignon Fogarty ever want to walk away from it, it will be much easier to replace a "character" than her.

Your podcast can be bigger than you, if you're open to that. It can live longer than you, if you're open to that. The first step is putting the podcast, not you, front and center on its cover art.

CHAPTER 006

COMMUNICATING YOUR MESSAGE

When it comes to podcasting, "good" is subjective. What lights one person up is another person's cure for insomnia.

Without the rules and limits of traditional broadcast media, we have the freedom to create whatever we want, but lack of limitations is also one of the big downsides of podcasting. With so few filters, anybody can be a "podcaster" with very little work.

And a lot of people are doing just that … As *The Onion* once proclaimed in a headline, "250 Million Americans Still Need Guests On Their Podcasts This Week."

According to the article, "No podcasters will consider simply not releasing an episode this week, as not one of them wants to risk losing any of the 14 listeners they have been steadily cultivating for the past year and a half."

It's funny because it's true. And if you're somebody who considers podcasting more than just a hobby, it's also frustrating.

Fortunately, by following a few simple format rules, you can rise above the noise with quality episodes and content people will respond to.

Our Fragile Egos

Wal-Mart sells more clothing than any other retailer in the country. Part of this likely has to do with great distribution and low prices, which make its clothing easily accessible. But there's another reason people love to buy clothing at Wal-Mart that few talk about and many others are completely unaware of …

Vanity sizing.

In other words, the Size 8 dress you buy at Wal-Mart may very well have a tag that says Size 6, or even Size 4.

Which is bigger? Regular-size Trojan condoms or LifeStyles' "King XL" size?

Neither. They're both the same size.

Vanity sizing works both ways. But the label is only icing on the cake. The only thing that *really* matters when it comes to clothing, condoms, and podcasts is, "Does this fit me?"

Copywriters who write direct mail sales letters have a saying about length, "It's never too long, only too boring." But keeping people entertained is only part of the equation when determining how long your podcast episodes should be.

Yes, size matters in podcasting. Before even hearing so much as an intro, people will make judgments about it based on length.

They'll ask themselves questions like:

- Do I have time to listen to the whole thing?
- Do I want to commit to listening to the whole thing?

- Will I be overwhelmed by this podcast episode?

How long is too long for a podcast episode? For most people, it's much shorter than you think.

Brevity

There's a rumor – maybe it's true – that there are cultures who believe we are born having a fixed number of words to communicate with. This could mean:

1. A higher power knows exactly how many words you'll say before you die.
2. The more words you use to communicate something, the sooner you'll die.

Regardless of whether or not there is truth to any of this, when it comes to podcasting, nothing good comes from too much talking. If you want a successful podcast, you need the ability to get to the point.

People are busy. If you can't get to the point quickly, they'll stop listening to you and go find somebody who can.

A focus on brevity forces you to focus on what's really important about your message. Comic Rik Roberts, host of *School Of Laughs* podcast, has a great exercise for aspiring comedy writers to help them do this — transcribe your joke word-for-word, then go through it one word at a time, removing all unnecessary words that don't add to the joke and delay you from getting to the punchline.

Standup comics, even those who are established, often perform as part of a multi-person show and have a limited amount of stage time. It's not uncommon for an upcoming comic to be on stage for just three to five minutes and, during this time, he wants to deliver as many jokes as possible.

The same concept applies to you and your podcast. Listeners have a limited amount of time with you, so make the most of it.

Rik's "write tight" philosophy will help you cut unnecessary elements from *your* message and keep your podcast moving forward. Listen to and transcribe the intros, the outros, and the segues of your last five episodes. You'll be amazed at how many of the words you've said that don't need to be there.

When podcast listeners get exhausted, they stop listening. Forever.

You won't make fans by wearing them down with long episodes. You make fans by being deliberate in the content you create and getting to the point as quickly as possible.

Respect listeners by creating episodes that easily fit into their busy lives. Consider brevity as you are outlining and recording episodes. And if you find something when editing that doesn't move your podcast forward, cut it.

Your listeners will thank you.

25 Minutes Is Best (For Most Podcasts)

According to the U.S. Census Bureau, the average travel time to work in the United States is 25.4 minutes. Because most podcasts are consumed in cars, if you want to give listeners a complete experience, an episode length of around 25 minutes is the best way to do that.

Other reasons to consider a 25-minute episode length:

- Entertainment consumers have been trained to focus for this length of time. If you were to take out commercials from a "30-minute" television show, which we do via DVR, Netflix, and commercial-free torrent downloads, you're left with roughly 21 minutes of content.
- Most treadmill workouts in the gym, another place where podcast listening is prominent, are equal to either 30 or 60 minutes, enough for listeners to listen to one or two complete episodes.
- 25 minutes is long enough to have valuable content, but short enough for you to outline, record and edit frequent episodes.

A 10-Minute Podcast?

The more frequently you release episodes of your podcast, the more downloads you'll get. This is due largely in part to subscribers who choose to receive new podcast episodes automatically and increased search engine traffic, since search engines have more content to work with.

This "daily podcast" genre has brought with it two things:

1. The highly-scripted interview or Q&A format
2. Shorter podcasts (10 minutes or less)

For most podcasters, this is the only way to keep up with a high release frequency.

Highly-scripted interviews allow guests to prepare answers ahead of time, which speeds up the recording process and reduces the need for editing. It also speeds up recording and editing even more by making episodes shorter.

A Q&A format, where the focus of each episode is answering a simple, very focused question, either prepared ahead of time or sent in by a listener, is equally formulaic. Read a question, answer the question.

It's possible to answer a question or do an interview in a short period of time, but the shorter your episodes are, the better you need to be at getting to the point. Even with great hosting skills, standard podcast content, such as introductions, outros, and advertising can take several minutes to get through. If you only have 10 minutes per episode, these elements can be a substantial chunk of your available time.

Will listeners stick around to hear a podcast that is 30 percent (or more) filler?

How will the people you want to listen to your podcast feel about short episodes?

Many listeners equate length with quality. A podcast considered to be "too short" may not ever get a shot at being heard, regardless of how great the content or host is.

Is a 10-minute podcast too short? Do you have the skills to produce an effective 10-minute episode? That only way to know is to produce some 10-minute episodes and test the reaction.

60+ Minutes

There are always exceptions to every rule. One exception for a successful podcast where each episode is over an hour long is Dan Carlin's *Hardcore History*. With the average episode length being between three and four hours, *Hardcore History* is one of few successful podcasts to consistently release episodes this long.

But keep in mind that new episodes are only released every two to five months — something else that breaks common "best practices" and is also a reminder that making such lengthy episodes compelling takes time.

Also keep in mind that, before he was online, Dan Carlin was a professional radio host. He has years of broadcasting experience.

There are other exceptions. Several podcasts, based on traditional morning radio shows, do very well with an extended episode length.

And many podcasters who were celebrities *before* they got into podcasting can get away with episodes that are very loose, very long, and on the verge of rambling, simply because they're famous.

Anything is possible in podcasting … For somebody.

Is it possible for you? Maybe.

If you're hell-bent on doing a long-format podcast, go for it. If you want to play the odds though, you're far more likely to reach a lot of people with your message by producing hyper-focused, shorter-length episodes.

But First, A Word From Our Sponsor

How long should ads within your podcast be? Like your podcast itself, brevity is important, but more important is that ads work within the main content of your podcast episodes.

Creative segues to ads that that are a match for your listeners and add something to the story you're telling will get listened to. Ads that interrupt a listener's experience will be skipped.

What's the big lesson here? Stop reading the sponsor-provided bullet points and ad copy verbatim and make your sponsor part of the overall story you tell on your podcast.

Stephanie May Wilson of *Girls' Night* does this. Her ads frequently use variations of this format:

1. A quick transition letting listeners know an ad is coming.
2. Thanking the sponsor for supporting *Girls' Night.*
3. Why sponsorship is important to *Girls' Night.*
4. How she discovered (and connected with) the sponsor.
5. Why she loves the product/service being advertised and listeners will too.
6. How she uses the product/service and has personally benefited from this use.
7. How listeners can use the product/service.
8. General benefits and features of the product/service that add to the story.
9. A promo code that gets listeners a discount on the product/service.
10. A second "thank you" to the sponsor for supporting *Girls' Night.*

It's a lot of stuff, but amazingly, she's able to pack all of these elements in a 60-second ad.

I'm kidding. A single ad on *Girls' Night* can be three minutes or longer.

One sponsor, three minutes. If listeners find your ads helpful and entertaining, they'll stick around for them.

Organizing Your Podcast Episodes

Most people don't eat at McDonald's because they like the food — they eat at McDonald's because they know what they're getting. Whether you're in New York City or Big Arm, Montana, when you walk into a McDonald's, you're going to have pretty much the same experience each time.

You'll know how to order. You'll know where the restrooms are. You'll know what's on the menu.

People who listen to your podcast expect something similar — they want to know what they're getting before they hit play. To give them this, it's good to have a format and organization that is consistent between episodes as well as somewhat like other podcasts. You can be creative with your episode format, but work within boundaries that listeners are used to, so they'll be comfortable when listening to you — this isn't a time to reinvent the wheel.

The First 60 Seconds

Unlike radio, where listeners can tune in at any time during a program, podcasts are consumed from the very beginning of episodes. And because people listen to podcasts on their own time, without being tuned in to a specific "channel" that will clue them in to what they're listening to, you must be diligent about having a standard opening segment that will not only make listeners want to keep listening, but also let them know what they're getting.

Don't assume people are listening to your podcast on something like a smartphone, where show and episode data will be displayed on a screen or, if information is displayed on a screen, they'll be able to look at it. People consume podcasts in a number of different ways, and are often doing other activities while listening, such as driving, that prevent them from reading episode information.

People subscribe to *several* podcasts at a time, playing them in the order they're automatically downloaded. When an episode of your podcast starts playing, you want listeners know it's you without having to look at anything.

Make sure you have the following elements at the beginning of every episode …

Show ID

This is easy and important. At the beginning of each episode, have a short announcement letting the listener know that they're listening to your podcast.

The Productivityist Podcast, for example, has an announcement at the very beginning of each episode that says, "I'm Mike Vardy and this is *The Productivityist Podcast.*"

That's it. It takes three seconds, but it's invaluable when it comes to show branding and making it easy for listeners to know what's playing.

Episode Number

Also easy. Also important.

People like podcasts because they can listen to them whenever and wherever they want. If they don't like a specific section of an episode, they can fast-forward it, and if something needs to be repeated, they can rewind and hear that section again.

As with radio, people flip through podcast episodes to find exactly what they're looking for. Make it easy on them by announcing an episode number at the beginning of each episode, right after a show ID.

Something like, "This is episode number 153" is all you need.

Note that show ID and episode number can be combined. Pat Flynn of the *Smart Passive Income Podcast* does this.

"This is the Smart Passive Income Podcast with Pat Flynn, session number 157."

Episode Teaser

Don't assume that just because people subscribe to your podcast that they won't skip to other podcasts they're also subscribing to. To help prevent this, you need a teaser within the first 60 seconds of each podcast episode that makes people want to keep listening.

An episode teaser is a quick and to-the-point introduction that lets listeners know what's coming and gives them a reason to keep listening.

On *RED Podcast*, I combine a show ID, episode number, and episode teaser at the beginning of each episode.

> *"This is episode number 158. The subject? The Superfan! How to develop fans who give you more money and spread your message for you. That's coming up ..."*

> *"This is episode number 165. My guest has over 1000 people giving him money for something they could get for free. How does he do it? That's what we're talking about ..."*

> *"This is episode number 174. I learned some big lessons when I was in the music business. One of them almost got me arrested. That's coming up ..."*

Because I'm talking over intro music, with an announcer introducing the podcast at approximately 10 seconds in, the teasers for *RED Podcast* are *always* 10 seconds or less.

Dave Jackson of *The School Of Podcasting*, who teases upcoming episodes *without* music behind him, does something similar. For example:

> *"Today on episode number 460 of The School Of Podcasting. I want to give you my insights on finding more time to podcast. I've talked about this in the past and I've got a new dimension that I want to throw into this. And we've got Hani from Simple Podcast Press. Wait until you hear about the new feature. Hit it, ladies!" (Cue theme music)*

Music behind your teaser is optional, but can be good as it helps to listeners identify which podcast is playing.

Episode Teaser Blueprint

Teasers are often recorded *after* the episode itself, once you know for sure what you've talked about. Put the teaser at the front of the final episode file during editing.

Here's a three-part format for you to base your teaser on:

1. The Show ID and Episode Number.

"This is (show name) (episode number)."

2. Details about the episode.

If you're interviewing a guest:

"On this episode, my guest is (guest name) and we're talking about …"

Or, if it's just you:

"On this episode, I'm talking about …"

3. The topics you'll be covering.

OPTION A: "(Topic 1), (Topic 2) and (Topic 3)."

OPTION B: "(Topic 1), (Topic 2) and (Topic 3). And we'll be answering the question, (insert question about related topic here)."

General Teaser Advice

Get to the point. I suggest making your teasers 15 seconds or less.

If you've ever been to Costco, you've likely been asked by a product rep, "Would you like to sample some (insert food here)?"

If you say yes, she'll give you a little sample, not a full portion.

That's the tease. Don't give people the full meal, just a taste that makes them want more.

Podcast Intro

This is the "theme" to your podcast. It sets the tone of things, introduces you, and creates curiosity.

At most, this needs to happen within 20 seconds. People discover podcasts like they flip through television channels. If you don't work fast to grab their attention, they're not going to stick around long.

There are three important elements to a great intro:

1. Music (or Sound Effects)
2. Copy
3. Voice Talent

Use The Right Music

When it comes to music for your podcast, there are a couple of things to consider. First of all, you want the "right" music. That means music that adds to the message you're trying to convey through your podcast. It also means using music you have the legal right to use.

I'm not an attorney, so this is not legal advice. I did spend over 20 years in the music business though, doing hundreds of music licensing deals for film and television, so here's some "non-legal" advice for you when it comes to using music in your podcast ...

Legally, you can't use a song you don't have the rights to.

It doesn't matter if you're only using 30 seconds of it.

It doesn't matter if you don't charge for your podcast and don't sell advertising.

It doesn't matter if you consider your use of the music "promo" for the artist.

The bottom line is if you use music on your podcast, you must have the legal right to do so.

Want to use a popular song recorded by a well-known artist? Because technology innovates faster than our legal system and podcasts fall into a grey area of being able to be streamed *and* downloaded, using most songs legally is a far too complicated process that will make you think twice about doing it. Look up "performance royalties" and "mechanical royalties" on Google to find plenty of information.

Can you use music without permission? Not legally.

Will you get in trouble when you use music without permission? Probably not. The issue you're far more likely to face is from "podcast" companies that also happen to be in the broadcast radio business, like iHeart Radio or Spotify. If you use music on your podcast, including your theme music and bumpers, you'll have to have legal permission before these companies will distribute your podcast.

Here's the good news.

A quick search for "royalty-free music" will get you hundreds of thousands of songs you can use for a one-time licensing fee. Along with a high-quality download of the music itself, you'll also receive the needed paperwork should anybody question your legal right to use it.

How To Pick Good Intro Music For Your Podcast Intro

With hundreds of thousands of royalty-free songs to choose from, you're going to have to do a little digging to find music that works for you. Like a stock photo site, there's a lot of filler to work through.

Spend a few minutes listening to search results for common podcast subjects such as "inspirational" and "business" and you're likely to hear something you've heard other podcasters use. This is because most people either don't have the patience to go through enough songs to find something great or because most people don't think the music they use is important.

The music you use is *very* important. It's what sets the mood for everything you do.

What to listen (and look) for:

1. Real instruments.

This is important — especially with drums and horns. You want something that sounds like it was made by a human, not a machine.

What do "fake instruments" sound like? Imagine an employee-training video or network marketing sales pitch from the 1980s. Search "corporate" on major royalty-free music sites and you'll get dozens of examples.

Like your podcast, music connects with people because of its imperfections. Avoid music that sounds like it came from a sterile laboratory.

The one exception to computer-generated sounds and drum machines is if you're looking for something in any of the major electronic genres, such as house, techno, or dubstep. This works because music within these genres is supposed to be made on a computer.

2. Number of downloads

Major royalty-free music sites let you know how many times the songs on their sites have been licensed. Like the charts on Apple Podcasts, this can be a good way to find something of quality, because cream rises to the top, but it's also a good way to end up with something being used by a competitor.

When you license music from a royalty-free music site, other people using that same music is always a risk, because royalty-free music isn't a custom product. Although most of the music licensed on royalty-free sites will be for non-podcast applications that none of your listeners will ever find, there is always a chance that a competitor will use your song, whether by accident or on purpose.

3. Stylistic Similarity

You don't hear circus music before a funeral, even if the dead guy is a clown.

Music sets the mood. If you have a lot of energy, you want the music that introduces you to be upbeat. If you're laid back and mellow, that needs to be reflected in the music you choose. You also need to consider how the music matches the topic you talk about as well.

Imagine this … You download a new podcast. The intro music is high energy, arena rock with big drums and screaming guitars.

The voiceover guy comes on … and he's *shouting*!

"YOU ARE NOW ENTERING THE HOUSE OF EXCELLENCE!!! GET READY!!! HERE'S YOUR HOST … THE MOST EXCELLENT MAN IN THE WORLD!!!"

Then the slickly produced intro fades out and a thin voice cuts through the background hiss…

"Ummmm ... Hello everybody. Ummmm ... Welcome to House of Excellence, the podcast about being excellent."

Not a match.

This is an extreme example, but similar stylistic mismatches happen in podcasting all the time. Everything about your podcast should be congruent. Don't be like that guy who wears jeans in the gym.

4. Simplicity

You want music you can talk over. Avoid songs with vocals, even simple background hooks.

An example: You've got an inspirational podcast, you looked up "inspirational" on a royalty-free music site, and you found an upbeat song with the catchy vocal "You can do whatever you want" repeated over and over again.

It's a good stylistic match for the subject, but anything you say while somebody is singing in the background will get lost. People can only pay attention to one person "speaking" at a time.

5. Get To The Point

Like your podcast itself, your music needs to get to the point. Nobody is going to sit through a long music intro in order for you (or a voiceover person) to have a place to break in.

Play your music, make your point, and get on with the episode. Unless you're doing an "episode teaser" over a song's intro, there should be no more than three seconds of music before an announcer comes in.

As a side note, the music you use also needs to complete the point. That means a strong beginning and strong ending that listeners can count on. Don't use something that could go on forever and just fade it out whenever you need to talk.

Your Podcast Intro Copy

While music sets the mood, the copy you use for your intro enforces it.

Intro copy should tell listeners three things:

1. Who are you?
2. What are you talking about?
3. Why should somebody listen?

Here's an example from *RED Podcast* ...

"This is the RED Podcast – the marketing podcast for experts. How to reach more people. Expand your authority. And deliver your message. Here's your host, David Hooper."

Rik Roberts' *School Of Laughs* uses this ...

"Welcome to The School Of Laughs Podcast. Whether you're an aspiring comedian, a part-time pro, or a speaker who wants to become funnier, this is the podcast for you. We'll break down tools, tips, and techniques to help you get bigger, better, and more bookable."

The Most Ripped-Off Podcast Intro Copy

If you listen to podcasts about business, you've likely heard Pat Flynn's *Smart Passive Income*. Founded in 2010, it's one of the most popular business podcasts online, getting as many as 350,000 downloads *per episode*.

Pat's intro: *"Welcome to the Smart Passive Income Podcast, where it's all about working hard now, so you can sit back and reap the benefits later."*

Anytime something is successful, people copy it. We all do this — we take great ideas and improve on them. That's how business and innovation work.

But don't just copy something almost word-for-word, neglecting to add your own spin and style. For example, *"Welcome to the XYZ Podcast, where it's all about _____, so you can _____ later."*

Using somebody else's words in an intro doesn't set the proper stage for *you* to deliver *your* content.

Voice Talent

Your introduction is the first thing listeners hear and sets up the rest of your podcast. Don't cut corners on voice talent by using your friends and family. Bring in a professional who can deliver your message with authority.

Like music from a royalty-free site, voiceover people are hit or miss. Like the music you choose for your intro, the person who voices your intro copy needs to match the feel and style of what you're doing.

And like music from royalty-free sites, you don't want to use the same voice talent everybody else is using. Your podcast deserves its own, unique sound.

A Simple Alternative

Sometimes less is more. If a "slick" intro isn't a match for your podcast intro, an alternative option is to introduce your podcast yourself.

Jeff Brown of *Read to Lead Podcast* has a "worldview" formula that works perfectly for this.

Here's how he introduces himself:

I believe that intentional and consistent reading is key to/for success in business and in life.

Using Jeff's formula, you can do something similar to create your podcast intro.

This is [PODCAST NAME], [PODCAST SUBTITLE].

My name is _____.

I believe that [KEY BELIEF] (OR: I believe that doing [KEY ACTION])

is _____ (key? instrumental? a must?)

to/for _____ (success/overcoming X/achieving X)

in _____ (this and/or that endeavor).

Personal Segue

There are thousands of podcasts about business. There are thousands of podcasts about parenting, thousands of podcasts about marriage, and thousands of podcasts about relationships.

And success. And making money online. And religion.

What's the "secret weapon" to make your podcast stand out from the crowd?

You.

You're the only thing about your podcast people can't get anywhere else.

Once you've set up your podcast episode by delivering a teaser to keep people listening and an introduction that announces who you are and what people can expect from your podcast, before you deliver the main content of an episode, I suggest having a "bridge" to get listeners connected to you as a person, not just a podcast host. Just a short introduction story on each episode to warm things up, not every single detail of what's happening in your life.

This short story should showcase and help explain the following things to listeners:

1. Who you are beyond the host of your podcast.
2. Why you believe what you do.
3. What your thoughts on current events or other situations are.

When you know the history behind something, it becomes more interesting. That's why coin collecting is so fascinating to people. Coins aren't just pieces of metal we use as currency — each one is a story of a civilization and culture.

When people know you and your history, *you* become more interesting. Episodes should always focus on listeners, but by sharing a small piece of yourself before getting into the hard content of episodes, that hard content will be better received.

Here's why …

People listen to your podcast because they want the content you provide, and they want to be entertained. Pure content doesn't connect well — it comes off like a college lecture.

If you want people to connect with your content, they need to connect with you. This is done with a combination of personality and stories.

Your personality. Your stories.

Everything we do (and have done) affects who we are and the work we do, including our podcasts. You don't have to share every intimate detail of your life, but if there are elements of your life that relate to the focus of your podcast, why not?

When I retired from music marketing and started to work with creative professionals other than musicians, my plan was to make a clean break. I no longer had the desire to work with musicians and didn't want to attract any more of this work by broadcasting it.

But as you've read in the examples within this book, there are plenty of "music business" experiences I've had which apply to the similar work of marketing podcasters that I'm currently doing. You can't just shut off a big part of your life and pretend it never happened.

Don't take personal experiences for granted. As long as you keep the focus of your podcast on the people listening, sharing these elements of yourself are a great way to bring a unique viewpoint to what you do as well as relate to people in a way that only you can.

Episode Core

This is the meat of your episode, whether it be content from an interview you're doing, a panel discussion, or a monologue.

Your podcast is *your* podcast, so the core of your episodes can be whatever you want it to be. It can be simple, just a couple of big ideas perhaps, or more complicated, with different segments covering different elements that are of interest to people listening.

Regardless of how simple or complicated the core of your podcast is, it must stay focused on the main topic (or related topics) and keep on track to be of interest to listeners. If you jump around too much, you'll lose them.

Your core also needs to be consistent between episodes. In general, people don't like surprises, and listeners to your podcast are no exception. When somebody turns on your podcast, she wants to know you'll give her what she's expecting.

Call-To-Action

What's the purpose of your podcast? This will be the deciding factor on how you end it.

The problem for information-heavy podcasts is that listeners often fail to act on anything that is discussed. This is usually because it's easier to listen to something and think about it than it is to do it, but it can also be because "what to do next" isn't made crystal clear.

Remember, people who listen to your podcast are often doing so in cars, at the gym, or while doing other things. They're physically distracted. Beyond that, depending on where they are in their lives, they're often *mentally* distracted.

For example, let's say you have a podcast about health and fitness. Almost nobody listening to you for the first time hasn't already thought *a lot* about that subject and gathered a ton of related "how-to" information.

So why would somebody listen to your podcast if she already knows the information you're sharing?

It's because she's not looking for information — she's looking for related clarity and direction.

How can you help listeners to get the clarity and direction they're seeking? Advise them to take a single action at the end of every episode. For example, continuing on the health and wellness thread, you could advise listeners to take the next logical step to accomplish what you've talked about during that episode. Then, in future episodes, give listeners additional single steps to guide them down the path necessary to achieve your bigger goal for them.

For a good example of how this is done, listen to the "recap" segments that Dave Chesson does at the end of episodes of his podcast, *The Book*

Marketing Show. These segments summarize content delivered during the episode core, usually via a guest interview, into specific and actionable steps for listeners to take.

Call-To-Connect

Throughout your podcast, you're asking listeners to do a lot — take action on the subject you discuss, read book recommendations, go to sponsor sites, visit past episodes, sign up for your mailing list, leave a review of your podcast on Apple Podcasts, and more.

All of these things are fine within conversation. In other words, if you mention a past episode, it's ok to say, "That episode is available at MyPodcast.com/123." And if you have an ad in the middle of your podcast, it's logical to ask people to visit that advertiser's site.

But know this … A confused mind always says no. You want the same clarity and direction to listeners in your call-to-connect as you use for your call-to-action.

If you give people a ton of information and multiple options for opportunities to connect with you, your message gets confusing. "Too many options" can overwhelm listeners and, when that happens, they won't do *anything.*

Listeners want you to let them know the best way to stay in touch with you. To make things easy on them and get them the best results, like the call-to-action you give after the main content of your episode, ask them to *do one thing* in order to do keep connected and help others connect with you.

This means you pick one of these things:

- Subscribe via Apple Podcasts

- Tell a friend about the podcast
- Sign up for your mailing list
- Subscribe to your newsletter
- Download a free report or other lead magnet
- Visit your website
- Buy your book

It *doesn't* mean, "Leave a review on Apple Podcasts, then hit the subscribe button to make sure you don't miss an episode. Have any friends who would like this podcast? Tell them about it. And make sure you sign up for our mailing list, so I can send you all the latest updates. You can do that at MyPodcast.com. While you're there, make sure to buy my book."

You eventually want people to do *a lot* of things and keep connected with you in multiple ways. Your best bet to make this happen will be to give people the single request of going to your website. Once there, they'll have the options of signing up for your mailing list, subscribing to your podcast, or doing whatever else you want them to do in order for you to stay in touch with them.

This is what I do at the end of every episode of *Build A Big Podcast*.

Here's what it looks like:

"If you've got questions about this episode, feel free to reach out to me directly via BigPodcast.com. While you're there, be sure to download my free 'Audience Attraction Cheat Sheet' with 25 episode templates you can use to create compelling episodes for your podcast."

Once I get people on my site to start a conversation with me or join my mailing list, I can then ask for other things, such as reviews, referrals, and sales.

Call-To-Connect Options

1. Questions And Feedback

Having listeners reach out to you with questions and feedback is one of the best ways for you to further connect with them. As a bonus, it also helps them extend the good feelings they get from listening to your podcast.

The more interaction you have with the people listening to your podcast, the better. Questions and general feedback about your show will keep you better connected with what people want from your podcast, build loyalty and connection among listeners, and keep your show moving forward.

Questions and feedback don't just happen. If you want either, you must ask listeners to take action.

Want more frequent communication with listeners that isn't as overwhelming as email? Have them reach out to you via Twitter. It keeps both questions and feedback focused, as all messages are limited to 280 characters. And because correspondence is public, it invites others to be part of the conversation. Still, to do this, direct people to your website first – don't neglect building your email list.

2. Reviews

Reviews are not a magic bullet to podcasting success. They're nice to have, but probably not worth spending a lot of time pursuing. Most people don't know how to leave reviews on Apple Podcasts (or other podcast directories), so getting reviews can be tedious and time-consuming.

But good reviews can also be helpful for attracting new listeners (more on this below) and they also allow reviewers to feel more connected to you because they're contributing to your access.

Here are three reasons why podcast reviews are helpful:

- Reviews can help people looking for new podcasts decide what to take a chance on.
- Reviews (on many directories) help your podcast to be featured more prominently in search results.
- Reviews are "social proof" that people think your podcast is valuable.

If you want reviews, don't assume people know this. Ask listeners who like your podcast to leave you a review and let them know why reviews are important to you.

3. Tell A Friend

Most people, even those who already listen to podcasts, aren't actively looking for podcasts to listen to. People are busy and don't need more tasks to fill their lives with.

But people *will* listen to a new podcast based on the recommendation of a friend.

Our friends know us and they know what we like. And we know them, so we trust their judgement when they recommend things.

That's why word-of-mouth recommendations are so important. Beyond that, much like reviewing a podcast, when listeners share a podcast with their friends, they feel like they're part of the community surrounding it.

Some professionals live and die by recommendations (or lack thereof). Real estate agents, massage therapists, and others who fall into this category understand how important referrals are and will be quick to let their friends know about your podcast if they enjoy it. But most people don't think this way, because their careers aren't dependent on referrals.

Unless the core audience of your podcast is a group of people in a profession that counts on referrals for business, make sure you communicate to listeners why sharing your podcast with others is important to you and how it will help benefit them as well. This is something you should do, when appropriate, throughout your podcast, not necessarily just at the end.

How can a listener benefit by helping you share your podcast with others?

- It feels good to share something valuable
- Increased status among friends, since you'll be viewed as a tastemaker
- Increased status among members of the podcast's community since you'll be helping the podcast to grow

Coming Next

There are two distinct parts to your podcast — the podcast as a whole body of work and each individual episode as something that stands on its own.

Unless you're already an established celebrity in a non-podcast medium or your podcast has been recommended to a potential listener by one of his friends, an episode topic or person whom you're interviewing are the top elements that will draw new listeners to your podcast.

For a podcast to be truly successful, people must love the entire body of work, not just an individual episode. Individual episodes are a great way for people to discover what you do, but long-term success will require that they stick around for multiple episodes and become part of the community around your podcast.

Podcast downloads are not equal. It's far better to have a download from somebody who loves you as a host, loves your personality, and loves your point of view than a download from somebody who only wants to hear the guest you're interviewing.

Listeners who love you as a host, enjoy your personality, and are stimulated by your point-of-view are far more likely to download *every* episode, because you're the primary reason they're listening, not the episode topic or the person whom you're interviewing.

When you have people "on the hook" and listening to an episode, you need to let them know you have more episodes available. This can be done by mentioning previous topics covered and linking to past episodes as well as letting listeners know what's coming up on future episodes.

Two "Coming Up" Scenarios

1. You can use the "personal intro" segment of your podcast to tease future episodes. For example, when this book was in the process of being written, I gave a quick update on it, then segued into a tease about an upcoming episode I was working on.

   "Speaking of books, I got contacted by Pat Flynn this week. He just finished a book manuscript and is releasing that soon. I'm bringing him in to talk about his writing process in a couple of weeks. If you're interested in how somebody can have a successful blog, two successful podcasts, and run a business while getting a book done, that's coming up on RED Podcast very soon."

2. At the end of your podcast episode, simply mention what you'll be talking about on the following episode.

Here's how I did this on the same episode mentioned in the first scenario, *RED Podcast* #183:

   "Next episode ... This is going to be important for you if you're thinking about writing a book or already have a book in process. I'm talking about hacking the Amazon charts. About hacking New York Times. I learned this from the music business by hacking Billboard charts. I've got the

...cks, I've got the tips, and I'm going to show you how it's done. Maybe you should do it, maybe you shouldn't. I'm going to leave that up to you. That's on the next episode of RED Podcast."

Note that the main topic of the episode with both of these "coming up" teases, *RED Podcast* #183, is how to organize your work setup so you're able to get more done. It has nothing specifically to do with book publishing, Still, both these teasers were able to fit in without issue.

Having a clear focus for your podcast will help you with transitioning between different episode segments, such as "coming up" teases, because everything you talk about will be related.

Even if your transitions aren't flawless, always tease upcoming episodes. Listeners need to know you have more than just the episode they're currently listening to. Teasing additional episodes sets you up as a complete solution to the related problems your listeners are facing.

Consistently putting a tease at the end of every episode will train listeners to listen to the end of every episode, taking them through important aspects of your podcast, such as your call-to-action.

Basic Episode Outline

Here's how to put everything together:

1. **Episode Teaser** - What's coming up ...
2. **Episode Intro** - The "theme music" and announcer, letting listeners know what to expect as far as content and style.
3. **Personal Segue** - Something to connect listeners to you, the host.
4. **Main Content** - The "meat" of the episode and why listeners initially tune in.
5. **Call-To-Action** - A recommended, next-step action based upon the information you've shared.

6. **Call-To-Connect** - An opportunity for listeners to connect with you, to ask follow-up questions or otherwise build a relationship.

7. **"Coming Up" Tease** - What's coming up on future episodes of your podcast.

MODULE 2
PODCAST CONTENT

CHAPTER 007

YOUR PODCAST CONTENT

Content is the lifeblood of a podcast. With great content, you can make *a lot* of mistakes and still be successful. That's not to say you should neglect the basics of a quality podcast, such as editing, having a quiet space in which to record, or using proper microphone technique, but without a foundation of quality content, none of these things (as well as the other "best practices" of podcasting) will breathe life into a podcast.

Think beyond volume, such as episode length or frequency of episodes. Just because you release a new episode weekly (or even daily) doesn't mean your content is worth listening to.

Downloads of your podcast don't matter. People who listen to your podcast matter. If there's nobody on the other end of a downloaded episode, that "download" doesn't count.

Want more listeners for your podcast? Focus on quality content. When quality is your priority, dedicated, engaged listeners will emerge.

How To Never Run Out Of Great Content

Thanks largely in part to John Lee Dumas and his success with *Entrepreneurs On Fire*, more and more independent podcasters are releasing new episodes daily.

On one hand, daily episodes make a lot of sense. The more episodes you have available via podcast aggregator services like Apple Podcasts and Google Podcasts, the better chance you have of somebody discovering your podcast, the more pages you have announcing new episodes on your podcast's blog, and the better chance you have of Google putting those pages in search results.

If you put enough content out into the world, you'll generate traffic. And if you generate enough traffic, you'll be able to make money.

The problem with daily podcasts is creating something people want to listen to with such frequency is *a lot* of work. You have to find something to talk about (or people to interview), you have to plan and outline episodes, you have to schedule appointments, and you have to edit what you've recorded, so people will easily be able to consume it.

Don't shortcut episode creation. While it's possible to create an episode by just talking about whatever's on your mind, "interviewing" whomever you can schedule, and publishing a raw recording as-is, nobody has ever been successful doing this, and it's unlikely you'll be the first.

Daily podcasts are great. There's nothing wrong with taking advantage of the fact the more content you release, the better chance you have of somebody finding it. But you want your content to be *good*.

Consistency of good content is more important than frequency of episodes. If your content is good, people will wait for it.

What Your "Customers" Know

Collecting great content for your podcast is another reason to talk to listeners. Research what's really happening in your market instead of getting your topics third-hand or recycling the same things you've been talking about for years.

Your listeners have problems they're dealing with *now*, this very minute. They have stories of dealing with these problems.

Discover those stories and tell them. Then offer solutions. This is the secret to coming up with great content for your podcast.

Limiting Your Content Options

Just like when somebody with too many choices picks none of them due to being overwhelmed, having no limitations for your podcast content will stall your ability to move forward. Without focus, your message (if you can even call it that), lacks clarity.

Listeners want to know what they're going to get when they listen to you. Limiting what (and how) you discuss topics on your podcast will help to give your ideas focus and a sense of stability listeners are looking for.

Let's say you want to talk about business and entrepreneurship on your podcast. How can you narrow this down so that it will stick out in such a crowded market?

Two things entrepreneurs say they need more of are time and money.

Thinking like this, it's easy to come up with several interesting show (and episode) ideas:

- How To Start A Business With Only $500
- Zero-To-Profit In 90 Days (Or Less)

- Part-Time Entrepreneur — Run A Business Working Only 10 Hours Per Week
- The Weekend Business Owner
- One-Man Operation — A Podcast For Solopreneurs

When you brainstorm *specific* show ideas, content builds upon itself. For example, if you decided to go with the "One-Man Operation" idea for a show, every episode you came up with and every question within those episodes would go back to the specific topic of businesses with only a single person.

So you'd have topics like …

- Using automation to do tasks, since you don't have other people to delegate those tasks to
- Setting up systems to help you get your work done more efficiently, since you have limited energy
- How to get the maximum amount of money for every hour worked, because your time is limited

And *no* topics and questions related to:

- Getting along with co-workers
- Making payroll
- How to hire people

Specific topics help you to go deeper for good ideas that will work and avoid content that isn't a good match for your show.

CHAPTER 008

EPISODE TOPICS

Not all podcast episodes are created equal; episode topics can make or break your podcast. This is important, so listen up.

If an episode topic isn't focused, or your content within that episode doesn't relate to or connect with listeners, you'll lose them. The best possible outcome when this happens is that these people will stay subscribed to your podcast or otherwise listen to additional episodes, but if you lose focus enough times, people will stop listening to your podcast and never come back.

Never.

The good news is that just the opposite of this is true. When you consistently deliver the *right* episode topics and content, you'll dramatically increase your audience and connection with them. They'll listen to your podcast consistently and tell their friends how great you are.

The foundation of being able to consistently come up with quality episode topics is knowing your existing audience and the people you want to attract. If you're unsure about what this means, reread the section entitled "Know Your Audience."

What makes a quality podcast episode:

- Your point-of-view and personality
- A single focus
- Helpful and useful information
- Content that is entertaining, but also gets to the point and is focused on listeners
- Actionable takeaways (especially if your podcast is in the how-to genre)

A quality topic will allow you to have an episode with all of these.

There is no formula for coming up with great topics instantly. Topic creation, like inspiration, happens on its own time. This is especially terrifying when you're on deadline and must get an episode out.

To increase inspiration, remember this ...

Consumption = Production

The more you consume, the more you have to work with as far as content to create from. For example, if your podcast is about business and entrepreneurship, you should be consuming the following types of information about these subjects:

- Business and entrepreneurship blogs
- Non-fiction books on the subject
- Seminars and conferences
- Interviews with top business and entrepreneurship thought leaders
- Other podcasts in this genre

Beyond this, you should be having conversations with like-minded people, participating in online forums. And following people of interest on social media. And subscribing to online newsletters. And reading related magazines.

You don't have to read *everything* and follow *everyone*, but you do want to get good at skimming information and looking for patterns. This is what will give you the fuel to come up with appropriate content for your podcast, as well as know what you shouldn't cover.

Keep A Swipe File

In the advertising and marketing industries, a "swipe file" describes a collection of tested and proven advertising and sales letters. These collections, usually individually curated and for personal use only, are made when somebody sees a well-done piece of advertising or marketing and saves it for later reference.

Swipe files can be collections of anything you can use to get ideas from and podcasters can benefit from creating swipe files of successful episode titles and topics, to give them ideas for their own episode creation.

Your swipe file doesn't need to be fancy. I use a to-do list application called *Things* to organize my "episode ideas" list. When I see a good episode idea (or just think of one), I add it to *Things*. When I create an episode on that topic, I check it off the list.

In general, keeping a swipe file can be a helpful way to keep lists of ideas for your podcast as well as various examples of good podcasting. I have several of these list/collections, including swipe files for podcast art, podcast titles, episode titles, and examples of podcast marketing.

For examples of my podcasting swipe files that you can use to get ideas for your podcast marketing, visit BigPodcast.com/resources.

Ask Your Listeners

All new podcasters with an interview-format podcast can relate to having to approach potential people to interview when first starting out. Then, as their podcasts get more established, things flip and potential guests start coming to them.

The same is true for content.

When you're just starting your podcast, it's 100 percent up to you to come up with content. As your podcast becomes more established, and you develop a relationship with listeners, they'll let you know of good subjects to cover.

Episode Quality

When podcasting was in its infancy, you could get attention for an off-the-cuff show you recorded while walking or driving or without much thought to either quality of recording or quality of content.

Old-school podcasters still talk about this time. And many still release these off-the-cuff episodes.

But the days of podcasts like these getting any kind of significant attention are gone.

5 Ways To Come Up With Episode Topics

If you're publishing new podcast episodes on a frequent basis, you need a good system in place for coming up with topics that are both a match for your podcast as well as something listeners will find interesting.

Five ways to do this:

1. *Always Be Watching*

This sounds obvious (and it should be obvious), but you need to get in the habit of *always* being on the lookout for potential episode topics. These topics should be organized in a way that will let you easily access them when needed.

Your filing system doesn't need to be elaborate. A dedicated spiral-bound notebook is all you need. Alternatively, an online system like Evernote can work well, especially if you spend a lot of time reading blogs, forums, and other places related to your topic and find ideas that way.

Personally, I use the previously-mentioned app *Things* to organize episode ideas. I have it on both my desktop and phone. When I think of an idea, I input it into the software, tagging it "episode ideas." The software syncs the lists on both my desktop and phone, so I always have my ideas accessible when coming up with new episode topics.

2. *Guest Suggestions*

If you have an open dialog with listeners, they'll tell you the topics they want you to cover. The downside of this is listeners will often suggest things that aren't within your podcast's focus. Should this happen, resist the urge to proceed with those suggestions.

3. *Word Storm*

A word storm is a brainstorming activity you can do that is very similar to a word association. To do a word storm, start with a single word and list all the *related* words (not synonyms) you can think of.

For example, if "podcast" is your word, you might list:

- RSS
- Apple
- iPhone

- Apple Podcasts
- Google Podcasts
- Headphones
- Blog
- Interviews
- Radio
- Microphones

You could then take each of these words and do the same exercise.

Your job is to come up with as many related words as possible. For this exercise, you want quantity over quality. Refrain from judgment during a word storm — not everything you think of will be an appropriate topic for your podcast, but even the "bad" ideas can lead to things that work.

4. Mind Map

A mind map is created around a single word or idea, which is drawn in the center of a blank page. Related ideas are connected directly to the central concept, with additional ideas branching out from those.

The result is a diagram that can be used to structure and organize multiple topics in a way that visually shows how these topics are connected to the central idea.

5. Word Association

Word association is a great technique to generate ideas as well as a cool segment idea for your show. You simply take a word and think of things associated with it. You can do this by yourself or get help from listeners or others whom you work with.

For example, "podcast" might make you think of "microphone." Then you could take that one step further to ask the question, "What's the best microphone for podcasting?"

Podcasting is no longer a novelty, and your competition isn't just "ramblecasts" done by nerds with tape recorders. Today, you're competing against professionals who know how to create quality content and deliver it in a compelling way.

And your competition isn't just other podcasts. You also have to compete against non-podcast choices — video games, television, restaurants, sporting events, movies, sex, drugs, and rock and roll.

You can't control every part of the process it takes to have a successful podcast, but you can control *some* things. And the greatest thing you can control is the quality of the episodes you publish.

Quality episodes are paramount for long-term success in podcasting. You can rack up a lot of downloads by focusing on episode frequency and volume, but "churn and burn" will never have more impact than producing something of quality.

Think about top television shows that are no longer on the air — shows like *Mad Men, Breaking Bad,* and *Seinfeld.* Why were they successful initially? Why are people still interested in them, even though new episodes are no longer being made?

People don't tell their friends about television shows because they have high ratings. People tell their friends about television shows because they're good.

Was every episode of these television shows great? No. When you look at the body of work as a whole, though, there is greatness.

If you want a successful podcast, you need to strive for the same level of excellence. Not every episode you record is going to be great, but you should strive to make it as good as you can. This means that some episodes (maybe *many* episodes) of your podcast will need to be re-recorded before they're released. Some will need to be shelved entirely.

Never release a mediocre episode because you have a "schedule." You're producing a podcast, not running a train station.

The Quality Podcast Content Litmus Test

As your podcast becomes more successful, you'll have more opportunities for guests, sponsorships, and other content available to you. The more people you reach with your podcast, the more people you'll have contacting you about guests to feature, products and services to endorse, and episode topic ideas.

There is one primary question you need to keep in mind when considering people, advertising, or topics for your podcast.

"Will this help the people who are listening to my podcast?"

The people who listen to your podcast trust you. They're also there for a very specific type of content. If you break their trust by either endorsing junk or going off-topic, you're going to lose them.

Publicists are pushy. They're in the business of getting bookings for their clients, not worrying about the people who are listening to your podcast.

Advertisers primarily want a podcast (or host) with both reach and trust because that's what gets them returns on their advertising investments. To advertisers, your long-term relationship with your listeners is secondary to your *current* relationship with listeners, your ability to reach them *now* for the specific purpose of getting them to spend money on what's being pitched.

Not all people who listen to you are the same. This is especially true if you, like me, have a reputation based upon work you did in another business.

When I attend live events, whether they be speaking engagements, conferences, or personal events, I always try to connect with the people who are sitting by me.

"Why are you here?"

"How did you find out about this event?"

"How do you know the bride and groom?"

I attended a live event hosted by author Jon Acuff for a charity he partnered with. I asked the couple sitting by me if they had enjoyed his latest book.

Neither had read it.

The female half of the couple told me, "I like his *Stuff Christians Like* blog," referring to an older project he hadn't updated for months and has since moved on from.

Both were fans. Both thought enough of Jon to come to a live event. Neither, however, was interested enough in what he was currently doing to spend $20 on his latest book.

This is a dilemma we all face. On one hand, you have people who like *something* you've done. But on the other hand, not everybody is going to like what you're doing now.

Does that mean you should hold back on what you're doing now? Does it mean you should occasionally revisit what you've done in the past, even if you're personally no longer interested in it, to keep some fans happy?

No. However, these can be tough decisions to make when you're getting messages from fans with ideas on the direction you should go.

As I was writing this book, I posted an update on Facebook which said, "Wrapping up my book on how to market yourself (and your business) via a podcast. If you have anything you want me to cover, let me know."

One of the first responses asked, "Can you cover how to break into the national radio market as an independent musician?"

As a reader of this book, would *you* care about how to break into the national radio market as an independent musician? Only if you're a musician. And even then, that's doubtful, because you purchased this book wanting information on how to market yourself via a podcast, not how to get radio play for your music.

When you know who you are, what you want to say, and who your audience is, it makes identifying and rejecting content that isn't a match much easier.

CHAPTER 009

PODCASTING FREQUENCY AND CONSISTENCY

When you listen to a podcast episode, you're almost always hearing something that, at the very least, has taken several hours to produce. Some of the more popular podcasts take hundreds (or even thousands) of hours to produce a single episode, with the work extending over a period of months.

The time it takes to produce great content, whether it be a book, a television show, or a podcast, is largely invisible to the people who consume the final product. And it *should* be invisible.

When somebody is watching a movie, the producer doesn't want him thinking, "These are actors." The goal is for viewers to suspend disbelief, lose track of time, and be completely caught up in the moment.

Experiencing something from the inside is *always* different from watching it from the outside. This is especially true when what you see from the outside is a product created to sell a dream, which is the case with most "Make Money With Podcasting" content.

Podcasting isn't easy. The good news, though, is that even the most difficult aspects of podcasting have an element of ease. If you can find this ease, you'll be able to "make money with podcasting," just like the books, podcasts, and gurus promise.

What's the first step? You must be consistent.

Podcasting isn't something where you can come and go as you please – not if you want to get good results. And your success with podcasting probably isn't something that's going to happen right away, regardless of how consistent you are.

Thanks to the power of the Internet, it's easy to find examples of people who have "made it big in podcasting" without doing the work you're probably *already* doing. You don't know what's happening behind the scenes, though.

Do some people who really understand new media become successful (or famous) overnight? Yes, sometimes people get lucky. What we see on the outside is *always* different from what's happening on the inside, though.

Most of the opportunities that come from viral videos and something-for-nothing "success" don't last long. And most who do manage to squeeze out more than 15 minutes of fame are put on the same shelf as media train wrecks like "Balloon Boy" and "Octomom."

If you want big success and fame for yourself and your podcast, go for it. But don't attach this to the fantasy of long-lasting success with none of the work, because that doesn't happen.

Remember That Crazy Girl on The Bachelor? What Was Her Name?

It doesn't matter what her name was. You'll never hear from her again, and there's somebody else on television now who's basically the exact same person and is equally entertaining to watch.

This is the reality of "instant fame." Those who experience it are part of a churn-and-burn system that makes them disappear from our awareness as quickly as they arrived.

Compare that with "slow-burn" success, where establishing a core fan base can take months, or sometimes years.

People who find you on a slow-burn podcast are more loyal than those who simply follow what's hot at the moment. Because they've had to seek out you and your message, they're more connected to both, and because of this, they're more likely to spread the word about you and what you're doing.

With a slow-burn podcast, the focus is on quality more than quantity or intensity. And it's this quality that will lead to a long career and more money when all is said and done.

You won't get millions of downloads right away. But you *will* get millions of downloads.

To have success in podcasting, you only need a core group of dedicated fans who are willing to stick with you and support what you do again and again. You don't need to be known by everybody.

By being deliberate about developing and promoting your podcast over an extended period of time, you increase the chances of being successful. This is where consistency comes in.

Just as the slow burn applies to your podcast, it also applies to your podcasting career. This is perhaps the most important aspect to internalize when it comes to claiming your space within podcasting.

Regardless of how good at podcasting you are, you're going to have ups and downs in your career if you stick it out long enough. Most podcasters are fine at the beginning of their careers, when they have nowhere to go but up. But what happens when you finally "make it" and have to deal with drops in popularity?

This is where the real work happens, and it's why we rarely hear from people who were on reality television. It's also why so many podcasts (and podcasters) come and go.

Getting attention for spectacle is easy. The hard part is doing work that matters — idea creation, outlining, recording, editing, and publishing. And it's especially hard when it seems like people don't care about your podcast.

This is why you want to be clear on your message and why you're podcasting. It's also why you'll find it beneficial to embrace the slow burn.

Your podcasting career will be a series of peaks and valleys. Often, some of the biggest valleys are those that happen after your highest peaks. And the opposite is also true.

Knowing this, if you keep showing up and claiming your space, you'll be fine.

How Frequently Should You Release New Episodes?

Tripp Lanier of *The New Man Podcast* has waited as long as three months between episodes.

Dan Carlin's *Hardcore History* podcast has approximately four new episodes each year.

John Lee Dumas did 2000 daily episodes of *Entrepreneurs On Fire* before going to a semi-weekly release schedule.

How frequently should you release new episodes? The short answer is "frequently enough so that people don't forget about you."

How long does it take people to forget about you? For most podcasts, not long. If you're not releasing episodes on a regular basis, and listeners don't know you take a while between episodes, they'll unsubscribe, move on, and never come back.

To build a connection with people, they *must* consume your podcasts. If there are no podcasts to consume, you have a problem. This is one of the reasons I suggest launching new podcasts with no fewer than 25 episodes.

Launching with 25 episodes gives listeners a variety of content to choose from. People have choices with podcasts — they can pick what they want and leave the rest. The more options potential listeners have initially – as long as those options are focused and related to your core topic – the greater chance they have of finding something of interest.

Potential listeners want to know your podcast will be there when they need it, which is another reason to launch with 25 episodes — it shows potential listeners you understand what it takes to publish a podcast. It lets them know you have skin in the game and that your podcast won't fade away as quickly as it launched.

Even beyond your initial launch period, having a variety of content for listeners to choose from is still important. The more episodes you release, the more opportunities potential listeners have to download and listen to your podcast. The more infrequently you release new episodes, because listeners have fewer episode choices, the greater the chance they'll go somewhere else to find something they resonate with.

In this instance, podcasting is a numbers game. The more episodes you release, the better. Never neglect episode quality, though. A frequent release schedule won't help a bad podcast.

The Podcast "Cushion" - Don't Get Too Comfortable

Podcasting is an ongoing process. If you release new episodes daily, or even several times per week, it can be tempting to record and produce episodes in large batches, to give yourself time off from these tasks.

Resist the urge to give yourself too much cushion for your podcast. It's efficient to gang-record multiple episodes at once, and it's efficient to edit multiple episodes at once. But when you have episodes ready to go weeks in advance, you lose connection with your podcast and your audience.

You are not a factory. The podcast episodes you produce are not widgets.

Imagine you're a musician. Like a podcaster, you work in a studio to make recordings, so while you've got the studio booked to record your new album, why not record a second album to release in the future? Doing this will save you both time and money.

The only problem is the world is constantly changing. People change, trends change, and *you* change. These changes won't be anything drastic — especially if you're only recording a month or two ahead of time. But still, if you get too far ahead of yourself, the audience you recorded for will no longer exist by the time your recordings are released.

If you're looking for longevity in podcasting, you *must* stay on top of what listeners want. Podcasting is not a "set it and forget it" medium.

The Happy Medium

Record a week in advance. You'll have enough breathing room that you don't feel rushed or have to cut corners to release new episodes on time, but not be so far ahead in your publishing schedule that you miss opportunities to talk about current events or have timely interaction with listeners.

Churn And Burn

Urban Dictionary defines "churn and burn" as "cranking shit out."

Many of the top podcasts use this method to generate downloads. This works because the more episodes of a podcast there are, the more search engines and podcast directories have to work with. Also, the more episodes a podcast has for potential listeners to choose from, the better chance there is that they'll find episodes they're interested in.

Like tickets to a raffle, the more you have, the more likely you are to get picked. But just because you *can* do something doesn't mean you should.

This is podcasting, not a raffle. To have real impact on people, you need to provide them with more than just a link in a search result and you need them to do more than just click on it.

Never confuse making an impact with making noise.

CHAPTER 010

EPISODE NOTES

Think about how *you* discover and listen to podcasts.

Aside from word-of-mouth, the most frequent way the majority of people find out about new podcasts is via search engines such as Google. These search engines, while they have the ability to index audio, video, and other multimedia content, focus on text.

This isn't the classic, "trick the search engines" style of SEO – the purpose of it is to serve your listeners. By focusing on text-based episode notes, you'll increase your chances of being found by both search engines and the people who are looking for you.

What happens when somebody finds your podcast?

He does one of two things: He either commits to listening to a short clip at the beginning of an episode (which is why you want to tease what's coming at the beginning of every episode) or he looks through episode notes to see if the content within the episode will be a match for him.

Spending the time to properly edit your podcast and posting quality episode notes is a matter of respect for listeners, both new and existing. They are an extension of your efforts to connect listeners with the correct content.

Like your podcast itself, individual episodes of your podcast are not for everybody.

Even your most enthusiastic fans won't be interested in every episode you release.

Quality episode notes save listeners time by letting them know, *before* they listen, which episodes they'll be interested in and which episodes they should skip. The result of this is listeners are more likely to hear *only* the episodes they find relevant, making them more interested and engaged with your podcast than they'd be otherwise.

What To Include In Episode Notes

Daniel J. Lewis, host of *The Audacity To Podcast*, recommends creating a written version of *everything* covered within an episode.

Everything.

This is scary to most people and also counter-intuitive. Why would somebody download and listen to an entire podcast episode if he can get the same information via a quick scan of text?

Daniel doesn't worry about this. Here's why:

"If someone comes to my site looking for an answer, he can get it by listening to my 30-60-minute audio episode or he can very quickly get the answer from my notes. In either case, he got what he needed from me and thus will trust and respect me more for having helped him."

Detailed episode notes probably won't cause you to lose as many potential listeners as you'd think. If people are looking for specific information, it's unlikely they'll listen to entire episodes of your podcast hoping to find it, regardless of whether you have detailed episode notes or not.

How To Write Episode Notes

An episode outline is important, not just for recording podcast episodes, but also for streamlining the rest of the episode creation process. Taking a few minutes to organize your thoughts before you get behind the mic will save you hours during editing and other post-recording tasks, such as creating episode notes.

My basic episode plans are simple. I start with a main episode topic and a specific idea of how I want to communicate it. These two things combined are what I call the "hook" and are organized into an outline format using bullet points.

Here's an example:

I did an episode of *Build A Big Podcast* about hosting skills. That was the topic.

My approach to the topic was analyzing the delivery of a specific broadcast host – a sportscaster – and how he reported a specific event, a trio of motorcycle jumps by stunt performer Travis Pastrana that were recreations of well-known jumps by stunt legend Evel Knievel. I used a clip from each jump as examples and then talked about them.

On my outline, I had my big idea, what I wanted to get across during the episode, the list of clips, and what I wanted to say about each. I also had a personal story about Evel Knievel which I used as an on-ramp to the main content.

Everything was in a specific order, so I had a plan to follow as I was recording the episode.

Because of this preparation, typing up episode notes after the episode had been recorded was easy. I simply took the outline I'd already created and wrote episode notes based on that.

Creating episode notes based on your original outlines isn't a perfect solution. Even with a great outline, episodes you record *always* vary from your initial plan. An outline is a great starting point and framework to build upon though.

The best method of getting accurate episode notes that reflect what you've actually recorded is to create them as you're editing the raw audio of your episode. This allows you to be fully present while recording.

What to look for when creating episode notes:

1. Highlights

Focus on the meat. What are the main topics the episode covers?

How can you tease the content within an episode to inspire curiosity in the person reading your notes and make her want to listen to your podcast?

For great examples of this, look at movie summaries on Netflix and book summaries on Amazon. They sell the excitement of what happens within the content being summarized and give people a reason to consume it.

Here's an example of a summary I did for an episode of *Music Business Radio* with musician Jim Peterik.

Jim Peterik is co-founder of The Ides of March and Survivor. He's written songs for acts like Cheap Trick, 38 Special, The Beach Boys, The Doobie Brothers, and Lynyrd Skynyrd.

On this episode, we talk about songwriting, live performance, building a following, booking gigs, and more. Jim also tells the story of writing "Eye Of The Tiger" and performs some of his most successful songs live in our studio, including one that became a huge hit for Sammy Hagar, "Heavy Metal."

This summary is short and to-the-point. It piques the interest of listeners who are musicians, fans of Jim Peterik, fans of bands he's worked with, and casual music fans who simply want to hear in-studio performances of songs they know.

If the main focus of your podcast is a specific topic, rather than an interview-based conversation with a guest, talk about the problem your episode solves.

State the problem in your summary and let readers know listening to the episode will get them the solution. Be clear about this, don't just hint at it.

Make your summary personal. For example, if you have a fitness podcast, don't just talk about "how to lose weight." Instead, talk directly to the reader using statements like, "how *you* can lose weight."

Use the summary to frame your podcast as the only solution to their problems.

2. Opportunities For Bullet Points

If you only focus on doing one thing to make great episode notes, focus on writing great bullet points. Here's why, in bullet point form:

- People are busy
- They don't like to read
- Because of this, they skim
- Bullet points get to the point without excess filler
- Because of this, they are a great format for your podcast's episode notes

Bullet points are often used in sales copy to emphasize key features and benefits. Because people are busy and distracted, they're much more likely to read short, bulleted points than long (or even short) paragraphs of text.

While your summary lets a reader know exactly what he'll get by listening to an episode, it's the bullet points that boost curiosity and emotion in the reader and actually make him want to listen.

Here's an example of bullet points from Episode 150 of *RED Podcast*, which is on the topic of what to do when friends and family don't support your business ideas.

What You'll Learn:

- Why we didn't want a lot of "friend and family" support for Laurel's last crowdfunding campaign, Project X
- How to create momentum for your new project
- Why I "like" everything on Facebook (even though I recently lost a client by doing this)
- The downside of supportive family and friends (you don't want this part of it)
- Why we don't ask for "votes" or send emails asking you to "like" pages on Facebook

Copywriter Mel Martin called these types of bullet points, "Fascinations."

The "Fascination" Formula

Powerful bullet points happen when you combine three things:

1. Specific Benefit

What's the pain your listener needs a solution for? What's the outcome he wants to achieve?

2. Instant Gratification

People want results now. Don't focus on the work it's going to take the get those results.

3. Intense Curiosity

How is what you have new, different, pain-free, conflict-free or without friction?

Some examples of what this looks like:

- What you should never, ever eat on vacation.
- Make your car "invisible" to highway radar. LEGAL!
- Intensity of pain in dentist's office depends on time of day. New discovery: hours when it hurts least
- Two famous cold remedies that make you sicker if taken together.
- How to check into a crowded hotel *without* standing in line
- Numbers that should never be used for combination locks. Professional burglars try them first.

7 Templates To Create Great Bullet Points

1. How-To

Start with the problem and finish up with the remedy for that problem, but don't give the specific solution in the bullet point. Remember, the purpose of this is to make people listen to your podcast.

Examples:

"How to _____ in a way that _____."

"How to (tell/know/be certain/etc.) if _____."

2. Benefit / Pain

Lead with the benefit your listener wants and follow up with what she's afraid will happen.

Let's say you have a podcast about marriage and relationships …

"You're getting married! — What you *must* know to avoid a huge wedding bill!"

"Is he faithful? The *one way* to know for sure"

3. The Secret Code

Make the complicated seem simple.

Examples:

"*Exactly* what to look for when _____."

… hiring a new employee.

… evaluating a potential product idea.

Or, taking the same formula…

"*Exactly* what to eat when _____."

… trying to lose weight.

… trying to get pregnant.

4. Perfect Timing

When you *should* act to receive the benefit. When you *shouldn't* act to avoid pain.

Examples:

"When to _____ (and when not to)."

… invest in real estate …

… ask your girlfriend to marry you …

This template will work with just about any benefit. For better results, double up by adding some pain.

"When to invest in real estate (and when not to). If you get this wrong, you'll lose your shirt!"

"When to invest in real estate (and when not to). If you've played Monopoly, even if you've lost, you have all the skills you need to make a ton of cash!"

5. Where To Go

"Where to go to avoid _____."

"The one place you'll always find _____."

"The 'secret' location to save 50 percent on _____."

Like above, you can double up on any of these …

"The 'secret' location to save 50 percent on _____. And if you're quick, as much as 70 percent."

6. That's Impossible!

This is where you list something that sounds too good to be true, but it's not.

Examples:

"How to _____ (with/in/using) _____."

"How to lose 10 pounds (or more) in just 24 hours."

"How to record a podcast using a $10 kitchen appliance."

7. The List

If you're hitting more than a couple of solutions to a single problem, you have great material for a "list" bullet.

Examples:

"# ways your (boss/secretary/wife/husband/etc.) is trying to _____."

"# things you must (do/own/watch for/etc.) if you want to _____."

Time Stamps

A solution to help people quickly and easily find the information needed to solve their problems, and *listen* to your podcast, is to include a "time stamp" next to written episode notes. Give them a link to the exact point within the episode where they can get the solution they're looking for.

You'll often see time stamps next to episode notes in bullet-point format.

For example:

- The worst place to sit on a plane [5:43]
- This phrase will get you a better deal on a used car [16:37]
- One thing you should never feed a dog (Hint: It's not chocolate!) [9:19]

If you use WordPress, there are many podcast plugins that will automatically create time stamp links that take listeners from your episode notes directly to specific times within your podcast. Visit BigPodcast.com/resources for links to current recommendations.

Episode Photo Or Graphic

Podcasting, like radio, is "theater of the mind." When we hear audio, we imagine the visual images we don't have access to.

Sometimes it's better *not* to have a photo within your episode notes. You don't want a photo of something that's incongruent with the message of your podcast. For example, if you talk about being a millionaire, but record from a "non-millionaire" studio, such as your mother's basement.

Dave Jackson has a podcast called *Building A Better Dave*. The "About" page of the website starts out, "What a year I had. I filed bankruptcy, got divorced, and lost my home. My brother convinced me to move into his house, so I could pay off all the legal bills."

When you play an episode of *Building A Better Dave*, the announcer says, "Live from the basement, it's *Building A Better Dave!*"

If you have a similar situation, show the basement. It adds to the story you want to tell.

If you're interviewing or co-hosting with well-known people face-to-face, a photo of your recording session is helpful in capturing the moment. For example, we record *Music Business Radio* in a broadcast radio studio, which looks cool, plus we interview famous people and have them perform songs live. A photo of either (or both) of these things help sell potential listeners on downloading and listening to the associated podcast episode.

Again, these are things that add to the story being told. If you have a "moment," such as a live performance within an episode, take a photo and post it.

A standard headshot of a guest misses the mark for two reasons. One, it's a photo that has been seen elsewhere, so people are more likely to ignore it. Also, it doesn't add to the story of what you've done together – an interview, a co-hosted episode, or a performance.

Photos should *always* add to the story you're telling.

If you do interviews remotely and only have a standard headshot to work with, rather than posting it by itself, incorporate it into a custom graphic made just for that specific episode. This will showcase the moment you shared with your guest and take advantage of people's tendency to imagine the details they can't see.

Never use a staged or stock photo. You want an image of something that you were involved with and really happened, just like your podcast.

Not using a photo is better than the wrong photo.

I prefer using images within my episode notes that have the podcast name, the episode title, and the episode number. This gives readers of my episode notes something other than text to look at while making it easy for my podcasts to maintain a consistent look and feel.

You don't have to have *any* photos or images in your episode notes. Plenty of podcasts do this successfully. Marc Maron's *WTF Podcast*, one of the top podcasts in the world, has done hundreds of episodes with notes that are 100 percent text. Obviously, this is a lot easier to do than editing and picking photos or designing graphics for every episode you release.

While images and photos can make your episode notes more visually appealing, neither will make or break your podcast. Pick one (or none) and be consistent with it.

Guest Bio

Keep bios quick and simple. Listeners don't care where the guy went to high school or what his zodiac sign is, but they do need to know why they should push the download button and listen. For an example, let's revisit the Jim Peterik bio.

> *Jim Peterik is co-founder of The Ides of March and Survivor. He's written songs for acts like Cheap Trick, 38 Special, The Beach Boys, The Doobie Brothers, and Lynyrd Skynyrd.*

This is good for an opening paragraph that a potential listener will read first. It tells who the guest is, establishes him as an expert, and leaves *some* mystery.

A reader might wonder, "I know those bands. Which songs did he write? Anything I've heard?"

This is something to consider if you want to go deeper. Doing so will give you the opportunity to really sell the episode, hitting on the emotion of it and not just facts about the guest.

For example:

> *You might not recognize the name Jim Peterik, but you know his work. You probably have some of it in your music playlist.*
>
> *Jim has written some of rock's biggest and most memorable hits. "Vehicle" for Ides of March, "Eye of the Tiger" for Survivor, "Hold on Loosely" for 38 Special, and "That's Why God Made the Radio" for The Beach Boys are among the classic songs he's penned.*
>
> *He's co-founder of the band Survivor and he's sold millions of albums. He also has lots of stories to tell about his time on the road.*

A third option for guest bios is to put them in bullet-point format.

What this looks like this:

Jim Peterik

- *Co-founder of The Ides of March*
- *Co-founder of Survivor*
- *Wrote and recorded the fastest-selling single in Warner Bros. history*
- *Co-writer of arena rock anthems "Eye Of The Tiger" and "Burning Heart"*

- *Songwriter for top acts including Cheap Trick, 38 Special, The Beach Boys, The Doobie Brothers, and Lynyrd Skynyrd.*

Links And References

If you mention a book, resource, or anything else in a significant way, and there is more information about it online, your episode notes need to have a link to it.

The purpose of this is twofold. One, because most people listen to podcasts while doing other things, such as driving or exercising, they aren't able write down information at the time they hear it from you. Two, having a list of links to everything you mention on a podcast episode is a great way to get people to your site, where they'll be able to subscribe to your podcast, listen to additional episodes, or otherwise consume more of what you have to offer.

Things you need to link in your episode notes include:

- Books
- Related episodes of your podcast
- Other podcasts
- Websites and online resources
- Software
- Blogs

Advertiser Info

This is important. It not only adds additional value for the sponsors who support you, it's also great for listeners, for the same reasons having a list of "links and references" is.

Because podcasts are targeted to specific audiences, podcast advertising is often targeted as well. When this happens, listeners are likely to want more information on the products and services being advertised on your podcast, just like they want more information on non-advertised products and services you mention.

Call-To-Connect

Just as you put a call-to-connect within a podcast episode itself, episode notes should also contain a call-to-connect request.

Examples:

- Subscribe via Apple Podcasts
- Tell a friend about the podcast
- Sign up for your mailing list
- Subscribe to your newsletter
- Download a free report or other lead magnet
- Visit your website
- Buy your book

Pick the one that gives you the most leverage. For most podcasters, this will be a request for people to do something that gets them on your mailing list. Doing this will enable you to get them to act on other things, such as subscribing to your podcast, leaving a review on Apple Podcasts, or taking advantage of an opportunity to buy from you.

Bonus "Episode Notes" Content

Your Actual Notes

The episode you prepared for and thought would happen can be just as interesting to listeners as the episode you ended up with. This is how to take advantage of that.

Whenever I do an interview with somebody, I type out, then print, a basic bio I can reference during recording. I also write out a "roadmap" of how I think the episode should be organized — a basic flow of questions, potential segments and topics to discuss.

This outline is *never* followed verbatim, because you never know where a guest will go with his answers.

Still, as the guest is answering questions, I'm working from this outline, writing down elements of his answer that connect to the next things I want to ask and trying to come up with a way to seamlessly go from whatever the current topic is to the other topics that I'm hoping to cover.

The result, when you look at it after the interview, looks like a bunch of doodles on a textbook. The "printed" part of the initial outline is surrounded by handwritten notes made during the interview – keywords of big ideas, arrows to guide me from one segment to the next, circles around certain things I need to mention, and stars next to areas of topics I need to focus on.

These are episode notes. *Real* episode notes.

If you have something similar, rather than type up everything so it looks perfect, scan what you've got and upload image files. Many times, these are more interesting to listeners than something polished that you created after the interview was over, since scans of your actual episode notes show your plan for each episode and are a more authentic representation of what actually happened in the studio as well.

Transcripts

If you're going to post transcripts of your episodes, make them bonus content that complements your main episode notes, rather than a substitution for them. Transcripts by themselves are way too intimidating for most people to consume, and not the most effective way for listeners to find out what an episode contains or to find the links that were mentioned, in order to look them up.

If you're going to post transcripts, do so via a link from your main episode notes page to a dedicated (and separate) transcript page. This will allow you to keep your main episode page more focused and leaner, with the transcript only seen if somebody clicks on it.

Bonus PDF Downloads

A bonus document, either linked directly from your episode notes or sent via email in exchange for contact information, is a great way to provide added value to listeners who resonate with a specific episode and want more information on the topic covered. It will help to solidify your relationships with listeners, as well as set you up to be the obvious solution to their problems.

Suggestions for bonus PDF documents:

- Transcripts
- "Big Ideas" from the episode
- Related worksheets – for example, a "food tracker" document for an episode on weight loss, or a budget worksheet for an episode on budgeting
- Sample chapters from a book that is discussed
- A summary of a book that is discussed

- Sketches, diagrams, and images that can't be displayed via an audio podcast

Bonus Audio Content

Bonus audio content is great, because it's easy to produce and it's in a format that listeners of your podcast are already familiar with and enjoy. Like other bonus content, bonus audio can be linked directly from episode notes or given away in exchange for contact information.

Suggestions for bonus audio content:

- Outtakes and bloopers
- Content that was cut from the main episode, but still has value to hardcore listeners, such as extended stories and pre- or post-episode banter
- Post-episode commentary – your big takeaways from a guest, what you liked or didn't like, etc.

Bonus Video Content

If you have an audio podcast, but video would add to the story you're trying to tell, this is the place to put it.

Suggestions for bonus video content:

- Movie, television, and book trailers
- A tour of your studio
- Behind-the-scenes content

Final Thoughts

The purpose of your podcast isn't for you to hear yourself, but to help you share your message and increase your influence. Quality episode notes will help you do both by making it easy for people to find your content (and get the results) they're looking for.

Episode notes give you an opportunity to approach topics in different ways, adding content that doesn't work in audio format and expanding on content that does. They make it easier for you to be found via search engines and, once you're found, instantly let users know they're in the right place.

Remember, you're not just a podcaster, you're a media company. Take advantage of the different ways your content can be consumed. This will give you an edge over podcasters who focus solely on audio.

MODULE 3
DELIVERING YOUR MESSAGE

PART 1 – HOSTING

CHAPTER 011

THE FOUNDATION OF GREAT PODCAST HOSTING

The first time I saw her, it was in the parking lot of a yoga studio. I noticed her because she was *very* tall.

She was thin and had long hair. It was long and thick, like hair in a magazine shampoo ad. It bounced when she walked.

She looked like the kind of woman who got a lot of attention from men.

I followed her into the studio and got ready for class. She was in the back of the room, taking off her coat and shoes.

Then she took her wig off, revealing a completely bald head.

I was shocked. More than that though, I was amazed. Rarely do you see people with such confidence.

"That was one of the coolest things I've ever seen," I told her.

And that was the beginning of our friendship.

This is what true authenticity looks like. It happens when you no longer care, not in an "I'm going to let myself go" way, but from the realization that you know you're going to be okay regardless of what happens or what people think about you.

This is the quality you need to be a great podcast host.

But let's be honest about authenticity. It's a nice buzzword, but for most people, the definition is about as clear as the definitions of success, greatness, or excellence. And in the podcasting world, what most people refer to as "authenticity" isn't actually authentic.

It doesn't count as authentic when your "authenticity" is designed to sell more stuff, get more listeners for your podcast, or prove to the world you're somebody with his shit together.

To give them this, you need to be both vulnerable and strong. Vulnerable, because it shows you're just like they are, and strong, because it shows them what's possible.

When my friend Vivian took off her wig in the yoga studio, it gave everybody else who was there permission to drop their own facades. And the fact that she went first made her action even more powerful.

Imagine if she'd asked, "Would you mind if I take my wig off?"

The moment wouldn't have been nearly as powerful. And by worrying about somebody else's reaction, her authentic self would have been squelched.

Most people would have waited, though. They wouldn't have moved forward without getting permission from somebody else first, because they'd be worried about making other people angry or uncomfortable.

That's the definition of a follower.

People listen to leaders. So be the person people want to listen to by giving them the permission they're looking for, not by waiting for them to ask you or anybody else if it's okay to do something. Show them through your own actions that it's okay for them to do it on their own.

The Missing Piece To Successful Podcasting

Whether or not you're successful at podcasting has nothing to do with having a great voice, sounding "professional" behind a mic, or knowing which knobs on a mixer will give you a desired effect. You can easily hire other people to turn the correct knobs and make you sound good.

The one thing that can't be outsourced, which is essential for you to create and maintain a successful podcast, is your ability to connect with the people who listen to you.

Most podcasters screw this up big time.

These are the podcasters who don't prepare content, don't vet guests, and don't edit. These are the podcasters who are more interested in having a place where they can hear themselves talk than actually having a relationship with listeners or creating episodes that make impact on them.

And it's because of this that these podcasters *don't* connect with those who happen to listen to their podcasts (or keep those listeners around very long).

It's easy to get caught up in the "flash" — the big download numbers, the latest recording equipment, and the ego stroke of being on the front page of Apple Podcasts. That's not going to keep you in the game, though.

What keeps you in the game is a two-way relationship with the people who listen to you.

Think of it like an exchange of energy. Ball goes out, ball comes back. People on the receiving end of your podcast are just as important to its success as you are.

Don't listen to the guys who claim, "I'd be podcasting even if nobody listened." That's nice in theory, and looks good as a motivational quote on Instagram, but there's no reality in it.

"Nobody listening" sucks, and it's what makes podcasting a struggle for so many people. It's also one of the biggest reasons why most podcasts die before reaching their eighth episode.

If you knew a lot of people were listening to your podcast and you were making a real difference in their lives, you'd find the time to podcast. You'd find the resources to podcast. You'd do what was needed to be done to get new episodes out.

The irony is that doing these things is what attracts listeners.

The Podcast Triple Threat

To be successful as a podcaster, you need three qualities working together.

1. Personality

There's something about human nature that causes us to assign certain attributes to those who *appear* certain ways, without actually having verified these attributes to be accurate. For example, an executive who appears to be in high-demand may get multiple job offers, even if his job performance has been poor.

This is why good-looking people are more likely to get away with murder and "unattractive" defendants tend to get longer, harsher sentences.

Emotion trumps reason.

On the positive side of this, as a podcaster, people see you as an authority. Even if you podcast as a hobby or record with a $25 microphone into a hand-me-down laptop computer, it's still possible to be recognized as having a leadership position within your niche because you're "the voice" of the people who listen to you.

Don't leave your podcasting success up to the fantasy of others.

The most successful podcasters have a personality that is a blend of confidence, humility, and approachability.

True authority requires confidence, and if you want long-term success with your podcast and to positively affect the people who listen to you, being in this position is something you must be comfortable with. People are living vicariously through you.

Whether you podcast about science, politics, celebrity gossip, or television shows, don't leave people wondering how you feel. Standing for *something* is more important than being agreeable to listeners because a strong opinion gives listeners something to either embrace of push back against.

When you show listeners where you stand, it allows them to get clear on where they stand.

Balance this authority with approachability. When people see (or hear you), you want them to think, "If I saw him out in public, I'd feel comfortable introducing myself."

Think about top celebrities. The biggest ones have these characteristics.

Taylor Swift, for example, is confident. She's not afraid to try new styles of music, look a bit awkward on stage, or laugh at herself. She's beautiful, but not flawless. And you get the feeling that if you saw her out and asked for a photo with her, she'd be fine with it.

Your listeners want something similar from you.

2. Knowledge And Curiosity

Curiosity opens you to new worlds and possibilities. Curiosity lets you see beneath the surface of how things appear to find out how they *really* are.

James Altucher has one single criteria for the guests on his top-ranked podcast, *The James Altucher Show.* "I'm fascinated by some aspect of each person. I don't limit myself by saying each one has to be an entrepreneur or has to be a success. I just want to talk to anyone who makes me curious about their lives."

Knowledge is the result of being curious.

Are you interviewing people on your podcast? While curiosity sparks questions, it's knowledge that helps you to ask your guests the *right* questions. And when the person to whom you've asked the right question gives you the right answer, it's knowledge of this subject (and what you've yet to learn about it) that lets you know it's time to be quiet and listen.

Then the cycle repeats itself …

Be curious. Be quiet.

Be curious. Be quiet.

3. Work Ethic

Podcasting is, for the most part, very lonely. The work it takes to produce an episode, such as guest or topic research, scheduling, outlining, recording, editing, distribution, marketing, and promotion, is often a solo job.

Even if you have a co-host, a producer, or other partner working with you on your podcast, the work it takes to consistently release quality episodes can be tedious. At best, it's unrelenting, since every time you complete an episode, you're immediately back at square one to create the next.

Successful podcasters create systems and routines that allow them the necessary focus it takes to create great episodes while giving themselves the needed space to make sure they don't burn out.

Think of it as "crop rotation" for your podcast.

When growing the same crop in the same place for many years in a row, soil is depleted of certain nutrients. With rotation, a crop that removes a nutrient from the soil is switched to a different crop that returns that nutrient to the soil or draws different nutrients.

This rotation is what keeps the soil healthy and allows multiple crops to continue to grow.

You, like soil on a farm, can be easily drained. Some people have a higher capacity for "doing the same thing" than others, but if you don't take care of yourself, you'll eventually burn yourself out.

Consider these things when you design your podcast and the work it takes to publish it. Even if you like being alone, even if you get along well with the people you work with, and even if you like repetitive tasks such as editing, consistently doing the necessary work to create quality episodes can be exhausting.

Switching routines and taking time off will keep you from wearing out. If nothing else, develop systems of production that allow you to take breaks from intense work as well as rotate tasks, so you can stay fresh.

Recovery is where growth happens. Like a weightlifter, the work you do "in the gym" is only *stimulus* for growth. It's away from your work where you'll recover and have the experiences to take back into the studio later that will make you a better host.

Will it ever be easy? No. But you'll get better, which will help you find the ease.

You'll find your voice and develop your personality. You'll expand your curiosity and, because of this, your knowledge. You'll find new and more efficient ways of doing the necessary work it takes to create episodes that matter.

Pros Recognize Pros

Supreme Court Justice Potter Stewart described obscenity in the 1964 case Jacobellis v. Ohio as "I know it when I see it."

I feel the same way when it comes to a person's commitment to a successful podcast.

A committed pro can recognize another committed pro.

If your podcast isn't getting the level of respect you think it deserves, ask yourself this question: "How committed to this podcast am I?"

The best way to attract listeners is to treat your podcast like it matters and create something that's interesting, entertaining, and helpful to them. Without these things as your foundation, no amount of great marketing will help you.

Your podcast doesn't have to be a "business," but it helps to treat it like one. Show up fully, do the work, and take care of your "customers," even if your podcast is just a hobby.

Jump In The Pool

There's no "try before you buy" in podcasting. Until you commit to (and focus on) a specific topic for a while, you won't know for sure if it's a good match for you.

Until you record several episodes with a specific co-host, you won't know for sure how your on-air chemistry and ability to work together is.

Until you take on the responsibilities of booking guests, doing pre-interview work, scheduling recording time, getting episodes edited, and marketing your podcast, you can't be certain you're not being too ambitious with your episode frequency.

Jumping in is how you know what you want and how much you can handle. There's no other way to do it.

Auto racer Danica Patrick once said, "You're driving your car and you feel frightened a little bit. We bump up against that feeling as much as we can to try and push that limit further, get comfortable there, and then push it again. You're constantly on the brink of crashing, because that's the fastest."

The most important element to your podcasting success is that you keep moving forward. You don't have to be faster than everybody else, because the podcasting isn't a "race" and has no finish line. The only thing that matters to listeners is that you show up fully. If you're not already doing this, you can start now.

Always Remember Why You Started Your Podcast

Regardless of how much you love planning interviews, meeting new people, editing episodes, and all the dozens of small details that it takes to release your content, there will be times when you simply don't feel like keeping your release schedule commitments. It happens to everybody.

When this happens to you, it helps to know why you're podcasting. This is what will help you harness the motivation to do the necessary work.

CHAPTER 012

FINDING YOUR VOICE

If you listen to classic rock radio, you'll hear stations unaffiliated with each other doing similar things:

- "The Double-Shot" (or Two For Tuesday) - Back-to-back songs by the same artist
- "Get The Led Out" - Led Zeppelin for an entire hour (or more)
- Some guy with a deep voice who says things like, "TURN IT UP!! AND RIP THE KNOB OFF!!"

Every radio format has its own version of this, because that's how radio works. Every radio station borrows from other stations — playlists, promotions, bits for the morning show, DJ names, etc.

Podcasters do the same thing. For example, the equipment we use, the way we label episodes, and the design of our websites.

Watching others to see what works, and then using what works, is fine. Every industry does this.

But there's a downside.

When you're using the same equipment as the next guy, getting your music from the same place, and doing your audio processing using the same plugins, things get homogenous rather quickly. And it's even worse when you try to replicate the style and delivery of popular podcasters.

"Personality" is the only way to stand out in podcasting. And here's how to do it in a way that nobody can effectively copy.

Pace, Energy, And Delivery

What's the difference between Rush Limbaugh and Sean Hannity? When it comes to their basic political and social beliefs, not much. But the difference in how they deliver basically the same message is night and day.

Limbaugh has a smooth, laid-back style. And even though the Pulitzer-winning site PolitiFact has *never* rated any of his statements they've fact-checked as "True" (and only 6 percent as "Mostly True"), his delivery is so confident that his fans never seem to question him.

Regardless of how you feel about Rush Limbaugh's politics or his record of telling the truth, listen to his delivery. Whether you're podcasting solo, you have a co-host, or you're interviewing people, his laid-back confidence and ability to use just the right amount of energy to keep audiences engaged is worth modeling.

Hannity is an example of what you *shouldn't* be doing on your podcast.

Hannity yells a lot. He interrupts guests and doesn't let them finish answering his questions. And when he interrupts them, he yells even louder than he normally does.

He's like a little dog that barks all the time. And like a little dog, if Hannity feels like he's been backed into a corner, he gets defensive and makes even more noise.

Pace and delivery are important. You can get away with interrupting guests and not letting them finish their thoughts when you're in the political space with a show designed to agitate people, but it's not going to work in most situations.

It's good to be confident in your delivery. But don't confuse confidence with aggression. Limbaugh is extremely confident in his delivery, most of the time without raising his voice.

So why are so many radio and podcast hosts loud and aggressive?

One of the biggest critiques new podcasters get about their performance is "lack of energy." They *think* their delivery is exciting and dynamic, when it actually sounds more like a cure for insomnia.

How do you fix this? A common recommendation is to stand when recording. Use your hands. Get your body involved.

Unfortunately, this can cause you to go in just the opposite direction — too much energy. Add this to the fact that most podcast hosts, like Sean Hannity, don't listen to guests and talk over them, and it's no wonder there are so many bad podcast interviews.

There's also another, much bigger problem with standing while you record, which is detrimental to getting a great interview.

I stood up for years when interviewing people on the radio. Then I did an interview with a performance coach and "show doctor" who filled me in on why standing isn't a good idea.

Bill Cakmis has been in the entertainment business for over 30 years, and has worked as a professional actor, writer, and director. He's helped hundreds of actors, politicians, athletes, television hosts, and musicians to be better at media and connecting with the public.

I had him in to talk about interview etiquette, handling tough questions by the media, and stage persona. I wasn't there to get a personal critique of my hosting performance, but when we were done, I asked him for feedback.

"Sit down," he said.

We recorded in a small production room, about 8'x8'. It was packed full of recording equipment, plus chairs for the guest, the engineer, and the producer. To give everybody a little more breathing room, I stood up.

Not only did it help save space, "It helps bring energy," I thought.

And it did. But according to Bill Cakmis, it also brought something that negatively affected the interviews I was doing — it was intimidating to guests.

"You want to be on the same level as your guest," he said.

"Intimidating" is good for a host like Sean Hannity, but not for most people. And if you want to make guests comfortable so they'll be more likely to open up during interviews, it's not a good idea for you.

Since that recommendation from Bill, we've rearranged the studio, getting rid of excess equipment and making the most of our limited space. Today, I sit in a chair, across from my guest. And to make things even more comfortable, instead of overhead florescent lighting that makes it feel like you're in a doctor's office, we use table lamps that look like what you'd find in a living room.

It's a completely different environment and the resulting interviews have been completely different as well. It's no longer "me vs. them." It's a setup that allows everybody in the room to work together to create the best possible episode.

Pace, energy, and delivery are connected to everything about the way you record your podcast, not just your hosting ability. You don't want guests to think you're too laid back, but you don't want them to feel like they're at the dentist, either.

Your Big Personality

I spent some time working out of the same office as a booking agency that handled fashion models.

When a female model would walk through the door, her stereotypical traits, such as excellent posture, a slim build, and good angles, would let you know why she was there. For a layman like me, though, the "level" of work she was there for wasn't as easy to distinguish. Some were there for national print campaigns while others did local jobs.

Why? Because most of the models who came into the office looked completely different without makeup and in their street clothes than they did on a job. Yes, they were good-looking, many of them *great-*looking, but they looked different when actually at work — then, they were bigger, bolder, and more exciting.

This is not unlike what you want to do with the personality you present on your podcast. At its basic essence, it's still you, but it needs to be bigger, bolder, and more powerful to be memorable.

As a host, listeners expect certain things from you. They want authenticity, but they want something that separates you from average people on the street, including them.

The "Boring" Can Be Exciting

My friend Evelyn has 14 siblings. She doesn't think anything of it, because she's never known anything else.

I have another friend who grew up on a commune in Lewis County, Tennessee, known as The Farm. It was founded in 1971 by hippies who moved from San Francisco and still exists today.

To many people, the things you take for granted are fascinating. If nothing else, your experiences will add a unique perspective to your podcast, which can help to differentiate you from other podcasters.

Tennis Pro Vs. Bodybuilder

In bodybuilding, there's emphasis on developing a balanced physique with evenly distributed muscle mass. Without this, there is no symmetry.

A bodybuilder would look funny if the muscles in his right leg were noticeably larger than those in his left leg.

You are not a bodybuilder.

You're more like a tennis player. In tennis, there are a variety of "strokes" that can get the job done. And if one is good enough, nobody will notice your lack of the others.

Even the best baseball player isn't great at every position on the field. The CEO of a company would fail miserably at many lower-level jobs. Many successful self-employed people failed miserably at working for somebody else.

You're far better off playing to your strengths than focusing on weaknesses in an effort to achieve "balance." Focusing on too many things at once dilutes the results that focusing on a single task or goal will allow you to achieve.

You don't have to be good at everything to be successful at podcasting. If you're not good at particular tasks or you lack certain skills, your best bet may be to outsource that work to other people.

Who's The Boss?

One trend in podcasting is for hosts to be just like their audiences. This is especially prevalent in business and entrepreneur podcasts, where the host is often doing (or trying to do) the same things his audience is doing, such as making money online, growing a business, or quitting his job. However, this trend spans genres, with people sharing what they're doing to lose weight, their dating experiences, and other personal journeys.

This kind of "personal journal" is fine and can be very helpful to people. However, if you want to eventually be seen as an expert on the subject, you're setting yourself up for failure.

Think about a father who tries to be his kid's best friend. He's the "cool parent" who dresses like his kid, listens to the same music as his kid, and lets his kid drink beer, even though the kid is underage.

You can be your kid's "best friend" or you can be his parent — you can't be both.

Similarly, you can be a peer who is going on a journey *with* the people who are listening to your podcast or you can be a leader who's already been through an experience and has returned to the starting point to help others with their experiences.

If you're looking for friends, by all means run your podcast like a personal journal. If you're looking to be respected as leader though, you need to act the part.

The Best Kind Of Podcast Host

The best kind of podcast host balances authority with approachability. People want to be led, which is why you need authority. But people also want to feel like it's safe to reach out to you.

It's a fine balance. To find it, here are seven things you can start doing to better connect with listeners.

1. Assume Rapport Is Already There.

The people who listen to your podcast already feel as if they know you, so when meeting them in person or talking to them online, continue on this path. Skip the awkward, "getting to know you" phase when you're introduced and go straight into talking to them as if you've known each other for years.

2. Let People In.

Be open. For example, if you're having a conversation with somebody, whether in person or online, and you see another person "waiting on the side" or otherwise trying to interact with you, let him join that conversation. Be confident, yet humble.

3. Listen.

If you can make fans of your podcast feel good, they'll do anything for you. Simply listening to people during interactions with them is a great way to show that you care, build their confidence, and make them feel great about the experience of connecting with you.

4. Be Vulnerable.

Nothing is flawless. Even a slight "damaging admission" when something goes wrong shows you admit and accept imperfection. It will also go a long way to building trust with the people you interact with, since it humanizes you.

5. Let People Help You.

People want to be part of what you're doing. If you get an offer from a listener to help you promote your podcast, help you book space for a meetup, or introduce you to someone influential, don't automatically dismiss it. While not every person (or every offer) will be a good match for you, most people are honest, have good intentions, and really do want to help others.

6. Look for Things In Common.

People like people who are like them. Focus on the similarities you have with your listeners.

7. Remember Names.

If you're not good at this, figure out how to get good. Nothing makes people feel more important than being remembered.

Keeping Connected With Listeners

A podcast should never be thought of as a one-way broadcast of your voice to whomever is listening. Transmitting your content online gives you great opportunities for two-way communication with listeners, so take advantage of this to become more connected with your audience.

Don't be fooled by all the social media "experts" who appear to be attached to computers or mobile devices 24/7. Even if you were to do this, if you're promoting your podcast like you should, you'll have way too many fans to respond to every email personally, keep track of every conversation on Facebook and otherwise "be everywhere."

It's much better to pick one form of communication and do it effectively. I suggest Twitter, since messages are limited to 280 characters. This allows you to communicate personally, but nobody on the receiving end of your message will be offended by the brevity, because *all* messages on Twitter are limited.

Pick a time to respond to messages you receive, do it, and then let it go. You don't want to be tied down to a computer or mobile phone all day — that will keep you from doing important work. Beyond that, it will keep you away from *other* fans of your podcast, such as sponsors and guests.

Trying to be everywhere will only leave you worn out and the people you "interact" with (and later end up neglecting) pissed off. You should strive to be fully present when communicating with fans, not communicate with them as an afterthought or in a way that makes the task feel like a burden.

As you get to know your listeners better and better, communication with them will become much more effective. Because of the personal nature of Twitter, you'll also have the benefit of quality, making people feel as if you're "talking directly to them" with a personal message.

The Late Show Rule

In 2015, Stephen Colbert started a three-year contract to host The Late Show on CBS for a reported salary of $4.6 million per year. This was a pay cut from his previous job, hosting Comedy Central's The Colbert Report, where he reportedly made $6 million per year.

And his salary is on the low end for this type of work: Jimmy Fallon reportedly makes between $11 and $12 million per year as host of NBC's *The Tonight Show* and Jimmy Kimmel gets paid $10 million per year for *Jimmy Kimmel Live!*

Why do these host earn so much money? Because they're the reasons people watch.

The same rule applies to podcasting. People listen to podcasts because they connect with the hosts.

Guests you interview on your podcast may bring a few listeners in, but they're equally likely to repel potential listeners. This is especially true if you interview a guest in the middle of a big promotion, where he's on dozens of different podcasts to promote a book or other new product, basically repeating the same interview each time.

Popular and well-known guests on your podcast are not nearly as helpful bringing in new listeners or increasing episode downloads as most podcasters think. People listen to your podcast because of you, not your guests.

Instead of chasing down guests you think will help you to grow an audience because of their existing popularity, focus first on guests who will provide value to listeners. When you have a podcast that provides value to listeners, popularity emerges on its own.

Brand Match

If you look at an advertisement from Apple, you'll know it's Apple, even if the company name and logo has been removed.

Think of the most famous music acts and how defined their sounds are. Or the most famous visual artists and how defined their work is. When you hear a Van Halen song, there's no doubt it's Van Halen. When you see a piece of visual art by Andy Warhol, you know he's the creator.

This is the kind of clarity your podcast should have. Everything about your podcast must match its message. *Everything.*

Six elements to focus on:

1. *Story* - How did you get here?
2. *Purpose* - Why does your podcast exist?
3. *Position* - What do you stand for?
4. *Promise* - What promise are you making to listeners?
5. *Personality* – In what way do you deliver your message, position yourself, and deliver on promises to listeners?
6. *Emotion* - How do you want people to feel about you and your podcast?

These elements should come through in your podcast itself, your website, graphics and imaging that you use, and correspondence with listeners and the media. Everything you do should back these things up, because inconsistency will confuse listeners.

Finding Your Voice – Start Where You Are

You want to be yourself on your podcast. You need an image, voice, and energy that you can consistently bring to every episode of you show.

Every episode.

With that said, this is a *performance* — you need to do a little something extra.

Think of your favorite entertainer. It's unlikely his public image is a total fabrication. It's far more likely that what you see is his real self, but exaggerated.

This is who you should be on your podcast. It's still you, but with a bit more power, a bit more authority, and a bit more excitement.

A quick story …

Jeff Sanders hosts *The 5AM Miracle Podcast.* He talks about healthy habits, personal development, and how to increase productivity.

That's the kind of guy Jeff is. He wakes up at the crack of dawn with intention and a solid plan for the day.

A radio host in the personal development space saw what Jeff was doing and reached out to him, hoping to work together on a project. While discussing this, he told Jeff that his tagline, "Dominate Your Day Before Breakfast," was intimidating and scaring away potential listeners.

And he was right. Jeff's tagline *is* intimidating, at least to some people.

Jeff had two options:

1. Change his tagline and general approach to something softer in hope of increasing listener numbers.
2. Keep the harder tagline, keep the approach that was a match for his personality, and focus on listeners who connected with it.

He chose number two.

This is podcasting, not radio. You win in radio by blasting your signal everywhere and dumbing things down in hope that the people who receive it don't change the channel or turn you off. You win in podcasting by creating something that people like enough to search for.

Try to please everybody and you'll please nobody.

White Tigers, Black Republicans, And Christian Swingers

If you've ever seen the Republican National Convention on television, you'll notice a lack of racial diversity. You'll see a few shots showing black people in the audience, sure, but don't be fooled — that's the same couple of guys being shown over and over again.

I kid, I kid. But let's not bullshit here. The GOP is made up of mostly white people.

With this said, there *are* black Republicans in the world.

There are also Christians who share more than just Bible verses. They believe "Thou shall not covet your neighbor's wife" doesn't apply if that's what your neighbor wants.

Like white tigers, Christian swingers exist, but they're not common. And it's these "not common" subcultures that are a great match for podcasting.

Smaller Niche = Bigger Podcast

Jesse Dollemore is a "conservative atheist" who lives in Los Angeles whose podcast *I Doubt It* caters to that market with episodes that talk about news, current events, and politics from that perspective.

He doesn't fit the mold of FOX News. You'll never see him in a church.

But just because you don't see conservative atheists (or any subculture) on media or where you hang out doesn't mean they don't exist.

They do exist. And they're waiting for you to fly your flag so they can have a place to gather and find each other.

Play your game and let people come to you.

Finding Your Voice – How Long Will It Take?

Hitting "publish" takes guts. When you release anything into the world, whether it be an email, a blog post, or a podcast, you open yourself up to criticism from the people who can now access it.

It's normal to be scared when you release something. Being scared simply shows that the work you're doing is important to you and you want it to have impact on people.

Everybody comes to the table with different skills when we start podcasting. Before you ever picked up a microphone or stepped into a studio, you were working on finding your voice and developing your world view.

Because of these things, it's impossible to give the accurate length of time it will take for you to "feel comfortable" coming up with episode topics, outlining episodes, getting behind the mic, and publishing your podcast. It's also impossible to know how long it will take for you to become completely clear and comfortable with who you are and the worldview you share. Some people, maybe most people, never get there.

Sounds depressing, doesn't it? It's actually a great gift – it means that where you are now with your podcasting comfort is exactly where you need to be.

People are constantly changing and developing (or should be). We learn as we go, gathering new and different knowledge along the way.

As we learn more, we also realize how little we actually know. We also learn there is no "finish line."

But it helps to have a defined goal. Because of this, I'm going to give you something to work on, which will allow you to focus on the process of getting more comfortable with yourself and getting clearer on your worldview: You should record and produce 100 episodes.

This means coming up with topics, outlining everything in a way that will make sense to listeners, and actually recording. It means self-editing, so you can get an accurate feel for your organization and delivery.

This doesn't mean that you must publish *everything*. Some of the episodes you create may not be made for publication.

It also doesn't mean you have to complete 100 episodes before you publish *anything*. You can publish episodes as you go.

Your 100 F*cking Episodes

Some of the episodes you create may be solely for the purpose of getting comfortable with specific elements of podcasting, such as sharing your worldview.

Tim Grahl, in his book *Running Down A Dream*, talks about a technique he used for finding his writing voice that you may find helpful in finding your podcasting voice.

I found if I put lots of "fucks" and "shits" in my writing,

I would say what I really wanted to say. Because I was breaking the taboo of cursing, it allowed me to overcome other things I was afraid of saying. If I thought the message was strong, I would just edit out the cursing in the second draft.

The important thing about the 100 episodes exercise (and why it works) is that you actually do what it takes to create episodes rather than simply thinking or talking about the process. Action trumps talk. If you want to talk, by all means talk, but organize what you want to say, get behind a mic, hit record, and make an episode out of it.

Everybody is scared to release their first episodes and even pros are scared to release *some* episodes — that fear never totally disappears.

Pros don't let that fear stop them from hitting "publish", though. And if you want to have a successful podcast, you'll ultimately have to hit "publish" on the episodes you create.

Worried about people hearing your early or non-polished work? Don't be. First episodes rarely get a lot of listeners when they're released and, even if your podcast later takes off, most listeners will never go back to hear Episode #1.

If listeners *do* go back in your archives, they'll likely find your early episodes encouraging. It's nice for listeners to hear that a slick-sounding podcast wasn't always so polished, the confident-sounding host didn't always sound so confident, and the flawless episode organization heard on current episodes was anything but organized in the early days, because this shows that improvement is possible when you put in the necessary work.

You also receive benefits by publishing your first episodes. Finding your voice and otherwise getting good at podcasting takes a while, and improvement happens in small increments that aren't easily noticeable until you go back months, or even years, where you'll be able to easily hear for yourself that the hard work you've put into becoming a better podcast host has paid off.

A Word On Profanity

Should you use profanity in your podcast? This is a great debate among podcasters.

Blogger (and podcaster) Michael Hyatt posted commentary his blog titled "How Much Business Is Your Profanity Costing You?" In this post, he gave three reasons *not* to use profanity.

1. Profanity alienates people

2. Profanity hurts your brand
3. Profanity gets less effective over time

Profanity *can* alienate people. This is why I don't use profanity on my podcasts.

It *can* hurt your brand. But if you're somebody with an edge, it might also help it.

Yes, it gets less effective over time. *Anything* you rely on too heavily gets less effective over time. You could say the same thing for common business buzzwords like "transparency," "authenticity," or "excellence."

Curse words are just words. Sometimes they're the right words for the job, sometimes they're not. Let's not give them any special powers.

CHAPTER 013

IMPROVING YOUR PODCAST HOSTING SKILLS

Want to get good as a podcast host? The foundation to do this is built upon your ability to embrace failure.

Just like you can't learn a new language without speaking, you'll never become great at podcasting without actually making podcasts.

You can't just read books about podcasting. You can't just listen to great podcast hosts. You can't just take a course or talk about podcasting on Facebook.

The only way to become great at podcasting is to get behind a mic, hit record, and make podcasts yourself. You must make mistakes, because that's the only way you'll know what doesn't work and improve on your skill set so those mistakes are less frequent.

In the radio industry, an aircheck is a demonstration recording intended to show off the talent of an announcer to prospective employers. I have a series of 1973 and 1974 airchecks from a jock named Jeff Christie that are especially interesting.

Jeff had a show on KQV in Pittsburgh called the "Jeff Christie Rock and Roll Radio Show" and you can hear him announce songs from The Stylistics, Stevie Wonder, and Rick Nelson. He announces the weather and stumbles over the amount of money in the "Cash Call" contest. He gives away two six-packs of Carefree Sugarless Gum and flubs a line announcing The Carefree Rock Concert Contest.

"That's a tongue-twister," he says.

It's nothing special — except for a couple of trademark lines Jeff Christie still uses today, like "serving humanity" and "Excellence in Broadcasting."

Jeff Christie was fired repeatedly and told by station management that he would never make it as on-air talent. Today, known as Rush Limbaugh, his syndicated show is the highest-rated radio show in the United States with a listenership of over 15,000,000 people each week.

Want to hear these recordings? Visit BigPodcast.com for three different airchecks from Rush Limbaugh's early days of radio.

Hard work beats talent.

But first, a warning ...

Pretty Girl Syndrome

There's an affliction affecting podcasters. It's called Pretty Girl Syndrome.

Have you ever seen a woman so beautiful that you can't believe she's still single? Yeah, she dates a lot, but she's never with one guy too long.

What's the deal?

It's called Pretty Girl Syndrome and it happens when a woman is so attractive that she changes the energy of every room she walks in — normally intelligent guys stop thinking clearly and this changes the interactions she has.

She's shallow and superficial? No worries — *she's pretty!*

She's mean? You can put up with that because *she's pretty!*

She's not very intelligent? Who cares?! *She's pretty!*

It's not her fault. The problem is that men started noticing her beauty, possibly when she was just a teenager, and because of this, she never had to develop the same skills average people do.

She never had to learn to talk to people because men just approached her and they did all the talking. She never had to learn how to be rejected because she hasn't been rejected yet. She never had to learn how to be alone because she's never had to be alone.

Don't let Pretty Girl Syndrome happen to you.

Pretty Girl Syndrome occurs when women (and men) believe their own hype. It occurs when they surround themselves with "yes men" and others, like family members, who think they can do no wrong.

Imagine if Rush Limbaugh, broadcasting in the early 1970s as Jeff Christie, had been told by station management patronizing comments like:

"I think it's great. I can really hear the passion."

"You sound very excited about music."

"You have a great voice for broadcasting."

This is exactly what's happening in podcasting forums online — way too many people are afraid to offer constructive feedback. They're afraid of being seen as trolls, hurting feelings, or acting like podcasting is a business. They want to be liked more than they care about offering honest opinions.

Feedback like this is not doing you any favors. And it's one of the main reasons podcasting has been stagnant, and that so many people feel, like Steve Jobs did in 2010, that it's "amateur hour."

So how do you know if you're *really* good? How can you make sure you're not suffering from Pretty Girl Syndrome?

Surround yourself with people you trust. Do it now, *before* you start getting popular. Once you're popular, whether it's through a book, a blog, or the podcast, it's harder to get honest opinions about what you're doing because so many people want something from you.

The Modeling Agency

Can I tell you another story about models? It has *a lot* to do with podcasting, I swear …

As I mentioned earlier, I once worked out of booking agency where there were *always* models in the office. These weren't run-of-the-mill catalog models doing work for local department stores and car dealerships — they were top-shelf talent working on projects for Victoria's Secret, Abercrombie & Fitch, and other national brands.

They were so good looking, you'd think, "If I looked like that, I'd never have *any* problems." And if you didn't know better, you'd think "Pretty Girl Syndrome" would be an issue.

It wasn't.

Why? They were constantly getting "airchecked."

It's tough to have your job performance critiqued, but I want you to imagine what these models went through when they received feedback. It got really personal — too short, too fat, too tall, too black.

Many people, when they hear the word "aircheck", think about something like these models went through. They think about having to open themselves up to a critique that's very personal and possibly hurtful.

This isn't the case.

Airchecks in radio and podcasting aren't meant to make you feel bad about yourself — they're a tool designed to help you get better. Don't be scared.

A quick (and related) side note ...

Almost every interaction I've ever had with creative talent, such as models, actors, and musicians, has been positive. I've found the majority to be well-rounded, easy to get along with, and humble.

My theory is that people in creative industries develop these characteristics for two reasons:

1. The constant judgment and rejection from agents, clients, and others who decide whether they get hired or not.
2. Having to successfully work with so many different types of people, not only to get the job, but to do the job — stylists, makeup artists, producers, photographers, other talent, etc.

Podcasters are in the same situation. Like the people in other creative industries, people see our finished product and think what we do is glamorous. But rarely do outsiders understand the work that goes into what we do.

The judgment and rejection that comes with podcasting can make you bitter, or it can make you better. Your choice.

How To Aircheck

Airchecking is more than a critique or opinion of a show or episode — it's a tool to help develop and improve your talent as a host. With that said, as a podcaster who owns his own show, it's important that you not only review yourself during an aircheck session, but also review the entire presentation — the music beds, the guests being interviewed, the voiceover talent on your intro, commercial breaks, sponsor matches, and more.

You want an entire "overview" of the podcast you're producing.

Imagine you're the singer in a rock band. If you were to record a song, the first thing you'd notice about the recording is yourself. An outsider would be listening to the band as a whole — you, the guitarist, the bass player, and the drummer.

Think like a listener when airchecking. All aspects of your podcast are important.

Jeff Brown of *Read To Lead Podcast* spent over 25 years in radio before transitioning to podcasting. He listens for two things when evaluating podcast hosts:

1. **Delivery** - Is the content consistently succinct, straightforward, and easy-to-follow? Is there forward momentum throughout each episode, or numerous rabbit trails and tangents in an attempt to arrive at your destination?
2. **Content** - Is it personable, engaging, and thought-provoking? Does whatever's being discussed have relevancy to the typical listener's life today, right now?

Stu Gray, a 20-year broadcast radio veteran, has a three-part criteria for airchecking — "Be On, Be Good, Be Gone." He advises to listen for good preparation (Be On), listen for clarity of thought and purpose and the ability to say what you need to say without meandering (Be Good), and listen for the ability to "land" thoughts well (Be Gone).

Here are some specific things listen for when airchecking:

- Talking over people
- Transitioning to and from commercials
- Introducing guests
- Questioning / interviewing guests
- Responding to guests in a relevant way
- Reading content (news, listener feedback, etc.)
- Reading / announcing commercials
- Telling stories
- Interaction with co-hosts
- Jokes / humor

External Airchecks

It's a good idea to listen to and critique podcasts and radio shows other than your own. You'll get both inspiration and new ideas.

You'll also learn what *not* to do. Other podcasts are perfect for this, as we're often able to hear "bad habits" in the recordings of others which we miss in our own recordings because we're too close to them.

When listening to the podcasts of others, whether for critique or pleasure, be sure to listen at "normal" speed, not 1.5x or 2x rate. Although quicker playback will save you time listening, you're hearing things in a different way than people actually talk, and this can cause you to pick up bad habits, most notably talking too fast and not pausing between thoughts and words as long as you should for maximum impact.

How To Give Aircheck Feedback To Other Podcasters

You will find it helpful to connect with other podcasters to aircheck each other as well as aircheck third-party podcasts and radio shows together.

When giving feedback to other podcasters, you want to balance positive and negative comments. A good way to organize aircheck feedback is the CRE format — commendation, recommendation, encouragement.

First, let the other podcaster know what he did right.

Next, give any recommendations you have. Note that there are *always* things to improve upon, so *never* say something like, "This episode was great from front to back. I can't think of anything you should do differently."

The worst thing you can tell somebody you're reviewing is "your performance was perfect." There's no such thing as a perfect performance, and not letting somebody know where there's room for improvement won't help him to get better.

Finally, end your aircheck with some encouraging words.

Deep (And Deliberate) Practice

Podcasters aren't bad because of something random. Podcasters are bad because of their lack of deliberate practice.

That's good news — it means good podcasters are made, not born that way.

If you want to get good at podcasting, you must practice in a very specific way. Getting behind the mic and hitting the record button isn't enough, although that's part of it.

Not all practice is equal. And simply recording a bunch of podcasts isn't enough to make you great.

Simply asking questions, if you have an interview-format podcast, isn't enough to make you great. Asking questions is easy — the talent lies in bringing out a conversation that people want to listen to.

This is why the skill of so many podcasters stalls after a certain point. The more you do anything, the more comfortable you'll be.

And it's easy to confuse comfort with talent.

But you want to be *great*, not just comfortable. You're not a technician, whose only worry is mic placement, and this isn't a factory job. You're a human who wants other humans to connect with what you're doing. To do that, you need to focus on certain things.

CHAPTER 014

HOSTING SKILLS TO FOCUS ON (AND HOW TO FOCUS)

There are four main areas you need to focus on if you want to be great at podcasting:

- Listening
- Talking
- Planning
- Adjusting

This sounds simple. You may think you're already skilled in these areas, and you may be right. But remember what I said about comfort — it's easy to confuse comfort with talent.

How many times have you heard podcasts where the host pretty much does the same interview each time? I'm not talking about asking the same questions each time, although that has certainly been a trend — I'm talking about hosts who cover the same basic story.

In the business/marketing genre, these episodes usually go something like this ...

The Introduction

Oh my gosh!! Thanks so much for listening!!

This guy I'm about to interview is so great!! Seriously, he is just awesome!! I just met him, but I'm going to refer to him as "my good friend."

Okay, here's the interview.

[STINGER SOUND EFFECT]

The Build Up

How did you get started? / What's your background?

Really, you worked a day job you hated?

You were in debt? Wow.

Your marriage failed? Oh no!

The Redemption

You read *4-Hour Work Week*? I love that book!!

Let's talk about how you ... [PICK ONE]

Used your last dollar to put up a WordPress blog with Adsense

Spent the entire weekend writing an ebook that you sold on Amazon

Put ads on Facebook and turned a $10 investment into $100,000 monthly recurring revenue

The "Actionable" Advice

If you had to start all over again, what's the first thing you would do?

If you only had $100, what's the one thing you would do?

What's your favorite iPhone app?

The Offer

I had to beg you to do this, but you've agreed to give a special offer to my listeners …
This is a one-time deal that is only good for the next 10 minutes.
OMG!!! A free ebook?! Seriously?! That is so awesome!

Sound familiar? Every podcast genre has its own version of this.

It's easy to fall into this rut for a few reasons. For one, so many people are following this basic format (or a version of it), you see it done so often you start to think it's the way things *should* be done.

It's not.

Beyond that, as you already know, creating good content on a regular basis takes effort. It's much easier to phone something in than actually do the work needed to create something more — something compelling, something different, and something people would actually miss if it wasn't there.

Let's talk about the four areas of podcasting you need to excel in — listening, talking, planning, and adjusting — and exactly what you need to do in order to master them…

1. Listening

There's a difference between listening and hearing. Hearing is perceiving sound — that's it! Hearing is a physical act that happens when vibrations in the atmosphere strike our eardrums. It is happening all the time, even when we're sleeping.

Listening is an active behavior. It's a developed skill in which hearing is the foundation. It happens when we attach meaning to the sounds we hear. To attach the "correct" meaning for your listener, at least as far as interviewing somebody is concerned, you need to be skilled at interpreting things from his point of view.

Not listening can lead to misunderstandings and missed opportunities.

2. Speaking

You've likely been doing this for a while, without much thought. But there's a big difference between speaking to a friend who's next to you and speaking in a way that hundreds of people (or more) will want to listen to.

A good podcaster talks in a way which is authoritative, but also personable.

3. Planning

If you want people to listen to your podcast, you can't waste their time. People want to listen to episodes that are well-thought-out and organized. This comes from good planning.

4. Adjusting

A podcast with more than just you, whether that additional person is a co-host or someone being interviewed, is constantly in motion and constantly changing. The way you keep multi-person episodes moving forward in an organized and methodical way is by adjusting your performance as it's happening.

To become a great podcaster, you only need the four skills above — listening, speaking, planning, and adjusting.

There are two primary ways to become great at these skills. One, creating solo episodes, and two, creating interview-format episodes.

Solo Episodes

All podcasting requires both speaking and planning, but it's working on solo episodes that will enable you to really develop these skills. With a solo episode, speaking and planning is about all there is.

Solo episodes are scary. It's easy to hide behind interviews and co-hosts, relying on other people to cover for you and make what you're doing entertaining and informative.

When you're solo, all your bad habits are at the forefront. The stuttering, awkward timing, and filler words are obvious.

Your first solo episodes are *always* awkward. It's easy to fall into the belief that those who are great at solo podcasting are naturals, or write yourself off as unskilled talent. Remember, though, great podcasters are made, not born. If you put the time into doing the focused work of creating solo podcasts, you'll get better.

When it comes to creating content, remember that solo podcasting, just like solo radio, is similar to speaking one-on-one with a friend, except your friend isn't there to immediately respond. That's where planning comes in — as you plan episodes, you have to consider what listeners' responses will be as those episodes are heard, even though you're not there to see these responses in person.

When it comes to how you deliver content, there's a fine balance. Podcast listeners want to listen to somebody who sounds authoritative, but also approachable. You don't want to sound like a hyped-up stereotype — no strip club DJs or 1970s FM rock jock. But you don't want to sound like you're timid, either.

You want to connect to people who are listening, not simply talk *at* them. You want to communicate in ways listeners understand and relate to, using the language they use.

Ultimately, the podcast "personality" you create is up to you, and should be based on who you are and the genre of your podcast. As there are as many personalities and voices as there are podcasts, I can't give you advice on this that is any more specific, but I've never seen anybody go wrong with a mixture of "authoritative and approachable."

To become great at solo podcasting, focus on planning and speaking. Write an outline on your topic, hit record, and let it rip. If you make a mistake, take a breath, and start that sentence again. This is focused practice.

As you edit the recording, notice these technical elements:

- Stuttering
- Awkward pauses
- Double-words (For example, "I really, really like that.")
- Connector words (but, so, you know, and …)
- Coming in "too hot" at the beginning on sentences
- Fading out at the end of sentences
- Plosives (popping "p" sounds is the most common one)
- Lip smacks, pops, or clicks
- Heavy breathing

Also notice these elements that keep episodes from moving forward and can cause you to lose connection with listeners:

- Jokes that don't land
- Off-topic content
- When you spend too much time on a topic or repeat content

Look for holes in your outline. Were there things you should have explained better? Were there things you explained too thoroughly?

Brevity and clarity go hand in hand. You want to communicate your thoughts in a clear way, using as few words as possible.

Dale Carnegie said, "There are always three speeches, for every one you actually gave. The one you practiced, the one you gave, and the one you wish you gave."

The same is true for podcast episodes. Working on both planning and delivery of solo episodes, then editing them, is how to have less differentiation between the three.

Practice Reading Aloud

The ability to accurately read and deliver listener correspondence, quotes, ad copy, news, and guest introductions is essential to your podcasting success. If you do it well, you'll sound like a confident authority. If not, you'll sound like a telemarketer on his first day at work.

You know how you always got a little nervous when you were in elementary school and your teacher called on you to read something aloud? It's time you get over that.

How? Practice reading aloud.

What should you read? News articles are a great place to start as they're often written at a very basic level with short sentences and words. The best things to practice are what you're actually going to be reading during your podcast — for example, emails, social media messages, and news headlines.

What to listen for:

1. **Pronunciation** - Are you getting sloppy or pronouncing words the wrong way? For example ... not "fer" example.
2. **Enunciation** - Are you mumbling or slurring words together? If you're unsure, record yourself with software like Audacity and view the waveform that's created.

3. **Projection** - Are you starting strong, but fading away at the end of sentences? Is your projection consistent?

4. **Inflection** - Do you use "vocal variety" or speak in a monotone style? Are you emphasizing the correct words when speaking?

5. **Pace and Cadence** - How quick (or slow) is your delivery? Do you sound rushed? Are you dragging? Are you consistent?

6. **Pauses** - Are you giving enough time (or too much time) between sentences? How much are you pausing between listed items?

Ready to move beyond news articles? Try reading children's books and scripts as these are meant to be read aloud and will provide you the opportunity to play with dialog and different voices. A search online for "commercial transcripts" will also give you a lot of material to work with.

CHAPTER 015

GET BETTER AT PODCASTING (WITHOUT PODCASTING)

Something dancers, yogis, and weightlifters know is that you can get better at a specific task without actually doing it, if you do a related task. For example, dancers will get better at Quickstep by dancing Foxtrot, students of yoga will get better at full-arm balance by doing downward-facing dog, and weightlifters will increase the amount of weight they can curl by doing chin-ups.

This also applies to podcasting. The skills you need to be a great podcaster – mainly the ability to tell stories, think on your feet, and organize your communication – can be greatly improved through activities which also require these skills, but in a different way.

As a bonus, working on related tasks will also provide you with experiences that will help you establish a strong voice and perspective listeners will connect with.

Blogging

Blogging will help you to develop the ability to organize content in a linear and cohesive manner.

Writing blog posts will improve your ability to:

- Create an outline
- Craft an attention-getting opening
- Transition from one section to another
- Conclude your message in an effective way

In addition, blogging will:

- Drive people to you through improved search engine results
- Fortify your message (and other branding elements)
- Help you build your mailing list

You don't need a dedicated blog to take advantage of the skill improvement you'll get from blogging. Third-party platforms such as Medium and LinkedIn will allow you to get the same experience as writing for your own blog with the extra benefit of a pre-existing audience.

Speaking

Like writing a blog post or organizing a podcast episode, speaking in front of a live audience will help you:

- Find a topic people are interested in

- Organize your presentation in a way that's helpful to an audience (and easy to follow)
- Deliver your message in a compelling way

You'll also learn important podcasting skills that easily become neglected when you have the ability to go back and edit what's been said or written. The main one is how to think on your feet while presenting information.

I once gave a presentation at a conference in Atlanta. The audience was made up of record label executives and managers with a few ambitious musicians sprinkled in.

"You don't know what the fuck you're talking about," came an angry voice from the audience.

Not all audience interactions you'll have when speaking are this dramatic. The guy who yelled from the crowd in Atlanta was frustrated with lackluster ticket sales for his shows and, as frustrating as that is, most people in that situation would have kept quiet or waited to ask questions at the end of the presentation rather than interrupt it.

Still, whether an audience is yelling things during your presentation or asking you questions afterward, you need to know how to handle either. And only in a live setting will you have the opportunity to learn how to respond appropriately.

CHAPTER 016

PODCASTING CONFIDENCE

You've likely noticed this when you've recorded your voice and played it back — what you hear when you're speaking is totally different than the playback.

Why? Because when you speak you hear your voice in two different ways — you hear vibrating sound waves hitting your eardrums and through vibrations inside your skull.

Bones in your skull conduct lower frequencies better than air. As the vibrations travel through these bones, they spread out and lower in pitch. This is why, when you speak, your voice sounds lower and fuller than it does when you simply listen to it on a recording.

If you don't like your voice, it's only because you're not used to hearing it the way others do. The more you hear recordings of yourself, the more you'll get used to hearing your voice through just your eardrums instead of both your eardrums and bone conduction.

The "Radio Voice"

If you listen to recordings of radio disc jockeys from the 1970s and 1980s, you're likely to hear big, deep "announcer-style" voices. On some radio formats, you'll still hear this style.

You know the voice I'm talking about — it has the bass of a Don LaFontaine movie trailer with the energy of Rod Roddy from *Price Is Right*. It's slick and *everything* is enunciated.

When you hear a voice like that you think, "That guy should be on the radio."

The average radio announcer today has a voice that is more casual and conversational. He speaks clearly and with enthusiasm, but it's not over the top.

"Radio voice" doesn't mean you have to sound like an announcer. But that kind of feeling is a good place to start when figuring out the energy you want to bring to voicing your podcast.

The biggest issue most podcasters face when it comes to an energetic delivery is just the opposite of a "radio voice" – they don't have enough energy. They're so worried about sounding like a guy who reads commercials for a monster truck rally that they keep things too laid back. They sound like a nervous sixth-grader reading announcements over his school's PA system.

In normal conversation, we don't think about the finer details of our voices. The majority of people start talking at a very young age and, because of this, most have never had to analyze what's happening.

Then we get in a situation, such as creating a podcast, where we're analyzing *everything* we say and how we say it. And putting that much thought into something we've done so long without thinking about it can be stressful.

The extra attention on your speech can make you feel like you're speaking much louder than normal. Or enunciating too much. Or speaking too slow.

Maybe you are. But probably not.

The more episodes you record and edit, the more comfortable you'll become with your voice and the better you'll be able to use it to create the sound (and deliver the message) you want.

This Affects 75 Percent Of People (And Probably Affects You)

Glossophobia, also known as speech anxiety, is estimated to affect about 75 percent of people in one form or another. Surveys have shown that most people fear public speaking more than they fear death.

Symptoms of glossophobia include:

- intense anxiety prior to, or simply at the thought of having to verbally communicate
- avoidance of group events where there is focused attention on individuals by others in attendance
- physical distress, nausea, or feelings of panic in speaking, performance, or attention-receiving situations

We often call these symptoms "stage fright."

It affects different people in different ways. I know musicians who can get on stage and sing in front of tens of thousands of people, but clam up when playing for small groups. I know comics who can perform flawlessly on stage, because they know their material so well, but get weird when talking to somebody one-on-one.

Personally, I'm good speaking in front of a live crowd or via a radio broadcast, once things get going, but I get nervous before doing either. This doesn't happen every single time, but it happens enough that I'm aware it's always a possibility. When it does, my heart beats faster and it's like I'm outside of my body, watching somebody else as I wait to go on stage or begin recording. I get coughing fits.

You're Not Going To Die (But You May Wish You Would)

A few years ago, I did some stand-up comedy work, not because I had the desire to be a stand-up comic, but to get better at the three things great stand-up comics must master — delivery, brevity, and timing. My goal was to successfully get through a showcase performance at a comedy club in Nashville called Zanies.

To prepare for my performance, I wrote (and rewrote) material, I did private performances for other comics, and I did public performances at other comedy clubs to see how general audiences reacted. I worked closely with my comedy mentor, veteran comic Rik Roberts, who helped me to reduce my learning curve. Still, even though the final set was only five to seven minutes of material, the entire process took about three months as I was constantly tweaking the set on paper and on stage — testing new jokes, reworking existing jokes, and dropping things that didn't work.

I put in *a lot* of time.

The evening of the showcase, I was nervous. I'd seen comics bomb and it's painful. When you're on stage with just a mic stand, there's nowhere to hide if things go wrong.

My performance was scheduled later in the lineup. Instead of hanging out backstage, I got a seat in the audience.

I ordered a ginger ale, hoping to calm my stomach.

It didn't work.

I went to the bathroom and started coughing uncontrollably. I sounded like I was about to vomit. When a guy came in and checked on me, I acted like I'd had a few too many beers.

You know things are bad when you're in a public bathroom pretending like you're sick from drinking too much, and it seems like a better option than admitting you're nervous about getting on stage.

This was a comedy club with a tight schedule. I was lucky to be there and, without Rik to get me in, I wouldn't have been.

When it was time for me to get on stage, I had to be on stage. And it was time.

I was introduced, I did my set, and that was it. Instantly, I felt normal again.

I've been asked a few times if I'd do it again. I would. And because I've already done it successfully, I'm positive I could give a better performance.

Would I have less fear? That, I'm not so sure about.

You may be in a similar situation when it comes to releasing your podcast. If so, I've got good news for you.

Stage Fright Solutions

If you're anxious about getting behind a mic, you can reduce your anxiety by doing the following five things.

1. Know what you're talking about.

One of the biggest reasons people don't like public speaking is because, unlike writing a book or blog, your message goes out instantly — you don't have the option of *not* publishing what you've said.

Podcasting is different. Yes, some podcasters also stream live, but that's optional. And because of this, you always have the opportunity to edit what you record before anybody hears anything.

Anything you release to the world, whether it be a podcast, a book, a blog, a video, or a live speech, is fair game for criticism. Editing may help you feel better about what goes out, but a better way to reduce anxiety about your podcast is to know what you're talking about.

If you're not comfortable with the topic you want to podcast on, one of the best ways to get comfortable is to start having conversations with people who are in that world. Reach out to people via social media, go to related conferences, and hire experts who can help you. Read books, listen to podcasts on the subject, and be curious.

Connection with others is the starting point that will get you going in the right direction. You'll learn new things, as well as discover how much you already know. Once this happens, you'll be more confident about what you're sharing with others via your podcast.

2. Believe in your topic.

Book launch expert Tim Grahl, author of *Your First 1000 Copies*, says the number-one thing that sells books isn't what most people think — it's not a great book cover, having the perfect launch, or access to millions of people via email or social media.

The number one thing that makes authors (and their books) successful is that they believe in the information they've written, and that people will benefit by reading it.

This sounds obvious, doesn't it?

But do you feel the same way about your podcast? Most podcasters, if they're really honest with themselves, don't.

How to measure your level of belief:

Imagine this scenario: You live in a great house, in a great neighborhood. You've been there for years, raised a family there, and you love your neighbors.

You receive notice from your city's planning board that a real estate developer wants to knock down a community center as well as several other houses in the neighborhood to build a complex called "Sin City" — it will include a seedy bar, a bingo parlor, and strip club.

If the developer does this, your neighborhood will be filled with drunks, blue-haired women with gambling addictions, and suitcase pimps. There will be more traffic. There will be more noise.

You like your neighborhood the way it is and want to keep it that way. What are you going to do?

Email your neighbors? Knock on neighbors' doors to let them know what's happening? Alert the local media? Organize a letter-writing campaign to the planning board?

You'd do all these things and more. You'd do whatever it took to keep this kind of development from moving forward.

This is the kind of belief you need to have about your podcast. You need to know, without any doubt, that what you've got is the right thing for people. When you do, "stage fright" disappears, you become immune to critics, and you find the energy to make things happen.

3. Script everything.

One of the biggest fears people have about speaking in front of an audience is forgetting what they're going to say. This can be solved by writing a script to read verbatim.

When I started interviewing people on radio, I scripted out *everything* — the intros, the breaks, the IDs. And I had enough questions for a two-hour episode even though the episodes we did were only one hour.

A decade later, when I started doing solo podcasts, without the crutch of music to play, guests to interview, or callers to interact with, I scripted episodes as well.

If scripting everything word-for-word is what enables you to get behind the mic and create a podcast, do it. As you get more and more comfortable, you can start working from an outline or use a less-scripted solution to organize your episodes.

4. Practice with a receptive audience.

When you speak in front of a live audience, it can be easy to forget that the audience wants you to succeed. The same is true with a podcast audience.

Still, *any* audience, whether they're staring at you while you deliver a live performance or listening to a recording you did in the studio, can be intimidating. Practicing your communication skills in front of a live audience can help this and it's for this reason that I recommend podcasters look into Toastmasters.

Toastmasters (officially called Toastmasters International) is a nonprofit educational organization with over 15,000 clubs around the world, each averaging about 20 members. The purpose of these clubs is to help members improve their communication, public speaking, and leadership skills.

Toastmasters is a peer-led organization. All members are in the same situation, so when you give a speech at a local club, you're performing to an audience of people who also give speeches. Because of this, there is a lot of empathy and understanding for those getting over stage fright.

A Toastmasters audience strikes a good balance between understanding and honest. You'll get feedback that will help you improve your speaking delivered in a way that honors where you are and the work you're doing to better communicate your message.

5. The Rewrite

Hunter S. Thompson typed out every word of F. Scott Fitzgerald's *The Great Gatsby* and Ernest Hemingway's *A Farewell to Arms* in order to learn about the writing styles of the authors. This technique was used by legendary copywriter Gary Halbert, who would copy classic ads by hand and later went on to create the most-mailed sales letter in history, sending out 600,000,000 copies over a period of 30 years.

A technique songwriters often use to learn songwriting (or get out of a rut) is to take an existing song and "rewrite" it. For example, taking a popular song about a love triangle, using the feel and story behind the song, and creating a new song that tells the same story in another way.

You can do the same with public speaking and podcasting.

Listen to a podcast on the same topic you want to talk about. If it's an interview-format podcast, write down the list of questions asked. If it's a solo or co-hosted podcast without any interviews, outline the main points.

Once you have a basic template from the podcast episodes you've analyzed, create something similar for your own podcast. Take what you like from other episodes, change it up so it works for you, and leave what you don't like.

How To Handle Criticism

Not everybody who hears your podcast will like it. Some people who hear your podcast, in fact, will hate it.

On a positive note, if your podcast is getting criticism, it means you're reaching people. The only podcasts that don't get criticism aren't being heard at all.

Criticism can hurt. And the fact that it happens to everybody doesn't make dealing with it any easier.

If you've ever been to a comedy club and seen a heckler attempt to derail a show, you know it usually doesn't last long. Professional comics are prepared to squelch verbal disruptions and are quick to use excessive force to take care of initial outbursts by hecklers before they get out of hand.

It's common to see other creators take a similar approach when somebody criticizes their work. You don't have to go through too many one-star reviews on Amazon to find one where an author tries to argue with a dissatisfied book reader or apologize because the book wasn't a match.

You're not a comic in a club; you're somebody spreading a message via a podcast. Aggressively going after one frustrated listener risks losing the goodwill you've established with other listeners. And apologizing for your message makes you look like you lack confidence in it.

Your podcast isn't for everybody. That's no reason to be hesitant about the message it contains or apologize when somebody it's not made for happens upon it.

Here are three ways to handle critics:

1. Ignore them. If you're not going to do anything with the feedback you get, there's no reason to waste your time or get upset.
2. Listen to them. If the criticism is valid, thank the critic and take it. There's no reason to apologize and you don't need to make excuses – just take the feedback and use it to help you move forward.
3. If the criticism is coming from a listener who is frustrated that the problem he thought you'd help him with isn't being solved, reassure him that you're with him, you want to understand his problem, and you want to help him with it. Do what you can do point him in the right direction. This may be creating additional episodes based on his situation or may be offering other services that can help him.

Regardless of which option you choose, don't be defensive when receiving criticism. You're a professional, not a five-year-old.

A Final Thought - The High Dive

When I was about nine years old, a friend of mine had a birthday party that started out at a local swimming club. At this swimming club was a series of three diving platforms, the highest being about 30 feet.

None of the kids in our group wanted to attempt it.

After standing around the base, looking upward, watching other people jump off, and talking about how high the top platform was, my friend walked away for a few minutes. When he returned, he told us, "My father says he'll give me $20 if I jump off."

We watched a few more minutes. Then he went for it, climbing slowly as he made his way toward the top.

Then he jumped.

He hit the water, swam to the side, got out of the pool, and immediately climbed the platform again to take a second dive.

He came over to our group and said, "It's not that scary. You guys should try it."

The same is true for your podcast. Like diving off the high platform, podcasting can seem more intimidating than it actually is. And, like diving off the high platform, podcasting is better with friends.

Focus on the community around your podcast and the people your message is helping. This will keep you and your podcast moving forward.

PART 2 – PODCAST GUESTS

CHAPTER 017

YOUR PODCAST GUESTS

Engel Jones started a podcast called *Twelve-Minute Convos* with the goal of talking to 1509 people in just three months, and setting a Guinness World Record.

When his time ran out, he'd completed just 1001.

While he didn't make Guinness World Records, he got something far more valuable. He made hundreds of new connections, rapidly increased his abilities as a podcaster, and put his podcast (and himself) on the map.

This is the kind of opportunity available to you as an interview-format podcaster. It's an opportunity to get "instantly" connected to new people and bring them in to what you do.

The first step of making this happen is having the right guests for your podcast.

Getting Clear About What Makes A Good Podcast Guest

Finding "guests" for your podcast will *never* be a problem. The problem is finding quality guests who are a match for your podcast.

If you have an interview-format podcast, you need more than just a warm body on the other mic. You need somebody who is going to provide value for the listening audience.

To do this, you need to think like a journalist. When a journalist is working on a story, he asks himself, "Who will help me tell this story?"

He doesn't approach random people. He doesn't approach "popular" people who might tell others about his work. He doesn't get sidetracked by those who have nothing of value to add to what he's creating.

Like a journalist, you're telling a "story" with your podcast. It's probably not a traditional story like you'd read in a novel, but like a story, your podcast should have a defined message.

As an example, a Christian podcast might have a message that focuses on hope and salvation or, going in the opposite direction, a message that focuses on fire and brimstone.

Just as journalists think through the basics of their stories and go to people who can help fill in the blanks, you want guests who can help convey *your* message.

If somebody can't help you tell the story you're trying to tell on your podcast, he's not a good guest.

4 Basic Qualifications For Guests

Just because somebody is successful or has lived an interesting life doesn't mean he's a good match for your podcast. Consider these basic qualifications for people you interview:

1. Guests Must Be Knowledgeable And "Walk the Walk"

If somebody is going to appear on your podcast, he needs to have a certain level of competence. Anything less isn't considerate of the people who listen to you.

What does competence look like?

If a guest is talking about making money online, it means she actually needs to be making money online.

If he's giving advice on the food *you* should eat, it means he needs to be eating that food himself.

If a couple is talking about how to have a happy marriage, it means they need to be in relationship that resembles one.

Nobody wants to hear advice from somebody who hasn't experienced what he's talking about. Just like you wouldn't hire somebody with a dirty car to clean yours, listeners don't want (and don't trust) relationship advice from a guy who's been married seven times, Spanish lessons from somebody who can't speak Spanish, or advice on nutrition from Ronald McDonald.

2. Guests Must Be Likable And Personable

Pick any random human resources department looking to fill a job and you'll see that the "decision to hire" comes down to only two things — qualifications and likability.

Like a company hiring employees, you want podcast guests who are qualified. Listeners want to learn and be entertained by those who are wiser and more successful than they are.

However, the ultimate selling point that takes guests from good to great, in the minds of listeners, is their likability.

Will a guest be perceived as likable? Look for the following traits:

- A positive and hopeful outlook
- Relatable
- Genuine interest in your listeners
- Open-mindedness
- Empathetic
- Depth and interests beyond his known expertise
- Generous

Also consider approachability when booking guests for your podcast.

What would happen if a listener saw the guest he heard on your podcast speak at a conference? Would he feel as if he could approach him afterward? If he were to approach him, would the guest be kind and welcoming?

The level of approachability your guests have is the level of approachability listeners consider you to have.

3. Guests Must Be Entertaining, Thought-Provoking, Or Inspiring (Preferably They're All Three)

While "entertainment" doesn't have to be the primary focus of your podcast, you want guests who have lived interesting lives and are able to communicate their experiences and knowledge in a memorable and entertaining way.

You can improve your chances of getting a great interview by starting with a guest who has a good story to tell.

A good story is like a mirror — you "see yourself" in it.

Susan Ruth, host of the podcast *Hey Human*, interviews people from all walks of life. When you listen to *Hey Human*, you'll hear guests with differing jobs, differing belief systems, and differing social statuses.

Her choice of guests is extremely varied — a private investigator, a cartoonist, and a white supremacist, for examples. She says, "I want listeners of *Hey Human* to hear themselves somewhere within the stories that unfold from the conversations I have with guests."

When your listeners relate to guests in such a personal way, they'll keep listening.

This connection is the same reason people love podcasts that focus on inspiration. Stories of losing weight, building successful businesses, or successfully navigating difficult times are just stories until listeners can see themselves in them. Then they become adventures.

People want to create better lives for themselves. You want guests who will help show them that this type of creation is possible.

What this looks like:

You tune into a podcast for an interview with a male stripper who entertains at bachelorette parties. He shows up to every gig dressed as a cop.

You've tuned in thinking, "This will be fun. He's probably got some great stories to tell."

Then the interviewer asks, "How'd you get into this line of work?"

That's when the male stripper starts talking about being overweight when he was a teenager and being made fun of when he took off his shirt for a "shirts and skins" basketball game during a junior high gym class.

Boys bullied him. Girls ignored him.

After spending years feeling worthless and unattractive, he was ready for a change. So he hit the weight room.

That's where the interview goes from being solely entertaining to something more. And if a listener can say, "I'm that guy," or "I want to transform my life too," it becomes something special.

4. Guests Must Be Able To Connect With Your Audience

If your guest can't effectively communicate her message on your podcast, you'll lose listeners.

This means good guests:

- Answer the questions they're asked
- Stay on topic and don't go off on tangents that don't add value to the discussion
- Avoid inside jokes and jargon that mean nothing to people listening

Part of being a good interviewer is having the ability to help somebody tell his story. A great interview is a two-way street and won't happen if the person you're interviewing doesn't show up with these basic communication skills already in place.

It's been my experience that the people with the best communication skills are creatives who craft and present stories for a living — songwriters, authors, publicists, entrepreneurs, writers, and speakers, for example. These people are used to communicating with emotion, not statistics or facts.

Listeners of your podcast aren't robots; they want to feel something, not crunch numbers. Because of this, be aware of guests whose work focuses on "facts and figures" — scientists, accountants, and statisticians, for example. People in these industries are often too close to the work they do to be able to communicate it in a way that the general public can understand.

Certainly, there are exceptions to these rules. There are more than a few creatives who are way too close to their work to effectively explain it to others. There are also "facts and figures" people, such as economists Steven Levitt and Stephen Dubner, co-authors of the *Freakonomics* book series and co-hosts of the podcast, *Freakonomics Radio,* who are excellent at explaining technical things to the average person.

Don't be afraid to take chances on people. The worst that can happen is you'll do interviews you never release.

CHAPTER 018

FINDING GUESTS FOR YOUR PODCAST

The more information you consume and the more conversations related to the subject of your podcast you participate in, the more you'll be aware of options for great podcast guests. If you're doing this correctly, a list of potential guests will "emerge" — you won't have to go searching for people.

When you read something interesting by somebody who would make a great guest, write it down. When a friend mentions a great book he really enjoyed that's related to what you talk about on your podcast, write it down. When you see somebody speak at a conference (or otherwise meet somebody), write it down.

If you want to make sure you never run out of great people to interview or always have great interviews in the can, make a list of people you think would be great guests for your podcast, research those people, and reach out to them about being guests on your podcast.

How big should your "potential guest list" be? At least 100 people.

Start With 25

If your podcast is dependent on quality guests to interview, it's a good idea to put together a "potential guest list" of *at least* 25 people. This will allow you to start approaching multiple people at once, which will give you flexibility in scheduling and more opportunities to release quality episodes.

Here's where to find your first 25 guests:

Your Inner Circle - Ask people you trust to recommend good potential guests for your podcast. Be specific about the type of person you're looking for.

Like growing your listener base, start your guest selection with people whom you already know and use that initial momentum to bring in others whom you don't know.

New podcasts take time to build and may not have the needed goodwill and influence to attract great guests on their own. By going to people whom you're already connected with, you can "borrow" their goodwill and influence via personal introductions and referrals, to jumpstart getting the attention of quality guests.

Your Current Listeners - Listeners of your podcast can be a great resource to leverage when looking for new guests.

The possible downside of this is you'll likely get a lot of self-recommendations. Can you handle saying no to the people who aren't a match? If not, skip this method.

People You Admire - Who are your ultimate guests? Go ahead and write them down. Most people aren't nearly as tough to get in touch with (and get an interview with) as you might think.

Related Blog Posts - Find at least 50 blogs related to the subject of your podcast. Using a feed reader, you can quickly go through new posts on these blogs to discover interesting topics to cover on your podcast as well as interesting people whom you can interview.

Facebook - Facebook, like all social media, can be a major time suck, but it's also a great way to find potential guests. You'll have the best results looking at the pages for specific groups and topics related to your podcast rather than your general feed (unless you want to do interviews with people who post funny videos, conspiracy theories, and cat photos).

Industry-Specific Publications - Who is writing articles for these publications? Who is being interviewed?

Offline publications can be especially good for finding qualified guests and other information to use on your podcast, as their limited space for articles and interviews requires they have a quality filter in place.

As a sidenote, many trade magazines have a "controlled circulation" business model, which means there's a filter on who can subscribe as well. This means only a specific set of people, such as business owners or those in the position to make buying decisions, get these publications.

Your podcast likely has something similar in terms of who you're reaching. Because of this, these industry-specific publications can be a great resource to find companies looking to advertise to your audience.

To find industry-specific publications in your market, search for the following terms:

- [MARKET] trade magazine
- [MARKET] trade journal

- [MARKET] professional magazine
- [MARKET] professional journal
- [MARKET] industry publication

Media outlets, such as podcasts, are usually eligible to receive subscriptions on "closed circulation" publications.

Related Podcasts - Other podcasts are a great resource to find potential guests as you can hear not only what they say, but also get an idea for their abilities to handle the needed technical requirements necessary for you to get a good recording.

Guests get good at doing interviews by doing interviews. The more podcasts they're on, the more other podcasters hear them and want to interview them. This leads to the guest being interviewed on even more podcasts, which leads to even more podcasters, like you, hearing them.

This can be a dangerous cycle. Listeners don't want "replica" episodes they can get elsewhere or have heard before. Make sure to keep the episodes you create, especially episodes with seasoned podcast guests, fresh and unique by asking thoughtful questions that inspire thoughtful answers. (More about how to do this later in this book.)

To find additional guests when reviewing related podcasts, consider the people hosting the podcast. They're often experts in their own right, but many rarely get to be on the interviewee mic.

Online Forums - Depending on how focused the community is, online forums can be a great way to connect with new people and get suggestions and ideas for potential guests.

You can get a good sense of whether an online forum is worthwhile by looking over past messages. Also look at the group rules to get a feel for whom the forum was designed and how it's moderated.

Forum owners (also administrators and moderators) are o[ ] best option for finding guests, either because they themselves are qualified guests or because they have a feel for which members of their communities would be qualified guests.

Amazon (And Other Online Book Stores) - One of the great things about using authors as guests is that the work they've put into writing and promoting their books has helped them develop both knowledge about their subjects as well as the necessary skills for delivering good interviews.

Reviews on Amazon will allow you to get a handle on an author's knowledge. A quick search on Google, once you find somebody interesting, will let you know if that author can communicate that knowledge via an interview.

YouTube – YouTube is full of "how-to" videos. The people who create these videos often make great podcast guests, not only because of their knowledge, but because they're good communicators who already own and know how to use the equipment needed to record themselves.

But "how-to" guests are just the start of who you'll find on YouTube.

There's a video genre known as "storytime" where people share their unique experiences like:

- I Got My Teacher Fired
- My Husband's Secret Family
- I Caught A Customer Stealing At Wal-Mart
- I Almost Got Kicked Out Of Jesus Camp
- I Cheated On My Boyfriend

If you're got a human interest or storytelling element to your podcast, these storytime videos are great places to find guests who not only have a story to tell, but can tell that story in an entertaining way. A search on YouTube for "storytime [PODCAST TOPIC]" will give you plenty of guest and episode topic ideas.

This is just the tip of the iceberg of what you can find on YouTube. A quick search for "Q&A" will give you dozens of episode ideas as well as guests you can interview.

For example:

- "Q&A: Gun Rights And Open Carry"
- "Q&A: Editing Audio For Podcasts"
- "Q&A: Teen Parents"
- "Q&A: Transgender Brother"
- "Q&A: The VIP Room"

You can also use it as a resource to find people who review certain products, people who answer "Dear Abby" style questions about specific topics, and people who show, via their videos, what they're experts at (such as cooking, oil painting, or fixing things around the house).

YouTube is the perfect site to get ideas for new topics and find people to talk about them. You can quickly and easily get a sense of what people know, what they've experienced, and how well they can communicate.

Twitter – Twitter is where busy people – like those you want to connect with – connect with each other. When making your list of potential guests, follow them on Twitter. When you do this, you'll see the conversations they're having, as well as the people with whom they're having them. This will introduce you to more potential guests.

Let's say you have a podcast on video games and want to do an episode on the *Call of Duty* franchise. A simple search for "Call of Duty" will bring up everybody talking about this topic, as well as give you ideas for unique ways to approach it. If you find somebody or something said to be interesting, you can join in the conversation.

You don't have to get on dozens of mailing lists or follow your ideal guests on every social media site they're on. But do what's needed to make sure you can keep up with the work these people are doing – and, if possible, what they're doing *outside* of work. An Instagram account, for example, can tell you a lot about a person's private life (at least what he wants you to know about it), and this information can be helpful in making a personal connection.

What Guests Will Look For

1. Market Match

The more general the topic of your podcast is, the tougher time you'll have getting the attention of great guests. For example, a podcast about "pets" isn't as attractive to a dog trainer as a podcast about "dogs." And if the dog trainer you want as a guest specializes in a specific breed of dog, you'll have an even better chance of getting him on your podcast if you also focus on that breed.

2. Connection With Host

You are your own best asset for bringing in great guests. The more status and influence you have, the most people will be willing to talk to you, even if your podcast isn't a perfect match for what they do.

Relationships go a long way in the media and entertainment businesses. If somebody is a fan of *you*, you've got a good shot of landing him as a guest.

3. Audience Reach

Quality (and loyalty) of your audience is more important than quantity. For guests trying to spread a message, just like advertisers, reaching a small audience of the right people is better than a much larger, but more general, audience.

4. Authority/Credibility Within Market

Almost nothing trumps authority and credibility in the market. If you have enough of this, even if you don't have a huge reach, your podcast is brand new, or you haven't even released a single episode yet, you'll still be able to book great guests.

5. Longevity (Number Of Episodes)

Lots of people record interviews for podcasts that never launch, and lots of podcasts only last a few episodes before they fade away. Experienced guests know this and look at longevity of a podcast before agreeing to be interviewed, because they don't want to waste their time on doing interviews that will never be heard.

Fortunately for new podcasters who are working on establishing longevity, there are still interview opportunities. While a brand-new podcast won't be a great match for everybody, there are those who do recognize the value of new podcasts, one of which is using them as an outlet to practice interview skills or test new ideas.

Think about how comic Chris Rock develops new material. What the large audiences of his tours and televised appearances see has actually been perfected from dozens of unannounced performances at small clubs.

These trial performances can be painful to watch. It's not uncommon to see him refer to handwritten notes and deliver jokes that fall flat because they're not yet polished. That's part of the process, though. The only way for him to truly know a joke won't work is to attempt it.

There's nothing Chris Rock does on a big stage that hasn't been tested in this way.

Even if your podcast is new or unknown, by having the fundamentals of a good podcast in place, you still have an opportunity to be a testing ground for experts, entertainers, and others fleshing out new ideas and practicing their media skills. These fundamentals include the other elements of a "good podcast" mentioned in this book, from the focused direction of your podcast, to quality imaging and audio, to a personable host who comes off as professional.

Pros recognize pros. If you're doing something that has potential, people will know it.

6. Consistency

How consistently are you releasing new episodes of your podcast? Consistency with your release schedule tells potential guests that you're consistent with other aspects of creating a great podcast.

7. Frequency

How frequently are you releasing new episodes of your podcast? A daily podcast doesn't give single episodes (or interviews) the same longevity as a podcast that's released less frequently. A "churn and burn" release schedule, where more emphasis is put on quantity than quality, will drastically lower the number of great interviews you're able to get.

8. Social Proof (Including Reviews)

People want to be part of a winning team. When you approach a potential guest about being part of your podcast, the first thing he's going to do is see what other people are saying about you. This could be via reviews within directories like Apple Podcasts, via social media, or anywhere else where people come together, both online *and* offline.

If you're reaching enough people, not everybody is going to say nice things about your podcast. You do want people saying *something*, though.

If nobody is talking about your podcast, that means nobody is listening to your podcast.

9. Social Media (And Related) Reach

You, as a podcaster, should have more than just a podcast — you should have a media company. This means a "headquarters" for your podcast in the form of a blog or website, an email newsletter, and various social media outlets to allow you to have a two-way conversation with listeners, as well as a feeling of connection with them.

Ultimately, guests aren't coming to you to be on a podcast. Guests are coming to you to reach an audience – to reach people who will be interested in what they have to say. Your podcast isn't the only way to help them do this.

How To Get On Somebody's Radar

1. **Do Great Work** - There are lots of gimmicks and creative shortcuts you can use to get in front of people, but without great work to back you up, this will only lead to a quicker rejection by the person you're trying to reach.

People who do great work recognize great work, and they're longing to see more of it.

2. **Hire Them** - If you want to get in front of somebody, the biggest shortcut you can take is to pay for it.

The downside to hiring somebody is that you're starting the relationship off as a client and it may be difficult to transition it to that of a peer. You can mitigate this risk by doing great work.

3. **Reach Out (When Appropriate)** - I've got a business contact who sends me handwritten cards for everything. Birthdays, holidays, after-meeting follow-ups ...

Everything.

It's so quirky. But there's something really amazing about it. She's not calling me up all the time or emailing — she's taking the time to handwrite a personal message to me.

It feels good to be appreciated. And it's so nice that I feel I should send her a card every time she sends me one.

While you don't have to go this far with keeping in touch with people, going beyond emails, texts and Twitter mentions can be a good way to let people know you exist and keep you on their minds.

How to do this:

- *Share relevant articles.* *Relevant* articles, not stupid things you see on Facebook. This works best if you physically rip the article out of a magazine and send it via postal mail.
- *Send a recommended book.* Read a good book lately? Send it. I have people who are important to me in my Amazon address book, so I can do this with just a few clicks.
- *Acknowledge people in public.* It feels good to be acknowledged publicly, especially if it's by somebody who does great work.
- *Congratulate people.* It feels good to be recognized for the work that you do. Facebook, LinkedIn, and Instagram are a great way to find out where people are and what they're doing. When something good happens, mention you've noticed it and send congratulations.
- *Send opportunities.* People are able to create great work because they're curious and open to new opportunities. If you have an opportunity you feel would work for somebody, send it to him.

None of these things are manipulative, unless you do them with the intention of being manipulative. Still, because so many people do these or similar things in a manipulative way, you may find successful people have their guards up. The way around this is to do great work.

CHAPTER 019

MAKING YOUR PODCAST APPEALING TO GUESTS

What do you think it means for somebody to be the host of *Saturday Night Live?*

Sure, it can help sell music, get people to movie theaters, or gather support for a political campaign. But something worth much more to *most* guests is that they're considered part of an inner circle.

Even after decades on the air, it's still a big deal to be asked to host the show.

The same is true for comics who are chosen to be cast members of *Saturday Night Live.* To have producer Lorne Michaels believe in you goes way beyond being given a springboard to commercial success — it shows others in the entertainment industry that your work is worthwhile.

When it comes to your podcast, like Lorne Michaels, you're a tastemaker. You pick who is important and who isn't.

You don't do this by booking anybody and everybody. If you want to play with the big boys, you have to learn how to separate the people who will be helpful to your audience from those who aren't a good match for what you do.

In short, you need to be selective when booking guests for your podcast. This should be done from the very first episode, and you should *never* compromise.

Of course, this is a two-way street. You need to have a podcast people want to be part of. Looking at this from a strictly guest perspective, to make this happen, the first thing you need to ask yourself is, *"What does a great guest want?"*

The simple answer is "to reach people," but the *real* answer is much more complex.

Many podcasters approach guests thinking it's the guests who bring "credibility" to a podcast. Not so. A podcast has its own credibility, and that credibility is transferred *to* the guest, not the other way around.

You are the primary reason people listen to your podcast. The people you interview are secondary.

Guests want to be associated with you because you have influence. When you allow people on your podcast, your endorsement of them and what they're doing gets them instant credibility with your audience.

This is how "celebrities" are created. They're just normal people who attach themselves to people, like you, and projects, like your podcast, that are considered worthwhile.

That's not to say a great guest won't help you build your reputation as a podcaster and increase your audience. The relationships you have with guests can be good for both you and them.

What You Need To Attract Quality Guests

1. Public Perception As A Tastemaker

Perception gets you in the door. Look like you deserve to be here.

2. Focus

Tastemakers have focus. They're not "something for everybody" kind of people and neither are their podcasts.

3. Gravitas And Relationships

You are your own best asset for bringing in great guests. The more status and influence you have, the more people will be willing to talk to you, even if your podcast isn't a perfect match for what they do.

What Would Andy Warhol Do?

In the late 1960s, artist Andy Warhol started putting together and promoting a clique of New York City personalities. These personalities, known as "superstars," appeared in his art and accompanied him during social engagements.

The superstars helped Warhol generate publicity while he offered fame and attention in return.

How did somebody achieve superstar status? Warhol would simply declare it.

Beyond this, he had a place to put them, so other people would declare the same thing. He founded *Interview* magazine. He made films, held live events, and produced music.

Like you, he had his own media company.

His belief system was simple — everyone wants to be famous.

Every group, no matter how large or small, has a hierarchy. The local PTA, neighborhood association, and church are all composed of members with different levels of authority, not equals.

The niche in which your podcast lives has a hierarchy as well. How can you increase your ranking within its pecking order? Beyond this, how can you increase the authority, influence, and prominence of the people you interview or otherwise associate with?

The answer to these questions is to, like Andy Warhol did, bypass the established and recognized organizations within your market and create your own scene, where you're the tastemaker, expert, and authority.

The Awesome 3

I've seen hundreds of people use The Awesome 3 technique to successfully establish themselves as tastemakers, experts, and authorities within their various markets. If you approach this technique from an honest place and have the skills and ability to back up what you promise, it will help you become more influential and well-known. When you have these things, you can provide more value to the people you interview.

The premise of the Awesome 3 is to create a group of "superstars," much like Andy Warhol did in the 1960s. With it, you appear to be everywhere.

How it works:

Connect with two other people in your industry who are at or above your level. These are people with whom you'll directly associate with and be recommending to others, so be sure they're ethical, honest, and will represent you well.

The Awesome 3 works any time and any place, including online, but you'll see the best results using it during a short, in-person, compressed-time event such as a conference or meetup.

To establish the Awesome 3, you and your two partners enter an event (or online destination) with the following action plan.

1. Separate from each other.
2. Meet as many people as possible.
3. When it makes sense, highlight and introduce your two partners to the people you're talking to.

When all three in the group do this, it will appear to the people you meet that you and your partners are "everywhere." And if done right, with both partners having something of value to offer to the people you meet, everybody wins with this strategy.

The power of the Awesome 3 isn't limited to live and limited-time events. It can be used throughout the year in every situation in which you and your partners come in contact with other people. Beyond that, it can be used to create podcasts, products, and events.

The entertainment industry does this kind of collaboration all the time. It's the opening act of a tour, the "feature act" on the recording by another artist, and the actor who does a one-off "guest star" role.

There's power in having other people talk about and collaborate with you. If done as part of an Awesome 3, it will bring all three of you to a greater level of respect and credibility within your community. It shows people you have something going on and makes them want to work with you.

People Want To Be Chosen

People want to be on the inside, even if the gate that's keeping them outside isn't very big.

The late actor Robert Culp, a long-time staple at Hugh Hefner's invite-only "Manly Night" at the Playboy Mansion, a weekly get-together of his best friends, invited guests, and inner circle, said it best:

"Gentlemen, gentlemen, be of good cheer, for they are out there, and we are in here."

"Manly Night" at the Playboy Mansion, by the way, is more or less a few old guys watching a classic Hollywood movie … *Casablanca, Maltese Falcon, North By Northwest.*

It doesn't matter what the "inside" actually is as much as it does that the "insiders" have been chosen.

How Far People Will Go To Be "Cool"

The Bachelor is an American reality television show that debuted in 2002. Hundreds of episodes have been produced. There have been multiple spin-off series, as well as international versions.

The premise of the show is this:

Everything revolves around a single man who starts with a pool of 25 women who are interested in having a romantic relationship with him. During the course of the season, women in the pool are eliminated from the competition, leaving "The Bachelor" with a single remaining woman to whom he proposes marriage.

Like all "reality" television shows, *The Bachelor* is heavily edited. Its creator, Mike Fleiss, has been criticized for admitting that the show has less to do with reality than it does making good television.

What makes good television? According to a 2010 interview Fleiss did on *20/20*, it's characters, specifically "villains."

Knowing the show will be seen by a national audience and knowing that producers are able (and often trying) to make contestants look bad, why would somebody choose to participate?

To be chosen.

And *The Bachelor* contestants have the opportunity to be chosen twice. To participate, they must be chosen by the show's producers. To win the contest, a single contestant must be chosen by "The Bachelor" himself.

Everybody wants to be part of the "in" crowd. And we want to this so badly, we'll risk national humiliation and embarrassment to make it happen.

Your podcast is not a top-rated television series. You don't have an audience of tens of millions. As long as you have some sort of an "inner circle" that people want to be part of though, you have something to offer potential guests.

International Drug Smuggler Seeks Employment

When setting the foundation for yourself, you don't have to be perfect, but you do need to be honest.

Brian O'Dea, a former drug smuggler from Newfoundland, Canada, had a problem. He wanted to go legit, but with a criminal record, who would hire him?

After being paroled in 1993, he published a long advertisement in Toronto's *National Post*, showcasing his executive management skills and being blatantly upfront about his past, arguing it was the greatest proof of his abilities.

FORMER MARIJUANA SMUGGLER

Having successfully completed a 10-year sentence, incident-free, for importing 75 tons of marijuana into the United States, I am now seeking a legal and legitimate means to support myself and my family.

BUSINESS EXPERIENCE: owned and operated a successful fishing business — multi-vessel, one airplane, one island and processing facility. Simultaneously owned and operated a fleet of tractor-trailer trucks conducting business in the western United States. During this time, I also co-owned and participated in the executive level management of 120 people worldwide in a successful pot smuggling venture with revenues in excess of US$100 million annually. I took responsibility for my own actions, and received a 10-year sentence in the United States while others walked free for their cooperation.

ATTRIBUTES: I am an expert in all levels of security; I have extensive computer skills, am personable, outgoing, well-educated, reliable, clean and sober. I have spoken in schools to thousands of kids and parent groups over the past ten years on "the consequences of choice," and received public recognition from the RCMP for community service. I am well-traveled and speak English, French, and Spanish. References available from friends, family, the U.S. District Attorney, etc.

Please direct replies to (National Post Classified, Don Mills, Ontario, Canada)

O'Dea went on to become a television and film producer. In 2012, he appeared as Kevin O'Leary's advisor and mentor to contestants on the CBC television series, *Redemption Inc.*, where ex-convicts compete for a chance to have O'Leary invest in their legitimate start-up businesses.

Bob Dylan once said, "To live outside the law, you must be honest."

Living "outside the law" is what you're doing with your podcast. This isn't traditional media — you're making your own rules.

But if you want to be successful when it comes to approaching guests, like Brian O'Dea, you've got to tell the truth about who you are and what you can offer.

If, like Andy Warhol, you've created your own scene and, like Hugh Hefner or *The Bachelor*, its participants and "winners" have to be chosen, the value of working with you is already obvious to potential guests. There's no need to exaggerate your reach or the benefits of being part of what you do.

Guests don't care about "download numbers" or the metrics used to measure the success of traditional media. They want an audience of tightly defined, highly loyal audience to choose them. Deliver this, and they'll say yes to working with you.

Quality Podcasts Attract Quality Guests

Don't chase people in the hope that they'll somehow make what you're doing more legitimate. Legitimacy of a podcast doesn't come from a guest any more than legitimacy of a woman comes from the man she's dating.

You are the foundation of your podcast. The best guest is worthless without you.

When you focus on being a great host, having great relationships with listeners, and otherwise doing what it takes to have a great podcast *on your own*, guests will emerge. If your podcast has even the slightest bit of professionalism, you'll be pitched by people looking for publicity for their businesses, books, films, albums, and various other endeavors.

There are thousands of interesting people you can talk to. Although you might be eager to interview them all, if you want your podcast to have longevity, grow your audience, and have impact on the people you reach, you need to focus on guests who will add value, not just noise.

A quality podcasts attracts quality guests. Keep at it and keep your standards high.

CHAPTER 020

HOW TO APPROACH POTENTIAL GUESTS

If you've ever heard somebody on a podcast and thought, "He'd *never* be on my podcast," you're probably wrong.

While some people are concerned about overexposure and the other issues that come from too much media, the truth is, most people are governed by ego. Benjamin Disraeli was right when he said, "Talk to a man about himself and he'll listen for hours."

At its most basic, being a guest on your podcast is an opportunity for somebody to talk about himself in public. If the average person receives an interview request from a somewhat professional podcast, he's not going to turn it down.

People are waiting for you to approach them.

But you've got to have the right approach.

At the 2013 new member reception for Academy of Motion Picture Arts and Sciences, actor Bryan Cranston offered some advice for aspiring actors on how to approach auditions:

"You're not going there to get a job, you're going there to present what you do."

As a podcaster, this applies to you and your approach to potential guests.

Your job when approaching people to be part of your podcast is to create a compelling opportunity and then present it. That's it.

You're not trying to get a potential guest to "do" anything, you're simply saying, "This is what I've done and I'd like you to be part of it."

There's no need to worry or be self-conscious. Authors, experts, entertainers, musicians, actors, comics, and other "celebrities" benefit from people like you just as much as people like you benefit from them.

This is why people want to be part of your podcast. If they know you, know of you, or want to be associated with something that you're doing, getting them on your podcast is easy.

How To Approach Potential Guests

Regardless of your level of authority within the podcasting space, there are some people who will never approach you to be a guest, even though they'd jump at the opportunity to be a guest on your podcast if asked.

Why?

Call it tradition. Maybe it's psychological. But just like many women wait for men to make the first move in a relationship, many experts and others you'd like to interview won't mention their interest in working with you until you've brought up working with them.

This is a good thing. Approaching potential guests gives you more options and puts you in control.

How to do it:

Conversations Start Relationships

One of the best things about social media is it allows you to easily jump into conversations that are already in progress. From the moment you start following somebody, try to do this in a way that adds value.

"How can I help this person?"

When you answer this question, you've started more than a "conversation" on social media; you've started a relationship.

How do you grow and strengthen a relationship? Keep going.

When you consistently demonstrate to somebody that you're interested in her well-being, she'll become more and more open to working with you. And when you can help somebody in a variety of mediums, it can speed up the rapport-building process by making your relationship seem more established than it actually is.

When communicating with people online, do so in different formats — tweets, photographs, emails, articles, YouTube video, podcast episodes, Facebook posts, etc. If possible, take things offline with phone calls, postal mail, and in-person meetings.

This is how friends talk to each other.

Most influencers have an offline element of their work, whether it's speaking, live performances, or just a meetup to connect face-to-face with fans of their work (and other like-minded people).

Attend something. And if you have opportunities to do this more than once, do it.

Friends also have an element of "give and take" in their relationships. This is another reason to provide value in your initial contacts with people – you don't want to come across like you're using somebody. You also don't want to come across like you're passive or putting somebody on a pedestal. Be bold and respectful, but avoid acting like a "fanboy."

Great guests, especially true celebrities, are so used to hearing praise from fans that they're immune to it. And if you dole out compliments to somebody for the sole purpose of getting something in return, you'll be resented for it.

When approaching somebody to be a guest on your podcast, it's fine to acknowledge you're a fan of his work. Have you read his book? Good. Let him know. But there's no reason to go on and on about it.

People want to be recognized by their peers. This is why peer-chosen awards, such as the Grammy Awards and the Academy Awards, carry so much weight among the music and film industries.

Pros know how much effort it takes to do great work. They know it's emotionally risky to release your work to the public. Pros know, every time you do this, it opens you to public criticism and critique, even if you're established and respected within your market.

You, as podcaster, know all about this too. It's not easy to create great work; there's a lot more to it than appears on the outside.

Acknowledge these things.

If Your Online Approach Isn't Working …

It used to be that getting a long-distance call at home was a big deal. If one came in, the person receiving the call would quiet others in the room with something like, *"Shhhh … It's long distance!"* Everybody would get quiet.

Email is inexpensive and quick, but because of this, you're going to have a lot of competition. The phone is good, but people are busy, so that might not be a good way to connect. If that's the case, you can cut through the noise and stand out with postal mail.

Is it old school? Hell yeah it is. But because almost nobody is doing it, it will get you the opportunities you're looking for.

How To Get Attention With Postal Mail

If you do postal mail right, it can't be ignored. You might not always get the interview you want right away, but even a failed postal mail campaign can help you to establish a strong connection that will help you with future opportunities.

How much do you want to establish a connection with somebody?

If you want somebody to immediately open your message to them, one of the most effective ways is to send it attached to a book. Beyond simply getting your message to somebody, this also activates reciprocity, a social rule that says we should repay those who do something for us.

People feel the need to return the kind of treatment they have received from you. This sense of future obligation associated with reciprocity builds relationships and sets up other exchanges.

There are a lot of ways to be nice to somebody. Why a book?

Successful people read books. Books come in big packages that are hard to ignore. The book sent says as much about you as the letter you're going to attach to it.

About that letter ... I suggest sending something like this:

> *Hello. I admire your work and thought of you when I read this book, so I'm sending you a copy to read yourself. I think you'll find it helpful.*

I'm not affiliated with this book or the author, by the way. I'm actually a podcaster. My podcast, RED Podcast — The Marketing Podcast For Experts is available at REDpodcast.com if you'd like more information on me.

I hope this book inspires you as much as your work has inspired me!

Notice that the note is vague. This is intentional. The purpose of this note is to inspire curiosity, not to sell. If done right, it will start a conversation that will make the recipient more receptive to opportunities in the future.

Why Potential Guests Are Skeptical Of You

In the two years after he was released from prison in 1995, boxer Mike Tyson earned $140 million. A year after that, he was broke.

How does a multi-millionaire go broke so quickly? Everybody Mike Tyson associated with, including his friends, was on his payroll. His manager, Don King, along with two co-managers, reportedly took $100 million of the money he earned during this time.

During a conversation with animal trainer Carl Mitchell, who was himself being paid $125,000 per year to train Tyson's two white Bengal tigers, the topic of so many people hanging around came up.

"They don't give a fuck about me," Tyson said. "They're just here for the money and to be with Mike Tyson."

Unfortunately, many successful people you'll want to interview on your podcast are in similar situations. Because of this, they're skeptical when approached for anything.

Having stand-alone credibility, not just "borrowed credibility" from the people you interview, can help negate this skepticism. By being established yourself, you're able to give something to the people you interview, and because of this, they're more likely to say yes to interview requests.

Asking For The Interview – The Process

You've established yourself as a tastemaker who provides value, even if only via association. Hopefully, you've established contact (and a basic relationship) with the person you want to interview and he knows who you are.

Now what?

When reaching out to people to ask for an interview, you must assume two things:

1. You have something of value to offer.
2. The outcome you want, to land an interview, will be successful.

Something you can't assume is that even those with whom you already have some kind of relationship will know what you do or what you have to offer them. Regardless of the level of relationship you've established with somebody, you need to have an "elevator speech" ready to go. This isn't necessarily the first thing you'll open with, but you'll have it if you need it.

Never describe yourself as simply a "podcaster." Everybody and his brother has a podcast these days. You need to describe what you do in a way that won't get you confused for a hobbyist.

A better approach is to say something like, "I produce one of the top podcasts about [subject] called [podcast name]. Every [frequency of release], I release a new episode that goes out to [number of people] [category of people]."

For me, this would be, "I produce one of the top marketing podcasts about audience-building called *RED Podcast*. Every week, I release a new episode that goes out to 10,000 authors, bloggers, and podcasters."

This is what you do. What you offer is access to these people.

Write this down. Memorize it. Work with different versions of it. It's easy to think we know what we're doing, and we do, but it's much more difficult to explain what we do (and what we offer) to others — especially when under pressure.

Approach potential guests with confidence. Remember, they need you as much as you need them.

Approach potential guests with knowledge about what they've done. For example, if the person you want to approach has written a book, read the book. If he's produced a film, watch the film.

This kind of effort (and respect) is rare. Most potential guests you approach are used to doing media with people who don't "get" what they're doing, so your knowledge of their work stands out. Not only will it help you get interviews, it also allows you to have more successful interviews.

Rapport and mutual understanding are the main goals of what you're trying to achieve. You have something to offer, the guest has something to offer. Give and take. Everybody benefits.

How do you actually finalize the deal? Make an offer that is direct and compelling.

"Direct" is easy.

People want to know what they're getting into before making a commitment. If you want somebody to be a guest on your podcast, say it. If you want to talk about something specific, say it. If you need 30 minutes to make it all happen, say it.

The important thing? Get to the point and give enough details that somebody won't have to go through a couple of emails just to find out what you want and need. If you're not clear on these things, chances are you won't get a follow-up email.

"Compelling" is a bit trickier.

As I've mentioned, people want to be understood. They want to associate with those who have an appreciation for the work they do. They want to be asked questions by those with the knowledge necessary to go deeper than the generic interviews often heard on morning radio and other mass media.

They also want to reach new people. That's one of the main reasons guests put up with generic interviews.

You can offer both — knowledge of a potential guest's work as well as a platform to get that work in front of new people.

By building rapport and making a potential guest feel understood during initial conversations, you show compelling evidence that an interview with you will be worthwhile. By establishing a solid foundation for your podcast — a level of professionalism, great production, consistency, social proof from others, etc. — you show your ability to reach people.

Rules For Interacting With Potential Guests (And Their Handlers)

Assume Friendship. Most of the time, when two people first meet, there's an awkward stage where each is feeling out the other one. Skip this stage of the relationship and assume your connection is already in place.

How do you do this? Be vulnerable. Be honest. Be open. This is what "real" looks like. When you're the first to act in this way, it gives the other person permission to reciprocate.

This doesn't mean over-sharing. It doesn't mean you have to tell your deepest, darkest secrets or personal information better suited for a psychiatrist. Being "real" simply means you trust the relationship will be great and you don't need play it safe, like so many people do.

Be Confident (Not Cocky). You've got a podcast. The people you're approaching can benefit from being exposed to those who listen to your podcast. That's worth a lot, and you should feel good about the potential value you're bringing to those you approach to be guests, but it doesn't justify acting like a jerk.

You Have Options. There will be times when you approach a potential guest for your podcast, and in the process of getting him scheduled, you'll realize, "I've made a horrible mistake."

When it comes to guests, you make the best decision you can with the information you have at the time. And there will be times when it's best to not do the interview you thought you wanted.

You're in charge of your podcast. Always think about what's best for the people who listen to you. If this means not doing an interview or not publishing an interview you've already done, by all means kill it.

Not Everybody Will Say Yes. If you're not being turned down for interviews, you're not approaching enough people.

People Have Lots Of Reasons To Turn You Down. People are busy, especially the type of people you want to interview on your podcast. Beyond that, people are self-conscious, they don't think they have anything to offer, they get nervous, they have conflicts of interest, and they get burnt out.

Sometimes a "no" is permanent, but being rejected is often a case of poor timing. If it's not obvious why you're being turned down, it's perfectly acceptable to ask if you can reach out again in the future.

Outsource Outreach. The best way to find and book great guests for your podcasts is via recommendations and referrals. After every successful interview, ask if your guest has recommendations for other people who might also be great guests. If the recommendation is somebody with whom you're already familiar and know you want to book, ask for an introduction.

Keep At It. The more interviews you do for your podcast, the more you're bringing other people into its creation.

Not everybody you approach for an interview will say yes. Not every interview you do will be something you want to publish. There will be technical issues with your recording equipment.

Thousands of things stand between you and getting a great interview recorded. If you attempt enough interviews, you'll see more than a few of them.

Don't let roadblocks keep you from getting good interviews with great people.

A Gentle Reminder About Podcast Guests ...

Guests are the lifeblood of a podcast, especially podcasts with interview-format episodes exclusively. Never lower your standards on guests just to keep a release schedule, because you feel you owe somebody a favor, or because you want somebody to owe you a favor.

Low-quality guests will kill your podcast.

If you're concerned about keeping up a release schedule, but not sure there are enough quality guests to interview on your podcast, either change your release schedule to something you can deliver on or learn how to do solo or co-hosted episodes that don't require guests.

PART 3 – PODCAST INTERVIEWING

CHAPTER 021

THE PRE-INTERVIEW

It's easy to hear another interview from a potential guest, swipe questions, and get ideas about where *your* interview can go. It's also easy to have a standard line of general questions that do little to give a listener anything different from what he can get somewhere else.

These are not the types of interviews listeners want and if you want a successful podcast, they're not the types of interviews you want. There's no point in asking generic, non-connected questions or repeating interviews that have already been done.

Pre-interviews are usually done via phone, but sometimes via email. Their purpose is to help you come up with an episode thread that's specifically for listeners of your podcast. As a bonus, a pre-interview is a chance to develop rapport with a guest, help ease jittery nerves, and get an idea of specific stories and experiences the guest has, which will help you to guide a narrative.

Even the best interviewers get caught up in boring and shallow interviews from time to time. If this isn't happening to you, you're not doing ιterviews. But don't let the fact that "oh, it just happens like ιναι sometimes" be an excuse for not doing your homework before an interview.

After doing your initial research on a guest, spending 15 minutes on the phone with him to have a casual, no-pressure conversation will make a world of difference to the quality of your podcast.

Before A Pre-Interview

Before connecting with your guest for a pre-interview, consider asking for help from:

1. Your Podcast Audience

Asking your podcast's audience for topic ideas to discuss and questions to ask guests is a great way to build rapport and make them feel part of an episode's creation process. This is especially helpful when interviewing well-known and celebrity guests with whom your audience is already familiar.

2. Handlers

Handlers and other people who work with the person you're interviewing are a great source of inside information that will help you to get a good interview. These people know why past interviews have failed or succeeded, and they have a deep knowledge of the person you're interviewing, one that often goes way beyond what that person is publicly known for.

Besides the standard "What should I ask?" inquiry, consider asking the following questions:

- What made you want to work for [guest]?
- What was your biggest surprise about [guest]?
- What's something that nobody ever asks [guest], but should?
- Tell me a memorable story about [guest]…

- If [guest] wasn't doing [career], what do you think she'd be doing?

The Pre-Interview

Depending on a guest's schedule, ego, and belief in preparation, you will find different levels of tolerance for a pre-interview. Unfortunately, many don't feel it's necessary to connect before an interview because they way overestimate their abilities to deliver the content you need for a good episode on the fly.

There are a lot of factors that determine whether you'll end up with a mediocre interview or a great interview. By far, preparation is the most important. And the best way to prepare is to do a pre-interview.

The best thing you can do to get buy-in from the person you're pre-interviewing is to take control, letting him know, "My job is to make you sound great. Think of me like your attorney when you're on the stand — I want you to have an idea of where my questioning is going, so you can answer my questions in ways that makes you sound your best."

You and your guest just want an *idea* of where the interview will go, which means you'll discuss possible interview topics, not the exact questions you'll ask. The job of a pre-interview isn't to come up with a script to read — that sounds stiff.

The first rule of pre-interviews is, "Let them talk." This is how you find out the good stuff. And if you're comfortable with silence, you can find out the *great* stuff.

I always ask a guest, "Is there anything you want to focus on?" The job of an interviewer is not to shill for a guest, but asking this question will help you to build rapport with him and let you know the aspects of his career, life, and knowledge that he finds important.

While *listening* is the key to a great interview, you're still in charge. Listening is not "passive" and your guest shouldn't be directing how you should do the interview. Directing the interview is your job.

If your guest isn't talking about something that's a match for the interview you want, it's okay to guide him in the right direction. For example, you can offer suggestions, rerouting the conversation by saying things like, "I just read an article I found interesting and I'd love to get your opinion on. It was about …"

The pre-interview is a balance. As you do more and more of them, you'll get better at knowing when to reroute the conversation and when it's okay for it to be loose. As long as you're always looking for an episode hook, side conversations can provide a lot of insight into your guest and give you a great way to tell the story of your guest in a way that nobody else has been able to tell.

CHAPTER 022

HOW TO GET A GREAT INTERVIEW

Great interviews happen because the interviewer listens to the interviewee and is able to adjust his next question based on the answers from previous questions. This is how you go deep and move the interview forward.

This is extremely important.

As an interviewer, you're not the only one asking questions of this person. If you're interviewing somebody who is notable in his industry, such as an author, a celebrity, or a politician, it's likely that person is doing dozens, maybe even hundreds of interviews about the same subject. It's also likely that person has answered the same questions, with the same answers, again and again.

This is what you don't want.

But if you ask the following questions, your guests are likely to switch into "automatic mode" and the "same interview" is what you're likely to get.

Questions like:

- Can you tell me a little about yourself?
- What do you like most about your profession?
- Who are your heroes?
- What do you do in your spare time?
- What's your biggest accomplishment?
- If you had to start all over again, what would your first step be?
- Where are you from?
- How did you get started?

These aren't necessarily bad questions, but know when you ask them to somebody who's interviewed a lot, you're likely to get a "pre-recorded" answer that's already been thought out and has nothing to do with you or the people who listen to your podcast. And this sets a bad precedent for additional answers.

How do you break out of this situation when it happens, or better yet, prevent it altogether?

1. Ask a question without having a follow-up question in mind.
2. Listen to the answer you're given.
3. Ask a follow-up question based entirely on that answer.

To keep your interview moving forward, you need *some* direction, but a single topic or big idea for each episode backed with bullet points that support that topic is enough.

Let me give you an example.

I did an interview with Ian Anderson, the driving force behind Jethro Tull. With over 40 years in the music business, he's played 3000+ shows and still does an average of 120 dates per year. He's sold 60,000,000 albums.

Obviously, with a guy who's been around that long and had so much success, there are a lot of places to go. Should I talk about the new album? How's the tour going? What's it like to hear your songs on the radio?

All this is great. It's worth talking about. But it can come off as stale and disconnected if you have things too planned out. So when I talked to Ian, I focused on a single thing — longevity. I then backed this up with preparation around three big ideas:

- **Personal vision** — keeping things moving forward in a changing industry
- **Energy management and work ethic** — why work so hard when you have millions of dollars coming in each year?
- **Connecting with an audience** — stories from the road, the process of making music people love

The questions, which hit upon everything mentioned above, came out naturally.

We're talking about podcasting here, not live radio or television. If you have a pause where you can't think of where to go next, that's okay. Pauses, just like mistakes, can be edited out.

What can't be edited out, at least not in a coherent way, is when your interview suddenly slams into the brick wall of an unrelated question. For example, your guest is talking about something deep, perhaps the death of his mother or how he went bankrupt and lost his home.

Don't follow that up with, "What's your favorite time management trick?"

Yeah, that will get you the interview length you're going for and get you through the checklist of questions you've prepared ahead of time, but you're missing an opportunity to really connect with somebody in a way that goes so much deeper. You're also disrespecting your audience by not going in a naturally flowing direction.

To become great at interviewing people, here's the exercise I suggest:

1. Find somebody who has something to say and set up an interview. This does not need to be somebody you could interview for your podcast, although it could be.
2. Get a bio from the interviewee, think of one major topic to discuss, and back that topic up with three supporting bullet points and one question to start the interview. The interview should be 30 minutes.
3. Connect with your interviewee via Skype (audio only — you're focusing on listening).
4. Ask your first question without thinking of a follow-up question.
5. Keep talking until you hit 25 minutes. Then wrap up the interview.

At this point, you want to transcribe the interview or listen to it and extract the questions you asked.

Upon review, can you see an overall flow and direction? If so, good job. But if you're bouncing around everywhere, this is something for you to improve on.

Need a blueprint to get your interviews in order? Try a story arc.

A story arc is a storyline, which in interview-format podcasts is told over a series of questions and answers. It's the "discovery" of a story that already exists within the interviewee, but has not yet been told to others.

As a podcast host, your job is to help mold the guest's story into something that makes sense to listeners. The story you create with the interviewee must have a defined beginning, middle, and end.

Think of the storytelling you've seen and heard in television dramas, comic books, comic strips, and films. The story you're uncovering from your guest is no different, although the speed and space in which you tell the story will likely be much quicker. A television series, for example,

allows the story to unfold over many episodes. Unless you ha
style podcast, you will need to tell a complete story in a single episode.

A complete story, of course, is *never* the complete story, regardless of whether you're able to tell the story within a single episode or you do it over a longer period of time. Details will always be missing, as they are in every story. However, as the name suggests, a "complete" story must feel complete. Your listener needs to walk away from your podcast episode feeling satisfied.

The purpose of a story arc is to move a character or a situation from one point to another. Classically, this change or transformation often takes the form of either a tragic fall from grace, or just the opposite. The first Star Wars trilogy is a great example.

Characters in this story arc go from a situation of weakness to one of strength. An example of this you might hear on a business podcast is, a wannabe entrepreneur gets fired from his job and, even though he has no money, starts his own business. In the end, he makes millions.

The Eight-Point Story Arc

The Eight-Point Story Arc was created by Nigel Watts. It was designed for novel writers, but it will also help you to create interesting nonfiction content, such as podcast interviews.

The eight points are:

1. Stasis
2. Trigger
3. The Quest
4. Surprise
5. Critical Choice
6. Climax

7. Reversal
8. Resolution

Nigel advises that the eight points are most useful as a checklist against which to measure the progress of a work. In other words, it's a good way to know where in the story you are.

What exactly are the eight points?

Stasis

This is the setup. In Star Wars, it's "A long time ago, in a galaxy far, far away …" In your podcast, it may be a guy who is 400 pounds and doesn't have hope, it may be a woman in a job she hates, or a couple on the brink of divorce.

Stasis is the very beginning of things, where your "hero" is before the story you're about to tell begins. It's the part of the story that shows the person you're interviewing now wasn't always in such a great place.

Trigger

This is where things start to happen. It's the part of the story that makes listeners perk up and pay attention. This is where the current story starts — the 400-pound guy having to buy two airline tickets because he's so large he can't fit in a single seat, the woman who hates her job gets laid off, and when the wife of the unhappy couple finds lipstick on her husband's collar and suspects something is going on.

The Quest

This is bulk of your story. It's the trials and struggle of your interviewee — the successes, the failures, the missteps, and the happy accidents.

This is where the guy determined to lose weight drops a few pounds and seems to be on the right track, but falls off the wagon during a vacation and gains it all back and then some. It's where the woman who lost her job starts her own business and is very happy, but she's not making any money and doesn't know how long she'll be able to keep her head above water. It's where the wife continues to see signs her husband is having an affair, but isn't sure if she should confront him because she's afraid of what her life would be like if she left him.

Surprise

Just as things seem to be moving forward in one direction, the tables turn. *"Wow! I didn't see that coming!"*

Surprises can be pleasant, but they can also be unpleasant, depending on your point of view. Regardless, they're always unexpected and, if you want people to keep listening, they can't be predictable. For example, "The 400-pound guy saved his money, got liposuction, and was instantly at his goal weight of 180 pounds. He lived happily ever after. The end."

This part of the story is where most podcast interviews fail. In the business genre, it's common to hear "rags to riches" stories of an entrepreneur who was laid off or fired from his job, started his own business, and within months was just fine.

It's a nice fantasy, but it's not the end. There's more to the story.

Why do we skip over the true reality of things or try to tie everything up with a nice bow? Because most of us are people-pleasers who want to give the audience what it wants, which is a fantasy.

People *like* fantasies — we want to believe that it's possible to take a pill and lose weight, instantly go from being broke to financially secure, and we can have an attractive lover show up in our lives without us having to do any work on ourselves.

But truth is more interesting than fiction. Also, your listeners know better. While people like fantasies, they value engaging stories they relate to even more.

Because of this, you want to tell a story that's plausible. When telling a story through an interview, don't forget the "sticky middle" that connects where people were and where people are now.

Examples:

The 400-pound guy's wife is sabotaging his diet by baking him cookies every night. She's got her own issues to deal with, and is afraid if he loses too much weight, other women will find him attractive and he'll leave her. Now, he has something else to worry about.

The entrepreneur's husband gets injured on the job and can't work. She's the only source of income for her family.

The wife finds out she's pregnant.

Critical Choice

The ante has been upped for your interviewee. What will she do? Will she give up after making it this far along? Will she push forward?

This is *the* moment when a decision must be made. It's where the game is won or lost.

Climax

This is where everything peaks. The intensity is at 11, even though the knob only goes to 10. It's the moment of decision, and it's anybody's guess as to what that decision will be.

The 400-pound guy decides to leave his wife because he's never going to get healthy if he doesn't. The entrepreneur goes for broke and dives even deeper into her own business. The wife decides to raise the baby on her own, and files for divorce.

Reversal

Our hero has become a new person and his "new life" has started. He's changed for the better. Even though the future isn't set in stone, he knows he's going to be okay.

This is the first glimpse of "happily ever after." A new sense of confidence, money in the bank, a new beginning.

Resolution

This ties everything up in a nice bow. Weight is lost, income is high, and love is all around. It's the payoff for all the hard work and years of plugging away, even when the chips were down.

This is the new stasis. And the end of your story.

The Interview Crapshoot

Sometimes the interviews you think are going to be great don't work out. And on the flip side, sometimes the ones you take a chance on are amazing.

Until you're in the studio, you never know. But it you find yourself getting more bad interviews than good, you likely have a problem with:

- Low standards
- Interview FOMO [Fear Of Missing Out]
- Your pre-interview vetting process
- Lack of preparation and pre-interview guest/topic research
- Pre-interview education for guests

Fortunately, all of these things are easy to fix; you'll naturally get better at working around them as you improve as a host. Remember, even the best host isn't going to hit it out of the park every single time.

CHAPTER 023

GUEST RED FLAGS

Things you should worry about when talking to potential guests:

1. No Pre-Interview

A pre-interview isn't always possible. Still, if you need one and the guest refuses, or doesn't see the importance of spending a few minutes to help you get what's needed to make him sound great, that's a sign that he may not be a very good guest.

2. Not Enough Time To Get What You Need

It's your show, and you know what it takes to put it together. If you have a long-form interview format and need an hour, make sure you get an hour.

People are busy. If you're working with a guest who is in the middle of a book tour, for example, that guest is going to have a lot going on. But don't agree to what will be an incomplete interview if it's going to short-change your listeners. Listeners come before guests.

3. Micro-Management And Control Issues

Everybody who has ever appeared on television, radio, or podcasts wants to come across as professional, but skip the guests who want to control the questions you ask or review final edits before anything is released.

If a guest doesn't trust you with holding up your end on the interview, he's not the right match for your podcast.

4. Some Topics Off Limits

Some guests want to talk about what they want, but not necessarily what you or the people who listen to you want. This is an extreme version of micro-management.

For example: a guest has a brand-new invention he wants to discuss, but he refuses to talk about (or even acknowledge) the existence of a previous invention, one which has a better story and more interest from your listeners.

Musicians with new material often don't want to talk about older material, even if the older material is better known.

Authors with new books often don't want to talk about older books, even if those books are more popular.

Business owners who have started new companies often don't want to talk about their previous companies, even if those previous companies are more well-known.

Understand their reluctance. Then talk about the older music, books, and companies anyway, if those are the things the people listening to you want to hear about. Your allegiance is to them, not your guests and their fragile egos.

Are there exceptions to this rule? Absolutely. Especially on topics that aren't the main reason people will listen.

I had a well-known guest who was a former member of a controversial religious group. When she left the group, it was newsworthy.

I was curious about this and thought it would be an interesting discussion. However, the publicist who booked the interview with me asked me not to talk about it because the guest was worried that doing so might get her cut off from family members who were still in the group.

I agreed not to bring up the topic during our interview because this element of her story was a sidenote, not the primary reason I was talking to her. Also, especially considering that many listeners had no idea about the story, the potential downside of talking about it for her was much bigger than any payoff for me.

5. Doesn't Answer Questions

Imagine if I were to go on a podcast about podcasting, but refused to talk about the subject, instead answering questions with, "I talk about that in the book."

This kind of behavior isn't fair to your audience. It also makes for a boring interview.

You want guests who are going to give good information that people listening can actually put to use. If somebody doesn't want to talk to you, there's no point in having her as a guest.

6. Inability To Get To The Point

I have a friend who can talk a lot and sounds really great when doing so. If you were to hear him speaking, you'd think to yourself, "This guy sounds like he really knows what he's talking about."

When he'd finally finish though, you'd realize you had no idea what he just said.

I have another friend who's very smart and knows a lot, but it takes him forever to answer a question. You'd think he's being paid on a per-word basis.

Some people talk a lot without saying anything. Others take forever to get to the point. Neither of these types of people are good guests for your podcast.

7. Excessive Focus On The Pitch

Unless you're in a hobby genre, most of the guests you interview will be in a business related to what they're talking about and have products or services to sell.

A musician talking about his new album will want to sell it (or tickets to the tour promoting it).

A book author talking about his new book will want to sell it (or tickets to a book signing or speaking engagement).

A business owner talking about his new company will want to bring in clients for it.

There's a tradeoff when talking to these people, one that has worked in radio for years, and also works in podcasting. A guest gives you a good interview, full of good information, then gets to plug what he's selling at the end.

A plug. Not a hardline, grab-'em-by-the-wallet sales pitch. Your podcast isn't a network marketing seminar.

8. Demanding Payment For Interview

In the world of podcasting, rarely does a "checkbook journalism" situation look like, "Pay me $X and I'll be on your show." It's usually something like, "If you buy 100 books, I'll be on your show."

Don't do it.

9. Wants An "Interview Trade"

Somebody calls you up and wants you on his podcast. Then he says, "How about an interview trade? You be a guest on my podcast and I can be a guest be on your podcast."

Would Howard Stern go for this? Would Jimmy Fallon go for this? Would Ellen DeGeneres go for this?

No.

Sure, you're not Howard Stern, Jimmy Fallon, or Ellen DeGeneres, but how do you think they got to that level?

CHAPTER 024

HOW TO TURN GUESTS DOWN

The more popular your podcast is, the more people you're going to have approach you about booking themselves or somebody else as a guest. This is great when you're interested in booking the person, but if you're not interested, you may find the situation awkward.

If you're pitched by somebody you're not interested in having on your show, *don't* use these three ways of responding.

1. Completely ignoring the pitch and not responding.

This is a problem for two reasons.

One, publicists and others who pitch to the media often have Jehovah's Witness-level immunity to rejection and don't stop their pitches with anything less than a firm no. Ignoring publicists only makes them stronger and more resilient.

Two, even if you're dealing with an amateur who isn't aggressive at long-term follow-up, if somebody thinks you didn't get the initial pitch, he'll start contacting you in multiple ways. That means you'll have to deal with the same thing via email, phone, Facebook, Twitter, and however many other ways you can be contacted.

If you know you're not interested in having somebody as a guest on your podcast, save yourself and the person pitching you time by letting this be known as soon as possible.

2. Passing the pitch to an assistant or producer.

You're at an event where you're innocently talking to somebody and he asks, "What do you think about having me on your podcast?"

Since most people aren't good with rejecting others face-to-face, a common response is, "Reach out to my assistant and she can help you."

This is a problem if you either don't have an assistant or your assistant does what I just advised *you* not to do — completely ignore the pitch.

It's common for podcasters to try to "delay" having to turn down a potential guest by telling him to "reach out to me via email" in hope that he'll never actually follow up. Not a good idea.

Few people follow up on "we really should get together" offers. We know how that game is played. But when you offer somebody an opportunity to be on your podcast, he's going to reach out. And keep reaching out until you tell him otherwise.

If you know somebody isn't a match for what you're doing, say so. If you're not sure, and you *really* think there might be something there, schedule a 15-minute call to get more information on the person. Never drag things out.

3. Saying yes to an interview, even though the person isn't a good match for your podcast.

I have a female friend who said yes when her boyfriend asked her to marry him, even though she didn't want to get married. She continued the facade for *months*, going through all the motions of preparing for a wedding as the date got closer and closer.

During her "engagement" period, she purchased a dress. She booked the venue and hired a florist. She went to pre-marital counseling. She announced the planned wedding to all of her friends and family.

She walked away from the relationship before she was married, but not until she'd spent thousands of dollars and wasted the time of dozens of people.

She was lucky. I have another friend who was in a similar situation except she didn't walk away until five years *after* she was married.

Saying yes to an interview isn't as extreme as marrying the wrong person, but the people listening to your podcast deserve better than having to sit through a bad episode because you weren't able to say no to the guest.

CHAPTER 025

WORKING WITH PUBLICISTS

Once your podcast gets basic traction, you're going to be approached by anybody and everybody looking for an opportunity to speak about their products and services. Many times, pitches are done by a publicist.

When dealing with a publicist, keep in mind who she works for. It's not you. Sure, most publicists are great people who want great matches between media outlets and their clients, but make sure your podcast isn't a dumping ground for publicity clients that couldn't be placed elsewhere.

Why would a professional publicist reach out to a small podcast?

Publicists want to make it appear like they're doing their jobs and worth the money clients are paying them. Securing interviews on small podcasts, because they're usually much easier to get, are easy wins.

The best way to make sure you get quality guests is for you to approach them. Don't wait around hoping that the people you want to interview will come to you — most of the time, they won't. Be nice to publicists, though. Just because a guest being pitched isn't a good match for you doesn't mean other clients these publicists work with, including future clients, won't be.

Be Picky

Some people are going to be pissed when you turn them down. So what? This is *your* podcast, not theirs.

What if a friend pitches you? It doesn't matter. The standards you set for guests on your podcast apply regardless of who is asking to be on your show.

Depending on your relationship with the person pitching you, you can offer various ways of helping to get that person up to speed. Still, you're not in the business of providing media training. Guests need to come complete and ready to go.

CHAPTER 026

YOUR PODCAST GUEST "CONTRACT"

When a guest schedules time to be interviewed on your podcast and sends relevant information, such as his bio, Skype username, and website, I suggest making him also agree to three things:

*I understand this:

Not all interviews on [PODCAST NAME] are published.

*I understand this:

My interview may be edited. [PODCAST NAME] does not send edits for approval.

*I understand this:

Audio quality matters. I'll be using a good mic (NOT a built-in computer mic or mobile phone headset) and I'll be talking to you from a quiet place.

These agreements alone will save you a lot of headache from people following up wondering why you haven't yet published their interviews, people showing up without the necessary equipment to properly record them, and people asking questions about edits.

It's not your job to explain to a guest how media works. But if you sense that somebody isn't 100 percent clear that you don't let guests approve final edits before you release them, this is a good time to let him know.

The purpose of the "three agreements" is to be 100 percent clear with guests about what you expect from them. This is not an interview release form.

THIS IS NOT LEGAL ADVICE

You don't need a signed release to use an interview. By giving an interview for the purpose of being published via your podcast, your guest has consented to the interview and your release of it. Because of this, there can be no claim for invasion of privacy or monetary compensation.

Of course, it's always a good idea if you can cover yourself. Because of this, I recommend having guests agree to the following release statement before doing an interview with you:

> *I agree to this interview. I understand [PODCAST NAME] has the right to reproduce and distribute this interview (in whole or in part) to the public using any current or future technology.*

This makes consent to the interview crystal clear. It also makes it clear that you have the right to use the interview for something other than a podcast and take advantage of any distribution format available, not just via online downloads or streaming.

CHAPTER 027

BAD INTERVIEWS, BAD GUESTS

Even Larry King had bad interviews. Below is an exchange he had with former Miss California USA, Carrie Prejean, who was stripped of her Miss California USA crown for alleged breaches of contract. At the time of this interview, she was promoting her book, "Still Standing," which told the story from her point of view.

KING: We're back with Carrie Prejean. She's the author of Still Standing. That book is available everywhere. We'll take a call or two for Carrie in a moment. You sued the pageant after they fired you. They counter-sued. And then you accused them of a number of things including religious discrimination, clearly an issue very important to you. Why did you settle? You don't have to tell me the terms of the settlement. But why settle, since you had a fight to carry on?

PREJEAN: Larry, everything that was discussed in mediation — I'll say it again— is completely confidential. I'm not going to be able to talk about that. So I'm just letting you know that ahead of time.

KING: So you can't even say why you settled? That's not — how does that break what you settled for. I'm not asking you what the settlement was.

PREJEAN: It's a confidential agreement and I'm not allowed to talk about that. So —

KING: So the agreement discusses the motive behind why each party agreed?

PREJEAN: Larry, you're being inappropriate. You really are. So I'm not going to —

KING: What? I'm asking a question.

PREJEAN: I'm not going to talk about anything discussed in mediation. It was a confidential settlement.

KING: All I'm asking — so — all right. So what you're saying is, in mediation, it was discussed why you were mediating?

PREJEAN: Larry, it's completely confidential. And you're being inappropriate, OK?

KING: All right. Inappropriate King Live continues. Detroit, hello.

CALLER: Hi, calling from Detroit. I'm a gay man and I love pageants. I'm sure that you, Carrie, have got great gay friends that helped you possibly win. What would you give them as advice if they wanted to get married?

KING: Did you hear the question, Carrie? Did she hear the question? Is she leaving because I asked what motivated the settlement?

PREJEAN: Excuse me?

KING: Did you hear the question?

PREJEAN: No, I can't hear you.

KING: You took the mic off. You put the mic on, you can hear.

PREJEAN: I think you're being extremely inappropriate right now. And I'm about to leave your show.

KING: Well, so I went to another area. I took a phone call. They asked a question of you. I left that subject. You feel it was inappropriate? I didn't mean to be inappropriate. I just thought it was a logical question. But you need to have a mic. Who are you talking to?

Hello? We'll be back right after these messages on LARRY KING LIVE.

(COMMERCIAL BREAK)

KING: We're back with Carrie Prejean. I did not certainly mean to ask you a question — you don't want to take phone calls, right?

PREJEAN: Yes, that was the agreement that you had with my publicist.

KING: No one told me. I didn't know we weren't supposed to take phone calls. And I meant nothing of the question.

PREJEAN: Right, and this is you and I talking and I appreciate that.

KING: OK. What are you going to do next?

PREJEAN: Oh, my gosh. I'm just so excited to be, you know, promoting this book. I'm so excited to be an author now. It's really great that — I'm 22 years old, and I think that I've accomplished so much. And I think that there is definitely a message out there to spread to young women and that is, you know, never do anything that you wouldn't want your biggest fans to see or, you know, never do anything that, heaven forbid, your dad would see.

Video of the entire interview is online. Search "Carrie Prejean Larry King" to find it.

Within the full interview, you'll find several things that should never happen. Among them:

- Hijacking questions to promote a product
- Walking off set
- Refusing to answer questions
- Losing your cool
- Not having a clear agreement about topics and questions ahead of time

Was Larry King inappropriate, as Prejean suggested? Could he have saved the interview in a way where she didn't walk out?

Maybe. But the show is called *Larry King Live*, not *Carrie Prejean Live*. And his responsibility was to broadcast the information his audience wanted to hear, not what she wanted to talk about in the exact way she wanted to talk about it.

How To Avoid Bad Interviews

You never know how an interview is going to turn out until you start recording. There are millions of little things that can affect an interview, most of which you can't control. For example, the guest gets bad news just minutes before you start recording, technical problems, or your studio floods.

So let's talk about what you can control:

You can control who you bring in. Focus on guests who are both knowledgeable about their subject matter and able to deliver this knowledge in an entertaining way.

You can give guests a list of guidelines to follow so you can get the best possible recordings of them. For example, if you're doing remote recordings, give them a list of mic recommendations and a recommendation to do the interview in a quiet and interruption-free space.

You can control your preparation to make sure that you're able to get the most out of what you're given.

You can control your environment. Is your equipment good enough? Do you have a quiet and interruption-free space?

These four things will take care of the majority of problems.

How To Let People Down

If you've done what I've suggested, all guests will have agreed that "not every interview is published" before you actually interview them. Unfortunately, because the standard for great episodes in podcasting is so low and a lot of sub-par content slips through the cracks, your rejection may come as a surprise for some people.

This can make the situation *easier.*

If you're taking a punt on somebody, you can let him know ahead of time that you're looking for soundbites and probably won't use the entire interview.

If you had no idea ahead of time you'd end up with something you can't use in its entirety, the time to let your guest know you'll be going through it for clips you can use on future episodes is one of the following:

1. While the guest is still on the line with you
2. Within a couple of hours after recording the interview, in your follow-up "thank you" email
3. After you've found the clip (or clips) you need and have released it within an episode

It's okay to take responsibility for the bad interview if you feel it's your fault. A statement like, "I feel like I wasn't able to bring what I wanted out of you" isn't a lie.

You Are In Charge

I've done hundreds of radio and podcast episodes. In that time, I can think of *two* where guests gave me (or the producer) a hard time about approving an episode before it was released. Those are pretty good odds.

Still, the number should be *zero*. I take responsibility for ever having this issue because I wasn't clear that once an interview has been recorded, it's mine to do whatever I want with.

If you're comfortable with these kind of odds, like I am, there's no need to make a big deal out of this. After all, guests should know better.

When you tell something to a newspaper reporter, what he does with it is up to him. When you let *20/20* or *60 Minutes* follow you around for a couple of days in order to do a short segment on you, you're not sitting with a producer in an editing bay, giving advice on what's important or not important for the story.

This is how media works: You give them raw content and they take over from there, packaging everything together in a way that works for their audience.

And this is how your podcast should work. Every. Single. Time.

From my experience, you're eventually going to deal with some people (fewer than 1 percent) who want to sign off on your final edit before its released.

Then what?

You have a choice. You can either lose the interview (and because of this, the episode) or lose the relationship with the guy you interviewed.

Lose the episode. Regardless of how great an interview was, it's not worth losing a relationship over.

But never back down on the fact that you're in charge of your own podcast. Letting guests have final say over what goes out compromises your credibility with your audience.

CHAPTER 028

CREATING A MEMORABLE GUEST EXPERIENCE

Very rarely will you have a guest who hasn't done interviews for other media outlets, some a lot more memorable than "just a podcast."

Most podcast interviews, if they're not recorded with both the host and the guest in the same room, are done via phone or an online calling service like Skype. Your guest is basically doing the same exact thing each time he does an interview — talking into his telephone or a microphone hooked up to his computer. He's in the same place, looking at the same surroundings, and talking about the same topic.

You want guests to have a *different* (and better) experience with you than they do elsewhere. And while you might not be able to do this via remote interviews, you can make sure working with you isn't forgotten by following up in a memorable way after your interviews are over.

There are three times you want to follow up with a guest:

1. Immediately

As soon as you've got something on tape and you disconnect from the guest, immediately send an email thanking him for taking the time to talk with you. As soon as this is done, send a handwritten letter of thanks in the mail. At the very least, send a handwritten postcard or "Thank You" card.

If the interview was booked by an agent or assistant, send that person an email and something via postal mail as well. Or make a phone call to thank him and let him know how the interview went.

Is this overkill? No. Not if you want the person you interviewed to remember you and your podcast. And as a bonus, showing appreciation like this acknowledges the work the guest (or agent) has done to help your podcast, which will go a long way in helping you to secure more top-shelf guests.

2. Within The Week

After your initial email and postal follow-ups with a guest, to make an even bigger impression, send a small gift. This doesn't have to be anything elaborate; it could be something branded.

No coffee mugs or water bottles — you can do better.

99% Invisible has custom "challenge coins" to give people who support the show. A challenge coin is a small coin or medallion, which bears an organization's insignia or emblem. These coins are carried by the organization's members to prove membership as well as given to people, such as podcast guests, to recognize something done for the organization.

If you want to keep things simple, books are a great gift for guests. And since books often come up during an interview (or pre-interview), they're an easy way to continue a conversation.

If a specific book was mentioned during the interview (or pre-interview) which your guest hasn't read, send him a copy.

Finally, food is almost always a good gift. If your guest works in an office with other people, send something that can be shared (and talked about) with co-workers for maximum impact.

And don't forget to acknowledge the work of publicists, agents, and other handlers.

3. When You've Published The Episode

Once an episode has been edited and published, email or call the person you interviewed as well as his handler (if applicable). Within this email or conversation, make it clear how the episode can be accessed and that you give permission for the guest to pass it along via social media or elsewhere, chop it up (e.g. take highlights), and use within his media kit or other promotion materials.

CHAPTER 029

PODCAST INTERVIEW ALTERNATIVES

There are a lot of reasons why you won't be able to get a guest on your podcast. Scheduling, technical issues, or rejection, are the most common.

There will also be reasons why you don't want a guest on your podcast. If you have a solo podcast, for example, and don't do interviews. Or maybe the potential guest is a jerk, or he isn't a good communicator.

Regardless of why you can't or don't have a great guest for your podcast, consider these "guest alternative" episodes.

The "Book Review" Episode

Exclusive content is important to listeners. Popular authors don't always provide this as they often hit dozens, if not hundreds, of media outlets when they release new books. Because of this, and because the same people who listen to your podcast are also listening (or watching) other similar media outlets, it's likely that any author interviews you ally during book launch periods, will be *very* similar to what listeners could find elsewhere.

People don't want to hear the same answers to the same questions again and again, even if the questions are asked by different hosts.

A "book review" episode is a great alternative to an author interview. It allows you to talk about the content of a great book without having to worry about waiting to fit into somebody else's schedule. It also allows you to put your spin on the topic, thus building your credibility and authority as an expert on the subject while giving listeners content not available elsewhere.

"Book Review" Episode Outline

1. Announce the book.
2. Give background on the author.
3. Explain why you chose to review the book.
4. Give a short summary of the book and who it's for.
5. Share three big ideas found within the book.
6. Give an "action step" from the book — something you're doing as a result of reading it.
7. Give information on where to purchase the book.

The Blog Post Commentary Episode

This is a great episode format as it helps you leverage an already existing discussion to generate traffic while giving you opportunity to be an authority on the subject.

THE CONCEPT: You see a blog post making the rounds of social media. Everybody seems to have an opinion on it, and your opinion goes against the grain. Rather than jumping in the discussion via Facebook, Twitter, or another site you don't control, you take it to your podcast.

This scares a lot of people, especially if you're disagreeing with a popular blogger who has a popular position. In situations like these, resist the urge to keep your mouth shut.

Your job as a podcaster (and influencer) is to stimulate discussion. Like an artist making controversial art, what you do should make people think, question, and react.

Will this type of content always be popular? No. I'm advising you how to impact people, not be the coolest kid in the high school lunchroom.

The "Frankenstein" Episode

When an interview is too short for a full episode or not as good as you'd hoped it would be, you still have options for using *some* of the content. My suggestion is to take what you like — answers to single questions, sound bites, funny stories — and put these elements together in a "Frankenstein" episode.

THE CONCEPT: You've got a lot of loose material from various interviews that hasn't been released for some reason. You group this existing but incomplete content together based on a single topic and stitch it together with your commentary to create a complete, full-length episode.

This is not a "best of" episode, where you use previously released content that worked well before. It's an entirely new episode with material that didn't fit elsewhere and couldn't stand on its own.

MODULE 4
PODCAST LAUNCH / RELAUNCH

PART 1 – YOUR PODCAST LAUNCH FOUNDATION

CHAPTER 030

PODCAST MARKETING PHILOSOPHY

The hardest part of podcasting (for most people) isn't anything to do with production — it's promotion and marketing.

Producing a quality episode can be hard work. Once you hit publish, you're done with that part. The necessary promotion and marketing to get people to listen to that episode and keep them listening as you release future episodes *never* ends.

Contrary to popular belief, there's no magic bullet to podcast success.

Jessica Rhodes of Interview Connections, a podcast booking service, has helped to launch dozens of successful podcasts by connecting podcast hosts with experts. In her words, "Podcasts are a long-term strategy with a compounding effect."

Success builds upon success. The more great episodes you have, the more opportunities you have for word-of-mouth referrals, social media mentions, and search engine traffic.

This foundation on which you'll build a substantial podcast doesn't happen overnight. And like the foundation of a building, it must be maintained.

For a successful podcast, promotion and marketing are paramount.

What Is Podcasting?

Podcasting, as popular as it is, isn't radio. Most people are clueless about podcasting.

"Does it have something do with an iPhone?"

"Isn't that on the Internet?"

"I've think I've heard of it."

If you were on the radio, you wouldn't get these reactions. People have not only heard of radio, they know how to operate one.

1. You turn it on via a power button.
2. You set the tuner to the station you want to listen to.

Done.

Podcasts are a bit more difficult to access, at least right now. That doesn't mean you have to make your explanation of podcasts difficult, though.

Do you understand the technology behind broadcast radio? Most listeners don't.

Do you *need* to understand the technology behind broadcast r order to listen to it? No.

Neither do your listeners.

Never give potential listeners long-winded technical definitions of podcasting like, "A podcast is a digital medium consisting of audio or video files associated with a given series. These files are maintained centrally on the distributor's server as a web feed, and the listener or viewer employs special client application software, known as a podcatcher, that can access this web feed, check it for updates, and download any new files in the series. This process can be automated so that new files are downloaded automatically, which may seem to the user as if the content is being broadcast. However, unlike broadcasting, files are stored locally and played directly from the user's computer or other device, such as an iPhone."

Nobody cares about the technical aspects of podcasting!

If you make podcasts seem complicated, nobody will listen. It's for this reason that I suggest you tell people podcasts are "like radio on the Internet" or "radio on demand" that can be accessed via a smartphone. Your job is to get listeners and make it easy for them to listen, not explain technical details.

The Majority Of People Are *Not* Like You

You're somebody who knows the power of podcasting when it comes to spreading your message. Because of this, you don't feel indifferent or even simply "like" podcasts, you *love* podcasts.

If I told you about a podcast that could really help you, how far would you go to get it?

If it wasn't available on Apple Podcasts, would you look for other options to access it? Of course! You'd search other podcast sites, download apps, or do whatever it took to hear it.

As somebody who understands how powerful podcasts are, it's easy to think others feel the same way about them. This happens with people all the time: we think "they're just like us."

They're not.

Projecting our personal qualities on others is part of our biology. It's a way for us to feel connected with people. And it's such a firmly established habit for most of us, we do it without thinking.

When I was a musician, I took a DJ gig playing a private party and wrongly assumed the people there were like *my* people, club people.

They weren't.

One guy requested a song. I played a remixed version of it designed for the club.

Before the song was over, he came back to me and asked, "Can you play the one on the radio?"

It was the same song, just a little different. Still, it was different enough to throw him off, and similar decisions that I made during that gig were enough for my booking agent to get complaints about my performance, which hurt my ability to get booked again.

I'd forgotten a foundational rule of marketing — know your audience. In this case, it wasn't club people; it was the general public — people who wanted to hear what they were already familiar with.

Remember who your audience is. And regardless of how comfortable they may be with technology, make it as easy as possible for them to access your podcast.

If you make things too difficult for people, they'll move on to something else that's easier for them. This applies to *everything* about your podcast, from describing it in a way that people can understand, to making it easy to access, to organizing the content in a way that is easy to consume.

CHAPTER 031

PODCAST ACCESSIBILITY

The easiest way for most people to access a podcast for the first time is through the web. Listeners go to a website, which is something most people are familiar with, and press a "play" button, similar to the ones found on CD and DVD players.

There are dozens of web-friendly podcast players. You want one with a big, easy-to-find button that make how to play your podcast obvious to new listeners. Visit BigPodcast.com/resources for links to the recommended options.

Podcast Apps

Like web players, there are dozens of podcast apps. What's the best one? That depends. From a marketing perspective, the "best" podcast app is the one people will use to listen to your podcast.

As far as simplicity for listeners, a custom app designed just for your podcast is the best way to go, especially if you serve a demographic that isn't comfortable with technology. This app does one thing and one thing only — play your podcast.

A custom app makes a bold statement about what you're doing. Like a hardcover book for an author, it shows that you're a professional, you take your podcast seriously, and that people take you seriously.

And if you have an audience who doesn't get technology, because of its simplicity, a custom app can be important in establishing your fan base.

Building a custom app for your podcast is easier than it sounds. All major podcast hosting companies, including Spreaker, Blubrry, and Libsyn have app options that are more or less templates which are customized using images and information specific to your podcast.

Going this route, a "custom" app is as easy as filling out a web form. All the technical aspects of getting your app online are handled, including the submission and approval processes to get in Apple's App Store and programming updates to keep the app working correctly.

If you want to make it as easy as possible for listeners to access your episodes, a custom app is the way to go, especially if your listeners are not already familiar with podcasting.

Your Worldwide HQ

You need a website to send everybody to. Preferably, you get to it via a domain that's the name of your podcast with .com after it.

Many will argue that "nobody goes to a podcast's website." And this is *usually* true. When was the last time you visited the website of your favorite podcast? You've probably *never* visited it.

Still, you need a website or, at the very least, a domain you own and control. Podcasting and other online businesses come and go; you don't want to be a casualty when a company you deal with goes out of business or otherwise disappears.

When you have your own domain, you can point it anywhere you want. This can be part of an existing blog, a social media page, or a custom site — it doesn't matter. What does matter is you're easily able to point listeners to wherever you happen to be.

Your podcast, if you do what I'm suggesting in this book, will be distributed through dozens of places. An "official" website will allow you to engage with listeners in a different way than listening to your show does, help you build a mailing list, and develop a social media following. All of these things will help to increase your connection with the people who listen to your podcast.

The Best (And Easiest) Way To Create A Podcast Website

WordPress is a free and open-source blogging system used by over 60,000,000 websites. There's a huge community of podcasters who use WordPress because of its great podcasting tools. It's easy to find somebody to help you when you run into a problem or need advice on how to improve your site.

Due to its popularity, many web hosting companies offer free (and automated) WordPress installation to customers. Visit BigPodcast.com/resources for a list of recommended web hosts.

CHAPTER 032

HOW TO ATTRACT (AND KEEP) A PODCAST AUDIENCE

Your podcast, regardless of how general the focus is, isn't for everybody. Too often, podcasters play it safe when it comes to narrowing their topics for fear of alienating people. A far bigger problem, which happens when you do this, is that you'll be ignored by everybody.

By alienating *some* people, you'll connect more deeply with others. When you try to please everybody, you please nobody.

You don't need everybody to like your podcast. A small number of people who *really* love you is all it takes to have be successful with podcasting.

People who are hated by some and loved by just as many:

- Donald Trump
- Rush Limbaugh
- Michael Moore
- Al Gore
- Sarah Palin
- Barack Obama
- George W. Bush

In podcasting, the best podcast examples of this are from shows that have specific religious or political philosophies. Any Christian podcast is going to alienate those who aren't Christians, at least on some level, but those who are Christian are going to buy in even more.

Think about it: if you're Christian, you'd much rather hear "Jesus is Lord" than a reference that could work for a variety of religions, such as "your higher power," since "Jesus is Lord" is a sentiment you can relate to. "Jesus is Lord" won't appeal to everybody, and may even turn off some, but a podcast that gives specific references to Jesus is going to connect with Christians in a very powerful way.

If you're a Christian podcaster, who cares if some people are offended or turned off by Jesus? You're a Christian podcaster! Focus on the Christians. Nobody else cares about you, so don't worry about them.

The same rule applies to any podcast. Embrace polarization. Anything else falls in the middle — and the middle is forgettable by everybody.

How To Double Down On Listener Attraction

If you're into baseball, you know and understand the language other baseball fans use. If you're a musician, you have something similar. If you're from Texas, there are certain aspects of your life oᵣₗᵧ ⌐⌐ Texans will understand.

These things can be said for *any* group, regardless of whether the shared interest or bond is religious, academic, social, philosophical, or geographic in nature. *All* groups have very specific words, phrases, jokes, rituals, traditions, and beliefs that people outside the group don't understand.

This "lexicon" is how you know an insider from an outsider.

People want to be insiders. They want to feel like they're part of something and that they belong. You can help establish and encourage this feeling among those who listen to your podcast by creating a podcast lexicon.

Your podcast lexicon may already exist, without you even knowing it. If you're connecting with listeners and paying attention to them, it will likely create itself.

Think about your best friends, your family, or your significant other. You have inside jokes, traditions, habits, preferences, and shared thoughts people on the outside don't get.

This is exactly what you want to do with your podcast.

Most podcasts, because they focus on a very specific and defined niche, have listeners who already have a very specific and common language. Build upon this by creating …

Inside Jokes

An inside joke is a joke shared by a specific group of people, one that only those within the group will understand. It's the ultimate mark of an inside, "Us vs. Them" lexicon.

Yes, you want *some* people to feel like they aren't part of your group. That's the only way you can have insiders who feel like they're part of something special.

This sounds counter-intuitive to many people. After all, don't you want as many people as possible to listen to your podcast?

Sure, but you want to focus on the insiders. This "status" is open to everybody, but you want people to have to work for it.

What you're doing isn't an elementary school field day where everybody gets a ribbon just for showing up. You're like the Olympics, where getting a medal actually means something.

Inside jokes make listeners work for status. If they listen long enough, they'll pick up on things and, because they've had to work to do this, they'll appreciate your podcast even more.

Vocabulary

Two-bagger means something to a baseball fan. Musicians know what an 808 is. Texans know what H-E-B is.

How is vocabulary established? It happens naturally, over long periods of time. If you don't want to wait that long, you'll need to come up with your own custom vocabulary and use it consistently within your podcasts to get others to pick up on it.

Podcasting legend Adam Curry is a master of this. His listener-funded podcast, No Agenda, has its own vocabulary to describe different levels of donations and status that comes from donating to the show. For example, a "double nickels on the dime" donation ($55.10) lets listeners become a "No Agenda Minuteman." A $999.99 donation (or $50/month over 20 months, if you prefer installments) gets you "Knight" status. There's also something in the middle, the "Quad Niner" donation level ($99.99), where Curry is obligated to say, "niner, niner, niner, niner" — a reference to his use of "niner" instead of "nine" in episode openings.

Even a single word or phrase used in this way can be a powerful. As an example, Jim Kukral and Bryan Cohen of *The Sell More Books Show*, a marketing podcast for indie book authors, often use the term "mahogany desk" to poke fun at outdated thinking within the traditional publishing world. This two-word phrase not only lets listeners know they're in the right (or wrong) place, it also showcases the forward-thinking beliefs of the hosts themselves.

Want a head start on developing a vocabulary for your show? Look at how people within your niche are talking about related products in reviews left on Amazon.com, notice the language used within discussions on Reddit, and read the comments on niche-related YouTube videos.

Rituals

When most people think of rituals, they envision things like worship rites and sacraments of organized religions, initiation into secret societies, oaths of allegiance, dedication ceremonies, and political inaugurations. And these *are* rituals. However, a ritual doesn't have to be nearly so serious.

When it comes to your podcast, a ritual is simply a set sequence of actions. It can be as simple and as informal as you want.

An example of this is a well-known ritual by financial guru Dave Ramsey that happens when listeners pay off their debts. A newly debt-free listener will call Dave during *The Dave Ramsey Show* and share the story of how he followed Dave's advice and, because of this, is now debt-free. Dave gives a 3-2-1 countdown, and the listener yells, "I'M DEBT FREE!!"

Running Gag

Somewhere between an inside joke and a ritual is the running gag.

ʒs are similar to inside jokes as they often start with an ιnintentional humor. Variations of the joke are repeated, leading audiences to anticipate them.

On my show, *Music Business Radio*, every episode ends with a standard list of credits. Something like, "Music Business Radio is a production of Tuned In Broadcasting. Your host is David Hooper. Engineering by Ryan McFadden. Gary Kraen is the producer."

At the end is a running gag with something like:

- "...and Lester turned out the lights."
- "...and Lester held the umbrella."
- "...and Lester programmed the drum machine."
- "...and Lester replaced the spark plugs."
- "...and Lester ordered the pizza."

None of these things has anything to do with the show. Lester, however, is the owner of the radio station, and has *everything* to do with the show. He voiced the original spots, which is how the joke got started.

A running gag is often humorous solely for how often it's repeated or its level of inappropriateness for the situation in which the gag occurs.

You may be familiar with "Keyboard Cat," an Internet meme which started as a simple video of a cat in a blue shirt playing an electronic keyboard.

The original video has since been taken and appended to the end of a various blooper videos to "play people off" after a mistake, accident, or uncomfortable situation, in a manner similar to a vaudeville performer. It shows up when you least expect it and at the most inappropriate of times.

Traditions

A tradition is a belief or behavior passed down within a group. Common examples include holidays or socially meaningful clothes, like old-fashioned barrister wigs or Christmas sweaters. Traditions also apply to the way we interact with each other, such as greetings and sign-offs.

Weekend Update is a *Saturday Night Live* sketch in newscast format which comments on and parodies current events. Hosts change every few years, as *Saturday Night Live* cast members come and go. Each host brings a new "sign off" used on every episode.

Original Weekend Update host Chevy Chase would sign off each episode with, "That's the news. Good night, and have a pleasant tomorrow."

Dennis Miller, host of Weekend Update from 1985 until 1991 would end each episode with, "Guess what, folks? That's the news, and I am outta here!" He would then scribble nonsense on his script, often throwing it into the air.

Seth Myers, host of Weekend Update from 2008 until 2013, would sign off each episode with, "For Weekend Update, I'm Seth Meyers! Good night!"

This tradition works in two ways that build on each other. One, there's the show tradition — a "sign off" from the host, which you can also find in "straight" network newscasts. And two, there's a host tradition — each host has an individual sign off.

An easy "podcast tradition" to put in place is an annual episode connected with a holiday or other event. An example of this is the annual "Things I Love" episode I do every Valentine's Day for *RED Podcast*. Each year, I talk about various resources I'm using on some aspect of my business — for example, resources I'm using to successfully grow an email list, to get more podcast subscribers, or to book public speaking gigs.

You can easily do something similar on a more frequent basis. For example, doing a "live" episode from a local bar on the first Wednesday of every month or segment with your spouse every Friday.

Beliefs And Convictions

Stand for something. The world doesn't need another milquetoast, "play it safe" podcast from a milquetoast, "play it safe" host.

When you fly the flag of what you believe in, you'll isolate *some* people, but you'll attract others. And it doesn't matter how popular or unpopular your beliefs are. Even the most popular beliefs have detractors, and even the most unpopular beliefs have supporters.

There are *zero* exceptions to this rule. In fact, the most "unpopular" beliefs often find the most loyal and engaged audiences.

When Indiana Senate Bill 101, also known as the Religious Freedom Restoration Act, became law, it gave individuals and companies the ability to legally discriminate against others using religious beliefs as a defense. The owners of Memories Pizza in Walkerton, Indiana, were among the first to publicly announce that they would refuse to cater a same-sex wedding.

The owners said that "if a gay couple was to come in, say they wanted us to provide them pizzas for their wedding, we would have to say no."

Not a popular belief. Within hours of this hitting the media, the business received hundreds and hundreds of negative Yelp reviews, as well as threatening emails and online harassment. Things were so bad the business had to temporarily close due to fake orders and threats.

Then somebody who shared the same beliefs as Memories Pizza started a GoFundMe campaign, asking for $25,000 to help the owners "stave off the burdensome cost of having the media parked out front, activists tearing them down, and no customers coming in."

By the end of the campaign, 29,175 donors had contributed $842,977 to the cause.

If a message that goes against the general tide of popular culture and basic civil rights can find support, *any* message can.

PART 2 – YOUR PODCAST LAUNCH

CHAPTER 033

HOW TO LAUNCH YOUR PODCAST

Launching your podcast isn't something to be timid about. You want to take full advantage of the extra exposure and novelty that comes from being new.

Like merging onto a highway, you want to get up to speed as quickly as possible. This is how to do it.

How Many "Launch" Episodes Do You Need?

While it's possible to launch with a single episode, doing this can slow down the relationships you're trying to establish with listeners, because one episode doesn't give people much information about who you are, the perspective you bring to podcasting, or what sets your podcast apart from other, similar podcasts.

Here's why launching with a high number of episodes works.

According to a study led by Lucy Hunt and Paul Eastwick of the University of Texas at Austin and Eli Finkel of Northwestern University, people appear more attractive to others over time. This study backs up what marketing people have known forever — the more time you spend with somebody, the more comfortable they are with you.

To take advantage of this, you want to launch your podcast with multiple episodes. The more episodes you have available to people who discover your show, the more episodes people will download and listen to. The more people listen to you, the more likely they are to become attached to you.

What it looks like:

When people discover your show, the first thing they do is play a single episode, sometimes just streaming a portion of it. If they find something of interest, they subscribe and start downloading all the episodes that look interesting to them. For example, episodes on specific topics they want to learn about, or episodes with interviews of people they're interested in.

If somebody listens to podcasts via Apple's Podcasts app, every subscription helps your podcast rank higher on the Apple Podcasts podcast chart. Better placement on the chart means more visibility via show rankings, as well as more visibility via search results. This extra visibility builds upon itself every time somebody downloads one of your episodes or subscribes to your podcast.

This is why I suggest you launch your podcast with 25 episodes. The more episodes you give Apple to work with, the more likely somebody browsing podcasts will find an episode topic she likes. And the more somebody likes a topic, the more likely she is to download and listen to the podcast attached to it.

Every podcast chart and directory works basically the same way. Amazon works in a similar way with books it sells. Google works this way with paid search.

Your aim is both popularity and relevancy. You can have both with a single episode, but it's much easier to achieve the big outcome you're looking for when you have a "body of work" for both people and search engines to work with.

CHAPTER 034

GETTING MEDIA ATTENTION FOR YOUR PODCAST

If you've ever been behind on a bill, you may have received a series of letters in an attempt to get you to pay up. These letters usually start fairly nice, but progressively get more and more direct and to-the-point.

For example, the first letter in the series, when you're just a little behind on your bill, will say, "This is a reminder that your account currently has a balance of $123.45. This amount was due to be paid in full on [date]. Please make full payment of the balance as soon as possible."

Then, a couple of weeks later, you'll get something that says, "We understand you are busy and may have forgotten to send us your payment of $123.45, which was due on [date]. Please pay this amount promptly."

And if you ignore the second message, you'll get an additional follow-up letter with a message like, "We have not yet received your overdue payment of $123.45. We have sent you several payment requests and have received no response. We urge you to protect your good credit by sending us full payment no later than [date]. If full payment is not received by this date, we will be forced to send your account to a collection agency."

Collection agencies use this type of mailing because it works. You can use a similar, multi-step technique to get the attention of people in the media, potential guests, and other people you want to connect with.

The Time-Released Podcast Promotion — How-To Guide

Instead of sending a standard single-package "media kit" about your podcast, take advantage of the power of a multi-step promotion by sending individual elements of your marketing material, one at a time, over an extended period. For an even bigger impact, send your messages via various methods — email, fax, postal mail, phone, courier, etc.

Yes, there are people who still use fax machines. Do what works. If that means sending your message via a singing telegram or a woman dressed up like a chicken, do it — don't make this precious.

The purpose of promoting yourself and your podcast using this method is to create excitement and desire in the person you're trying to connect with, so when you finally do reach out to ask for media coverage (or make another request), he'll be more likely to say yes.

Step 1 – Create Your Media List

Who can help you get the word out about your podcast? The people with the most power to do this are those who "buy ink by the barrel," meaning they're able to reach a lot of people with their messages.

For example:

- Newspaper writers
- TV personalities
- Online personalities
- Forum admins and moderators
- Conference organizers
- Podcasters
- Gurus
- Bloggers
- Journalists
- People who work for related companies that share your same audience

Create a list of *at least* 50 of these people who are actively creating content on the same topic as your podcast, organizing their contact information in a customer database program or spreadsheet. For recommendations on these tools, as well as software to help you find email addresses, phone numbers, and other contact info, visit the resource page at BigPodcast. com/resources.

Note that social proof works on people in media just like it does podcast listeners. Media coverage is affected by momentum, so that the more coverage you have, the more coverage you'll get.

To get momentum going, consider "media stacking." Start with independent people who will be easier to access than more established ones, then work your way up the media hierarchy.

Step 2 - Prime The Pump

People are busy. "Important" people, such as those who can help you effectively get the word out about your podcast via media, are especially busy. If you want to get their attention, you're going to need to do something to stand out. And if you want them to champion what you're doing and tell others, it helps if they feel connected to it.

You can get somebody's attention and start to build a connection in a number of ways. To do this with somebody who works in media and is actively publishing stories, articles, or other content, one way is to send a postcard with a quick message about that work.

Could you do this with email? Twitter? You could. But that's what everybody else does. And all emails and tweets look pretty much the same, which makes them even easier to be ignored.

A simple handwritten note of thanks directed at the recipient works well for letting somebody know you exist and appreciate his work. For example, "I really enjoyed your latest article on _____" or "Your article on _____ helped me to _____. Thank you!"

Don't make this too complicated. The postcard's only job is to "prime the pump." In other words, to get the recipient to be more receptive to future contact.

How does it do this?

First of all, because it's a postcard. Most postal mail comes in envelopes or packages. Postcards have little competition, so they automatically stand out.

But perhaps the most powerful aspect of a postcard is the recipient doesn't need to open it in order to get the message. If it's in your hands, the message on a postcard is easy to consume.

And the message on a postcard goes beyond just what you write on it. The "non-address side" of a podcast is like a miniature billboard. Putting your logo on it, which is what I suggest, will help get future non-postcard mail with that logo opened, because the recipient will recognize it.

It's not uncommon for people to follow up on mail they send, but how many send something beforehand? Almost none. This, combined with follow-up, will help to dramatically increase your ability to connect with people.

Step 3 - This Is Your Second Notice

If the first "collection agency" message didn't get a response, a follow-up message was sent. And like a collection agency, you're going to do the same thing – a second message that's a little bit bolder than the first.

Since the name of my podcast is *RED*, I have a lot to work with as far as interesting follow-up items that will stand out when sent through the mail — Red Hots, Big Red gum, Big Red soda, Red Vines licorice, etc.

These things are great, and they're effective at getting attention when sent through the mail, but if there was somebody I *really* wanted to get in touch with, I'd go bigger. To do this, I'd send the very first thing 90 percent of people associate with "red" — a stop sign.

You can get a metal, street-legal stop sign, just like the one on your street, for about $20. You can mail it anywhere in the country for about $15.

Like a postcard, one side of a stop sign has a graphic and one side is blank (plain aluminum). On the blank side, I'd tape an envelope containing the opportunity — either a request to be a guest or an invitation to "talk more" about working together. The recipient's address could be written on the outside of the envelope or directly on the back of the sign.

Imagine this for a second …

You get a knock on your office door. It's the postman. Or somebody from the mailroom. And he hands you a stop sign with an envelope attached.

You're going to open that envelope and read the message it contains. You're *probably* going to keep the stop sign in your office.

ιou re probably going to tell the people you work with about the experience.

"You'll never believe what I got in the mail today. A podcaster sent me a stop sign! And it had a message attached …"

What message do you put inside the envelope? That depends.

If I wanted to get the attention of a journalist who writes about marketing, I'd include something like …

> *Hello. I've been reading your marketing articles for years and really enjoyed what you've written about podcasting. As a podcaster myself, it's nice to see somebody in traditional media take this format seriously and acknowledge the opportunity we have with podcasting.*
>
> *I want to make you aware of a podcast with a similar message called RED Podcast — The Marketing Podcast For Experts. Each episode is downloaded more than 10,000 times by book authors, professional bloggers, podcast creators, and others wanting more information and advice on how to market their messages.*
>
> *Your article on _____ inspired me to record a related episode for RED Podcast. It's available at REDpodcast.com if you're interested in checking it out.*

Alternatively, if I were trying to get the attention of somebody at a company that shares the same audience as *RED Podcast* and could be a possible promotion partner, such a microphone company, I'd say something like …

> *Hello. I want you to be aware of RED Podcast — The Marketing Podcast For Experts. Each episode is downloaded more than 10,000 times by book authors, professional bloggers, podcast creators, and others wanting more information on marketing their messages.*

Since the very first episode in 2014, I've been using your microphones to create RED Podcast. Without you, what I do wouldn't happen, so thank you for creating such a great product!

I hope you'll drop by REDpodcast.com to take a quick listen to how "you" sound.

This is how you get people to respond to you. With that said, neither of these messages are asking for a response. Your initial message and "second notice" follow-up simply establish the foundation you'll need for the *possibility* of doing something with the recipient in the future.

Step 4 - This Is Your Third (And Final) Notice

There are a lot of reasons you won't hear back from people you approach about your podcast. People are busy, people are distracted, and people are skeptical. Plus, if you're following my advice, your communication so far has simply been to make the recipient aware of you; you're not asking for a follow-up or giving somebody a specific reason to follow up.

The best thing you can do to sell yourself and your podcast is to get people on the phone with you. A short, 15-minute call can work wonders when it comes to building relationships. It will also show the other party what you and your podcast have to offer and clear up misconceptions about podcasting, even if you these are not the primary reasons for your call.

"Third Notice" Ideas

A call that is both quick and powerful in terms of relationship-building is a "single-question interview." It says a lot about what you do and shows the person you've contacted what you do and how you work.

If you've done your research on who you're reaching out to, you should be able to come up with a specific and personalized question for each person that emphasizes something unique about them of their work, especially if you're reaching out to bloggers, podcasters, and others who create content based on their personal experiences. You can then use a combination of your questions, their answers, and your commentary to put together various single episodes or series of episodes based on related content.

For example, if you have a weight loss podcast, and you have a number of people on your list who talk about their personal experiences on the topic, you could reach out them and ask a question about one of the following topics:

- How the person personally lost weight
- A personal diet plan
- A personal workout plan
- What's working for people connected to the person (such as forum members or clients)
- Big mistakes the person sees in the people connected to him – why they're not having success

These basic topics could can be modified for most any subject.

- A personal success story related to your podcast topic
- A personal plan to achieve a specific goal
- A personal routine related to your specific topic
- What's working for members of a related community
- What's *not* working (common mistakes) for members of a related community

Once you've collected multiple answers, you can put them together in ways that allow you to tell a variety of stories related to your podcast topic, including:

- What's working now
- What's *not* working now

- Inspirational stories of people who have already had success
- A specific plan that allows listeners to achieve a specific outcome
- A "we're in this together" community-building episode that talks about the struggle (or successes)

This is only one idea of unlimited ideas to reach out to people for comment and to further a relationship. For example, if I were to reach out to somebody at a microphone company using this technique, I might ask about the following questions:

- What's your best advice for somebody with only $100 to spend on a microphone?
- How can you make an inexpensive microphone sound its best?
- When it is time for a podcaster to "upgrade" to a professional microphone?

Be creative. There are ways to make this technique work for anybody.

The "Third Notice" Call Process

Before The Call

1. *Do Your Homework.* You're calling to further a relationship, not catch up with an old friend, so do what you can to prepare yourself ahead of time. You don't want to waste time asking questions that could easily have been answered via Google or LinkedIn.

2. *Know What You're Saying (And Asking).* Your conversation should be specific to the person you're talking with, but there are also some basic elements that should be reviewed as well. Who are you? What do you do? How will you describe your podcast? Who listens to it? What are the benefits of listening?

During The Call

Respect the Other Person's Time. This means you need to get to the point quickly and end the call when you said you would, even if things seem to be going well. In other words, if you've asked for seven minutes, you need to end the call by the time your timer hits 7:00.

3. *Work From an Outline (But Be Flexible)*. Stick to your outline and make sure you cover everything needed to further the relationship you're building and fulfill the purpose of the call.
4. *Write It Down*. Keep track of the recipient's questions and comments. This will help you during the call, doing follow up, and on future outreach.

After The Call

1. *Follow Up*. Send a follow-up email thanking the person for her time and letting her know the next step in the process, even if it's just, "To make this episode, I'm going to put your comments together with some others and I'll let you know as soon as it's released."
2. *Keep In Touch*. Reach out when appropriate. Don't be a pest, but don't completely disappear.

Where's My Media Coverage?

By reaching out to people in the media, letting them know you and your podcast exist, and bringing them into the podcast creation process, you've started the ball rolling as far as media coverage for your podcast.

Media coverage emerges from quality work and relationships, and expands based on momentum. By continuing to reach out to the people on your media list about the episode you've put together and other helpful story leads (not just those with which you're involved), you'll strengthen your relationships and find yourself part of their coverage.

Some basic rules when dealing with media professionals:

1. Do your research on the person and previous work before reaching out. Always.
2. Pitch a story, not your podcast.
3. You don't decide what's important to cover – they do.
4. Be honest – never compromise somebody else's integrity.
5. Be respectful with follow-up.

Media is all about relationships. When you do the people on your list right, by sending them information that makes them look good, they'll do you right and make you look good.

How To Keep In Touch With Media (Or Anybody)

We've all had those people in our lives who come out of the woodwork whenever they need something. Unfortunately, this is how most people approach media contacts.

You want good relationships with people in the media. To make this happen, it's a good idea to make a habit of staying in touch.

Here are three ways to do this:

1. Send praise and positive feedback on articles and other content you see from your media contacts.
2. Share articles and other content from your friends via social media and on your podcast.
3. Be helpful. If you see something that would make a great story idea, share it. If you know somebody who would make a great source for somebody on your media list, introduce him.

CHAPTER 035

GROWING YOUR PODCAST VIA GIVEAWAYS

A giveaway or similar promotion during your launch period will help get you a lot of subscribers. It will help get a lot of people to sign up for your mailing list. It *may* help get you a lot of listeners.

Big downloads and lots of people signing up for your mailing list are great for your ego. Your focus during your launch period, or any podcast promotion, needs to be building an audience of people who will stick around and listen to future episodes, though.

"Numbers" without people attached don't matter. Listeners, real people who like your podcast, interact with you, and buy your stuff matter.

Listening to your podcast is a lot to ask of people.

It's easy to sign up for a mailing list, follow a Twitter account, click "Like" on a Facebook page, or hit the subscribe option in Apple Podcasts. And while all of these things will help you to build buzz and attract sponsorship, that attention will be short-lived if you don't do what it takes to turn these on-the-fence actions into something more substantial, like getting the people behind them to actually listen to your podcast and engage with you.

The first step to running a successful giveaway or promotion is to think beyond it. What will you do when the promotional period is over?

Everybody loves you when you're buying the drinks. Or, in this case, when you've giving things away. Use this momentum to turn potential listeners, many of whom are there primarily to get free stuff, into fans who will stick things out when your giveaway is over.

Giveaway And Promotion Best Practices

- What's the purpose of doing a giveaway? Are you simply looking to make a big initial splash? How important to you is attracting long-term listeners? Like any type of advertising or marketing, you should start with the end in mind.
- The prizes in your giveaway should be related to your podcast, as that's what will most appeal to the people you're trying to attract.
- Like a gift, the best giveaways are things people can use, but wouldn't necessarily get for themselves.
- A giveaway is the perfect time to do cross-promotions with other companies, since you can use related products and services as prizes.
- Is there something you can give away that can't be purchased anywhere? These are often the best kind of prizes. For example, letting winners come to your podcast studio and observe as you record an episode. Or custom voicemail greetings.
- Go to potential future sponsors for prizes. This gives your contest credibility, is a good way to start relationships, and may save you money on prizes.

- If your main goal of a giveaway is to get more listeners, announce winners during the episode, so prizes will go to your most enthusiastic entrants.
- Have well-defined terms. How long will you hold a prize to be claimed? What happens if a prize isn't claimed? Any restrictions on shipping?

General Giveaway Thoughts

There are various "raffle" and "viral giveaway" tools to automate this kind of promotion. The only software you'll absolutely have to have is something to manage your mailing list signups, because you'll use email to communicate with the people who participate.

For a list of giveaway tools, mailing list software, and other resources I recommend, visit BigPodcast.com/resources.

Remember, the purpose of your giveaway is to get people listening to your podcast and to make this a habit, so they'll continue listening after the giveaway is over. To maximize these things, it's best to give away prizes that people can use to listen to your podcast, like headphones or portable media players.

If you're an author with a book that's related to your podcast, that's a great giveaway. The same goes for any other type of offering you have, including services and live events. If your podcast is about travel, for example, and you own a resort, giving away a vacation package makes sense. This wouldn't make sense as a giveaway for a business podcast, though, because as nice as it is, it doesn't help the goal of having people consume what you do.

You don't want to attract random people who are simply looking for something free — you want to attract people who will benefit from what you have to offer.

Your giveaway should be an event — not a one-day event, but an ongoing event. I launched *RED Podcast* with 30 days of giveaways. You may want to do only a week or 10 days. Do something long enough that participating forces people to consume your podcast, but not so long that it becomes tiresome.

The *RED Podcast* launch had multiple prizes given away on each episode. Depending on your budget, you'll want to spread the "big" prizes out. For example, books or lower-end items, such as an Amazon Fire TV Stick would be given away more frequently than higher-cost items such as an Amazon Echo or Bose headphones.

A giveaway makes a great excuse to reach out to related companies and podcasts for sponsorship, but you need to set the pace and already have "prizes" in place before you approach either. People won't invest their money in your promotion unless you're willing to invest your money.

If you do your giveaway right, companies with complementary products and services will want to join with you. For the *RED Podcast* launch, I partnered with several "related" services, such as Blinkist, a book summary service. These partnerships, depending on how you negotiate them, will not only save you money on prizes, but can also help you reach a new group of potential listeners through email blasts and social media mentions.

Are there other podcasts similar to yours? These also make for great partnerships, with you exchanging "sponsorship" of goods or services being given away for mentions of your giveaway on the partnering podcast, in email blasts, and in social media posts.

CHAPTER 036

PODCAST LAUNCH PARTNERS

There's a saying music business executives use when describing music — "The more money it makes, the better it sounds."

Music fans, whether they know it or not, think something similar. For most people, the more fans an artist has, they more they like him.

We do this with electronic gadgets like iPhones. We do this with restaurants and coffee shops.

When somebody else likes something, it gives us permission to like it as well. This phenomenon is known as social proof, and it also applies to your podcast.

We're bombarded with choices in our lives. How do we know which one to make?

We look to what other people are doing.

Want to fill a club? Put a line of people outside the door. If you're really serious, rent a limousine with tinted windows and park it in the front, so it looks like something important is happening.

Want to fill a restaurant? Seat everybody who comes in by the front windows, where everybody else can see them.

Want to look better on Twitter or other social media? Increase your followers and keep the people you follow to a minimum.

50 Launch Partners

When you launch (or re-launch) your podcast, you want to get as many new people listening to your episodes as possible. By far, the best way to make this happen is through launch partners who will recommend your podcast to people they already have relationships with and influence over.

I recommend 50 launch partners because I want you to dig deep and put effort into coming up with a list of people who can help you. The final number of people on your list is arbitrary, though. Your main focus should be *quality* of people, not quantity. Not all launch partners are equal.

A quick story about a music business "launch" I was part of ...

I'd put together a huge music showcase. About 350 acts had come to Nashville to perform for industry executives as well as the public.

The kick-off party was at Warner Bros. Records. The building was designed for entertaining, with a huge outdoor terrace that overlooked the street below. Inside, dozens and dozens of Gold and Platinum records lined the walls.

It was a big deal for the musicians who were there. And one band, in particular, decided to make the most of the opportunity.

As hundreds of artist managers, radio people, and record label executives were at the party enjoying themselves, this upcoming (and unsigned) rock band had another idea. They sneaked past the catering staff, through an attached kitchen, and into the main part of the building.

Security soon caught them, but not before they'd been to dozens of offices, putting their music in the stereo systems of record label employees.

The music industry is full of stories like this. The reason why is the belief that, if you can get your material to the right person, it can change your life.

This is true. And if you can reach the right people with your podcast, it can change *your* life.

Unfortunately for the unsigned rock band that got loose inside Warner Bros. Records, the joke was on them. The executives whose offices they visited were in the payroll department, in charge of collecting and distributing royalty payments — they had nothing to do with getting acts signed.

Not all launch partners are equal. You don't need a lot of launch partners to be successful, but you do need the *right* launch partners.

Focus on partnering with the right people — the people who are also putting out great content and also have great relationships with their audiences. It's these elements that will make their endorsements of you mean something.

How can you do something for these people? Don't simply ask for an email blast or social media mention — provide value to their audiences. You can do this by sharing what you know via guest blog posts, specialized articles, and custom podcast episodes. You can do this with exclusive webinars and teleseminars with content made just for the audiences you're being promoted to.

Is it a lot of work? Yes. But it's worth it.

A simple endorsement is nice. Don't turn it down. Having a trusted launch partner endorse you by passing along your specialized content is so much more powerful, though.

Chicken vs. Egg

If you could get Barack Obama, Pope Francis, Oprah Winfrey, Bill Gates, and Jeff Bezos to help you launch your podcast, your success would be certain.

As long as you had a great podcast.

If you're going to get great launch partners, you *must* have a great podcast. People don't become influential by recommending mediocrity. And even if you could get these people to promote a mediocre podcast, your "success" wouldn't last long, because so many people would quickly discover how lacking your content is.

Don't rely on the hard-won influence of others to cover for your lack of quality.

CHAPTER 037

PODCAST REVIEWS

Reviews are endorsements. The downside is that they're often anonymous, and readers don't give good reviews the same weight as personal recommendations from friends or trusted influencers.

They do have a couple of upsides, though. One is the perceived trust that happens when somebody reading a review feels the reviewer is just like him. For example, a mother of twins who reads a review that starts off like, "I'm a mother of twins, so I don't have a lot of time to listen to podcasts …" will automatically feel a connection to the reviewer, even though the two don't know each other.

The biggest upside to podcast reviews is social proof – they show listeners and potential listeners they're not alone with their interest in a certain podcast.

What Makes A Good Review

Reviews don't have to be 100 percent positive to be an effective form of marketing. In fact, some average and bad reviews can be helpful for your podcast (or anything else) as they make the positive reviews look even more credible.

Reviews don't need to be perfect. People look for reviews that are real, and because of this, don't expect reviewers to have flawless spelling or grammar.

The best reviews address objections that would keep somebody from listening. Like a good testimonial, they tell where the reviewer was before discovering the podcast, and where he is now, after being helped by it.

Specificity of results achieved through your podcast is important. For example, "I lost 73 pounds using what I learned on this podcast" is better than "I lost some weight."

Specificity is also important when reviewers describe themselves or their situations. People looking at reviews actively search for stories and experiences they can relate to.

Here's a template you can pass to listeners that will make it easy for them to review you, as well as help to make sure the reviews you receive are compelling and helpful to potential listeners:

- Who are you?
- How did you find this podcast?
- What problem did you need to solve before discovering this podcast?
- How did this podcast help you solve that problem?
- What is your current situation? How has your situation improved since listening to the podcast?
- Would you recommend this podcast to others with the same problem you had?

A Word On Review Swaps

Reviews help with social proof, but in addition, *some* search engines also base results on product ratings and quantity of reviews. It's for this reason that many podcasters have created organized systems to the number of positive reviews for their podcasts.

If you search for "review swap" on Google, you'll find thousands of listings from authors and musicians who have done the same thing.

The basic concept of a review swap is "you review my podcast and I'll review yours."

Is this ethical? That depends on your ethics.

Is it a long-term strategy? For adding reviews, yes. It's not a very effective way to find new fans of your podcast though unless you have a podcast about podcasting and other podcasters are your target market. The fans you create from review swaps are from people who see how many reviews your podcast has and, because of this level of "social proof," decide to take a chance on it.

The Best Podcast Ever? Probably Not.

Every day, a new podcast is being launched, and every day, people are sucking up to that podcaster, regardless of how good his podcast is. These people will leave positive reviews, post great comments on Facebook, and help promote episodes

Why would somebody do this? Often, it's in hope of being interviewed on a podcast, getting an endorsement from the host, or getting a product mentioned.

You'll see comments on Twitter like, "Oh, this new podcast from [INSERT GURU HERE] is so great. It's like drinking knowledge from a fire hose. I can't wait to listen to every episode!"

Other podcasters will leave positive comments as well, with the hope you'll go to their podcasts and do the same.

Can you trust this feedback is honest? No. It's simply part of your hype machine.

Is there some value to reviews by other podcasters trying to be nice? Yes, any positive review helps as far as social proof.

But don't believe your own hype or the results of it. It's no different from you believing you're smart because your mother told you you're a genius. She's biased, and so are the reviews you get when you reward people with free stuff or promotional opportunities.

PART 3 - CONTINUOUS / ONGOING PODCAST MARKETING

CHAPTER 038

FOCUS ON YOUR REAL AUDIENCE

If you were a comic or musician, what would you do to get people to your first performance? You'd ask friends and family to come.

Doing this, you could get a few people in the audience. Those people aren't real fans of what you're doing though — they're fans of *you*. The primary reason they show up is because they're curious about what you're doing and want to support you as a person, not because they think your jokes are funny or they like your songs.

This works for a while. But if you're not expanding your audience beyond friends and family, you'll soon be playing to nobody, because "friends and family" aren't your audience.

It's common for podcasters to approach audience creation in a similar way, but with other podcasters instead of friends and family. And unless your podcast is about podcasting, it's the same trap.

You can get *anybody* to check out your podcast once. Your friends and family will certainly listen to an episode or two.

You can get other podcasters to review your podcast if you're willing to do the same for them.

You can hire people online to subscribe to your podcast for $5.

None of these people will stick around. None of these people will tell their friends about you.

Don't focus on the wrong audience. If you want to be successful at audience development for your podcast, you have to continuously target people who are a good match for what you do and will be helped by listening to you.

Podcast (And Television) Promotion

Saturday Night Live has been on the air since October 11, 1975. It was ranked 10th on TV Guide's "50 Greatest TV Shows of All Time" list and is one of the "100 Best TV Shows of All-TIME" according to Time.

A typical episode of *Saturday Night Live* features a guest host, many of whom are there because they have a film, album, or other work being released near the time of their appearance.

Just like many podcasts, *Saturday Night Live* has two audiences — a core audience that is there for every new episode, and a casual audience that tunes in only when there's an interesting event they know will be spoofed, such as a political debate, or a guest host they're fans of.

Saturday Night Live promotes individual episodes, not the show itself. For maximum results, this is how you should promote your podcast.

Like *Saturday Night Live*, you can let a targeted audience know when you'll be interviewing a specific guest. The ability to target specific demographics online gives you an ability to go much deeper than any broadcast media could do.

For example, if you do a podcast episode talking about how to sell goods on Etsy, it's easy to target people who are interested in the subject with search terms like:

- Etsy forum
- Unofficial Etsy forum
- Handmade market
- Selling homemade goods
- How to sell on Etsy

You can find people who would be interested in your topic by searching the following terms:

- _____ forum
- _____ community
- _____ marketplace
- _____ discussion
- _____ Facebook group
- _____ meetup
- _____ blogs

If your podcast topic is focused and you have episodes with content related to the single episodes you promote, people who discover you this way will also listen to other episodes. You can let them know these other episodes exist by mentioning them during your podcast or linking to them in episode notes.

CHAPTER 039

AUDIENCE ENGAGEMENT VIA SOCIAL MEDIA

If you've ever wondered why disco music was so popular in the 1970s, one of the reasons is that it enabled an audience, by dressing up and dancing, to become part of the show. Rap music, with its call-and-response style vocals, is popular for the same reason.

Social media outlets allow your podcast to have this same ability. A one-way broadcast message sent via social media can easily turn into a two-way conversation. Taking advantage of this is something that will not only help you spread the word about your podcast, but also allow you to form strong and lasting relationships with the people who listen to it.

Here are five easy options for how to start conversations on social media:

1. **Ask Two-Option Questions** – This is the easiest way to get a response from people. It doesn't take much time or thought for somebody to decide on one of two options and type a single-word

answer. These questions also have a very high interaction and discussion rate due to their polarizing nature.

There are three main types of two-option questions that I suggest:

- yes/no questions
- this/that questions
- true/false questions

Examples of yes/no questions:

- "Would you be interested in a podcast episode about _____?"
- "Have you ever seen a ghost?"
- "Should I grow a beard?"

Examples of this/that questions:

- "Which of these theme songs do you like better?"
- "Coke or Pepsi?"
- "David Lee Roth or Sammy Hagar?"

NOTE: This/that questions are a great way to "test market" things before you actually commit to them. For example, if you're working on art for your new podcast, posting two mock-ups letting people pick the one they like best. This will help you have more success when you release the podcast.

Examples of true/false questions:

- "Centipedes have one hundred legs. True or False?"
- "Gravity is weaker in North America than in Europe. True or False?"
- "One of the Bond Girls was born a man! True or False?"

NOTE: It's okay for *some* of the questions you ask to have nothing to do with your topic. You are trying to build a multifaceted relationship with listeners, and off-topic questions will help to do that.

2. **Ask Open-Ended Questions** – Make it easy for discussion ᴛᴏ ...
   You're looking for passionate answers from people that will start
   spinoff discussions. This is where the power of social media really
   takes off.

Examples of open-ended questions:

- "What was the first podcast you ever listened to?"
- "I'm looking for good people to interview for my podcast. Any
  suggestions?"
- "What's your favorite podcast?"
- "How do you find out about new podcasts?"
- "What's the last podcast you listened to?"

3. **Polls** – A poll-style question is great because it lets your audience
   get involved in an easy way (selecting from a choice of provided
   answers) as well as gives you a specific and measurable way to
   quantify how people feel about something.

Example of a poll:

"What's the top independent podcast of all time?"

    a. *Entrepreneurs On Fire* with John Lee Dumas
    b. *Smart Passive Income* with Pat Flynn
    c. *Keith And The Girl*
    d. *Stacking Benjamins*

4. **Caption Contests** – To maximize interest from a variety of people
   on Twitter, Facebook, or any other social media outlet, you'll
   need to communicate in a variety of ways, including, text, photo,
   audio, and video.

A caption contest, in which your audience suggests captions for the
photos you post, is the perfect way to encourage interaction.

How to do it: Simply post an interesting or funny photo with the description, "Caption this photo!" If you need help picking a winner, use a poll-style question to let your audience decide.

5. **Giveaways** – Everybody likes a giveaway, especially when it's from their favorite podcaster.

Examples of giveaways:

"PODCAST LIP-SYNC CONTEST!! First person to upload a video of himself lip-syncing the [INSERT PODCAST NAME] intro to YouTube gets a free T-shirt."

"First five people to respond to this message get an autographed 'episode notes' that I use to create [INSERT PODCAST NAME]."

"First 10 people to write [INSERT PODCAST NAME] on a piece of paper, take a photo of themselves, and upload it to Facebook win a copy of my new book. NOTE: Be sure to tag me!"

13 Tips For Social Media Success

Not all use of social media is equal. Do it right and you'll see a boost in your popularity. Do it wrong, though, and you'll actually repel people.

Most of what you see being done with social media is a waste of time. The majority of people are thinking very short-term, and, if you want success in podcasting, you've got to think bigger than that. This is not a "get rich quick" opportunity for you to get some quick publicity and a few extra listeners; it's a long-term strategy that will allow you to connect to people in a way never before possible, and you need a plan if you want to succeed with that.

When you post, think about the big picture. This means keeping your core message at the forefront of all your communication. This isn't the place to talk about everything under the sun or, even worse, air grievances. Your job with social media is to assist your podcast, so be focused on that.

Also keep in mind that part of the big picture is listening to the people who respond to you. The true power of social media isn't that you're able to blast your message at very little cost; it's that listeners can participate in the conversation. Being open to this will draw people in and make what you say on social media even more effective.

When posting anything online ...

- **Speak To An Individual** – Remember, although your messages are going out to hundreds, thousands, or even tens of thousands of people, each will be read by just one person at a time. Whether you're writing an email to your mailing list, posting something on Facebook, or updating your status on Twitter, use the same language you'd use as if you were talking to somebody one-on-one, just like you do in your podcast.

DO THIS: "I hope to see you at the podcast convention!"

DON'T DO THIS: "I hope to see all my fans at the podcast convention!"

Using the word "you" makes people feel included and recognizes that they're individuals, not a nameless, faceless mob that's part of your marketing strategy.

- **Keep Your Message Short** – Be brief and get to the point.
- **Mix Things Up** – Different people prefer different types of content. To connect with as many people as possible, alternate your communication style between photos, audio, videos, and text messages.

- **Be Human** – People are looking to connect with something real. Being too polished can actually hurt what you're trying to do, so don't worry about being perfect in your communication.
- **Recognize Specific Listeners** – If you have listeners who are doing something above and beyond normal, recognize them.
- **Target Via Location** – Filter location-specific messages, such as live events and meetups, so that people too far away to attend won't be bothered.
- **Be Timely** – One of the best things about social media is that it's instant. Take advantage of this by asking questions about current hot topics and responding to people as quickly as possible.
- **Push the Edge** – You're a podcaster with a point of view, not a radio host trying to please everybody. Don't be afraid to piss some people off. *Some* people.
- **Make Others Shine** – When you make others look good, they'll make you look good. Don't hog all the attention. Link to others, ask people questions about themselves, and let them have the spotlight from time to time.
- **Ask for Something** – Don't just talk, listen. Whether you need recommendations for a new episode topic or help finding a good Mexican restaurant in Chunky, Mississippi, your social media network can help.
- **Call to Action** – If you want people to do something, ask for it.
- **Tag People (When Possible)** – If you're posting photos of people, tag them to bring them into the conversation.
- **Keep the Momentum Going** – Don't do a "hit and run." When the conversation starts to move, jump in and keep it going.

CHAPTER 040

AUDIENCE ENGAGEMENT VIA OFFLINE EVENTS

Live events based around your podcast will set it apart from other podcasts and connect you to listeners in ways your podcast alone can't.

Live events engage *all* of a listener's senses. A person in the audience will hear *and* see you — and everything else around him. He'll touch things. He'll smell things. He'll taste things.

If an attendee likes others who are attending your event, he'll credit you for this feeling of connection. If he likes the way the venue looks, how the food and drinks being served taste, or how he feels being there, he'll associate those good feeling with your podcast.

This is how you speed up and intensify connection (and loyalty) with listeners.

Social Proof Revisited

Like naming the group of people who listen to your podcast, creating an event to be shared by people who have something in common (your podcast) builds camaraderie and class consciousness.

When you see somebody walking down the street with headphones on, you have no idea what he's listening to. When somebody attends a live event you host, that person is surrounded by others he knows listen to your podcast. This social proof helps your message to be better received, since it shows the message has already been validated by these people, and they're being helped (or entertained) by it.

As a bonus, the social proof of a live event will get an extra boost, since a live event is something people rarely attend alone. It's the perfect opportunity for listeners to tell others about your podcast and bring them into the fold, so they too can experience what you do.

Meetups 101

A meetup is simply an organized event where people get together. It can be as relaxed or as formal as you want, depending on your podcast, but should never be a general "networking" event.

For best results with your meetups, follow the Double-Single Rule, which has two elements:

1. A single person needs to organize the event and make related decisions. Not everybody is going to be happy with the details of when or where you do your event, so pick a venue, pick a date, and simply announce what you're doing. If you lead by committee, you'll lose valuable time that could be better used promoting your event and getting people to it.

2. Only one "presentation" per event. This can be a moderated discussion, a talk by you or another expert, or a live taping of your podcast.

Meetup Templates

It can take time to attract large numbers of people to your live events. Alternatively, you may not want large numbers of people to attend your events, as there can be diminishing returns on the direct contact you can have with them and the connections they can have with each other.

Here are three different formats for running live events using moderated discussion as the main presentation:

Small (10 people or fewer)

If we're honest with ourselves, it's a bit embarrassing to organize a live event and have just a handful of people show up. You'll wonder, "Don't I have enough juice to bring in more people?"

The good news is that, if you have the right type of podcast, such as a business-related podcast or a podcast that focuses on attaining a goal, a small-group moderated discussion can be extremely valuable to those who attend. If you have the right people present, even if there aren't many of them, attendees will have the opportunity to walk away with both deep connections and valuable insight into what they're working on.

Step One: Get everybody around a table.

Any type of table will do, as long as the environment isn't overly distracting and is quiet enough that attendees will be able to easily hear each other. You could meet at a local coffee shop, a coworking space, or an office.

Step Two: One by one, ask each person to introduce himself (in 30 seconds or less) and answer the following three questions …

1. What are you currently working on? (Or, for a non-business or goal-oriented podcast meetup, a similar question related to the focus on your podcast.)
2. What's working for you?
3. What do you need help with?

After the third question has been answered, allow the group to offer help. This can be in the form of a quick answer, but in the interest of time and moving the meetup forward, you may want to simply connect the two people to take care of the situation afterward.

Medium (10-25 people)

Similar to having a meetup with fewer than 10 people, a medium-sized group of 10-25 people is still small enough to provide an intimate setting for people to get to know each other. The format of a medium-sized group is very similar to a smaller group, with the main difference being a different question format to move the meeting forward more quickly.

Step One: Get everybody around a table or room.

Step Two: One by one, ask each person to introduce himself (in 30 seconds or less) and answer a single question related to the focus of your meetup/podcast.

What should you ask? Questions that facilitate attendees getting to know each other are best.

I attended a meetup of bloggers, podcasters, and marketers organized by marketers Brian Dixon and Mike Kim. The entire meeting, more or less, used the above format with the following two questions:

1. What book are you currently reading?
2. What are you currently excited about and motivated by?

These questions were asked one at a time, going around the group and getting everybody to answer the first question before the second was asked.

Large (25 people or more)

For meetups of over 25 people, the best way I've found to keep people on the same page and keep the group moving forward as one unit is to have a short presentation on a single topic followed by a Q&A. The presentation should be about something specific, and I suggest keeping it to 20 minutes maximum.

Remember, the primary purpose of a meetup is to get listeners of your podcast connected to each other. By doing this, they'll feel more connected to you and your podcast.

Before the presentation, take three minutes to have people in the audience meet one person they don't already know by swapping elevator-style introductions. This will prime the pump for people to reach out to each other after the Q&A segment and the "official" meetup has ended.

Meetup Best Practices

Venue

- Host your event in the city, not a suburb – people will commute from suburbs to the city, but not the other way around
- If using a restaurant, your meetup should be in a private room that's quiet and will allow your group to sit together
- Unless you podcast about religion or being a religious podcaster is part of your identity, *never* host your event in a church or religious institution
- You (and your guests) are the show — no noisy or distracting background entertainment, such as live bands or comics

- If hosting your event at a business, the business should be related to your podcast — don't use a carpet store if your podcast has nothing to do with carpet

General Organization

- Start on time (even if not everybody is there yet)
- End on time (but encourage people to stay later, if appropriate)
- No side conversations when the group is at a table together
- No mobile phones
- No laptop computers or tablets — if people need to take notes, they can do it on paper. If people need to check email, they can stay home.

No Social Media — THIS IS IMPORTANT!

You're using an in-person meetup to build rapport and trust between you and fans of your podcast. This happens through the sharing of information.

When doing roundtable discussions or Q&A, it's important that you have a NO RECORDING policy. People want a safe environment in which to share. If they feel what they're saying will be posted online or used elsewhere, they won't share it with the group.

Beyond this, you want to reward people for taking the time and effort to attend your event in person. You also want people at your meetup to be completely present for others in the room, not focusing on social media followers who aren't even there.

Leave some mystery. Like a closed-door session of a secret society, let people on the outside wonder what's going on inside. If they're that curious, they can come to your next meetup and find out for themselves.

Rather than have everybody take their own photos throughout the night, take a single group photo of everybody who wants to be photographed and distribute it to people who attended. By doing this, the same exact photo will be published on multiple social media accounts, which means shared followers will see it multiple times and be more likely to pay attention to it. *That* has power.

CHAPTER 041

YOUR MAILING LIST

Social media is great, but you want something you control access to, and with access that isn't dependent on a third-party company. Social media sites come and go, but email has been around for years, and nothing has come close to replacing it as far as ease and effectiveness of online communication.

You need a mailing list. A mailing list will allow you to go to listeners of your podcast whenever and wherever you want.

Which brings up the question, "How do you build a mailing list?"

We're bombarded with email. Because of this, it's getting more and more difficult to get people to sign up for an online mailing list. To help convince them to do this, you may want to offer a bonus for signing up.

I recommend that you build your mailing list using a "lead magnet" related to the topic of your show or something else that's a compelling reason for people to take a chance on you.

Lead magnets don't have to be lengthy or complex. As long as your lead magnet solves a very specific problem your podcast audience is facing, a short lead magnet will often be more effective than a long one.

Nine Lead Magnet Ideas

1. Special Report

This is the "classic" lead magnet that most people think of when you mention the term. Special Reports are short and to-the-point.

Some Special Report ideas:

For a destination-oriented show, such as a travel podcast that focuses on Las Vegas, something like "Top 10 Budget [insert destination] Hotels" or "Visiting [insert destination] on $50/Day."

You could rework these titles for a cooking podcast or healthy-eating podcast, doing reports with information on "Top 10 Low-Cost Meals" or "Family Grocery Shopping On $40/Week."

A podcaster who talks about cars could do, "7 Easy Car Repairs You Can Do Yourself" or "How to Save $1500 (Or More) On Your Next Car Purchase."

2. Cheat Sheet

This type of lead magnet breaks down a complicated process into short, easy-to-follow steps. Like a Special Report, Cheat Sheets are short and to-the-point.

Some Cheat Sheet ideas:

A personal finance podcaster could create a cheat sheet on how to negotiate with credit card companies called "3 Steps To Lowering Your Credit Card Rate" that takes readers through a process they can use when on the phone, negotiating with credit card providers.

A personal fitness podcaster could do a cheat sheet for first-time gym visitors that explains a basic workout, like "The 5 Quick Exercises To

Jumpstart Metabolism and Weight Loss," or one that calms nerves, such as "Beginner's Guide To Gym Etiquette."

If you want to see an example of this, I have a "cheat sheet" lead magnet for my podcast on podcasting, *Build A Big Podcast* called the "Audience Attraction Cheat Sheet" which contains 25 templates podcasters can use to easily create compelling episodes. Visit BigPodcast.com to download it free.

3. Resource List/Checklist

Resource Lists and Checklists are perhaps the easiest form of lead magnets to create. They're lists that help the reader solve a specific problem.

Examples:

"5 iPhone Apps to Double Your Productivity"

"Podcast Launch - What You Need to Do To Hit #1 on Apple Podcasts"

"Presentation Flight Check - A Step-By-Step Checklist for Delivering a Great Speech"

The Growth Marketing Toolbox Podcast, a podcast about attracting customers for your business through online marketing, has a lead magnet with the 50 tools that host Nicholas Scalice uses to run his marketing agency.

Daniel J. Lewis of *The Audacity To Podcast* has a "Podcast Pre-flight Checklist" with "20 things you should do before recording every podcast episode."

4. How-To Training

These show somebody exactly what it takes to successfully do a task.

The Science Of Success, a podcast about unleashing human potential, offers a guide on "How to Organize & Remember Everything" to help its listeners do just that.

An alternative to this is a "script" people can follow during a certain situation. Nick Murphy of *The Job Lab Podcast* offers a free "negotiation skills script" to help people negotiate job salaries.

5. Assessment/Quiz

If you've spent more than a few minutes on Facebook, you've seen these. They're the modern-day version of similar quizzes and assessments most often found in popular magazines for women, like *Cosmopolitan, Teen Vogue*, and *Women's Health.*

"Are You A Secret Bitch?"

"Why Are You Single?"

"Should You Get Back Together With Your Ex?"

The only way to know for sure is to take the quizzes.

These are popular. They get shared on social media a lot. And you can use this same strategy as a lead magnet for your podcast.

A great example of an assessment with a serious slant is Sally Hogshead's "Fascination Advantage Assessment," which will assess your personal branding and let you know how the world sees you.

An assessment doesn't have to be complicated, only helpful. Regan Starr, a software engineer, offers several resources to users via a daily email, including a "Podcast Rank Report."

6. "Insider" Access

In the podcasting world, listener access to the host comes in one of two ways — free and paid. "Free" is usually the podcast itself. "Paid" is often in the form of a seminar, training, or consulting.

Giving "Insider" access in exchange for an email address and/or other contact information is a powerful way to build your database. This doesn't have to be complicated. Access to a private conference call or closed Facebook group will work just fine.

7. Consultation

If you monetize your podcast with backend consulting or coaching, offering a free session can be a great way to get people aware of the kind of work you do and into your sales process. These free sessions, even if you're not a consultant or coach, are also a great way to have a deeper connection with podcast listeners and uncover what they really want.

8. Bonus Material

Content that's too long, too technical, or too niche to be released as a standard episode often makes a great lead magnet. This is what Eliot Wagonheim and Jodi Hume of *So, Here's My Story...* did with an episode that was too risqué for standard release.

Here's how they get people to sign up:

Once upon a time ...
we recorded an episode that we loved.
But ... we couldn't quite bring ourselves
to publish an episode on THAT!!!
So we deleted it ....
(or so we thought)
and forgot all about it.
... Until we got a VERY awkward call from our intern.
And while we STILL don't want to release it publicly, we have
decided we WILL share it with our community of listeners. Here's
a teaser ...

[TEASER GOES HERE]

We know, we know ... that was a really mean place to end it. But
the good news is that we'll send you a link to the whole thing:

[ADDRESS CAPTURE FORM]

9. Online Tool

What can you offer listeners that will save them time and money?

James Cridland of *Podnews*, a podcast for podcasters, has several online
tools for podcasters that he uses to encourage people who listen to his
podcast to visit his website and sign up for his mailing list. Examples
include an RSS link checker and podcasting job board.

How To Do Email

If you're on another podcast's mailing list, chances are you've seen plenty of examples of what you *shouldn't* be doing in your inbox.

Here are a few email marketing rules:

1. If somebody didn't sign up for your mailing list, don't put him on it.

Don't assume that, at worst, people won't mind you adding their names to a list. And don't assume that, at best, they'll appreciate the gesture. People are busy. If they want to get information from you, they'll let you know.

When it comes to building your mailing list, it's very easy to fall into the trap of thinking that 100 people is better than 10 and 10 people is better than a couple. This isn't true. When it comes to email, quality trumps quantity. It's far better to have 10 people who care, are waiting to hear from you, and will open (and respond to) your emails, than 10,000 people who have no clue who you are and will ignore anything you send.

You won't win people over with a bulk email, so don't bother.

This is important, so I'm going to repeat it ...

If somebody didn't sign up for your mailing list, don't put that person on it.

It doesn't matter if a listener (or anybody else) is already emailing you and says something like, "keep in touch." "Keep in touch" means they want to have a two-way relationship, not get added to a list to receive one-sided email blasts.

2. If you're releasing a daily podcast (or several episodes per week), you don't need to let people know every time.

You do a daily podcast. We get it. The reason nobody is listening isn't because you're not sending an email every time you release an episode; the problem is you're not making something worth listening to, turning episodes into "events" that people want to be part of.

3. You MUST have a one-click unsubscribe option.

Don't make people work to get off your mailing list. If they're not interested in what you have to offer, you want them off your list so you can focus on the people who do want to hear from you.

When people consider signing up for a mailing list, it helps to let them know you send messages through a service that allows them to unsubscribe at any time. Not doing this will cause you to lose signups from people who are "on the fence" about what you have, because nobody wants to sign up for a list they'll never be able to get off of.

4. You MUST use a reliable, third-party mailing list service.

Junk email is a big problem. Because of this, it's more difficult than ever to successfully send commercial email messages.

If you want the majority of your emails to land in inboxes instead of being blocked by spam filters, you need to send them though a reliable, third-party mailing list service that specializes in getting emails delivered. In addition to the benefit of getting your messages into the hands of the people who want them, these companies will also provide services to keep you from violating email marketing laws.

Beyond keeping you legal, a third-party mailing list service will also be able to provide you with marketing tools, such as the ability to track how many of your messages are opened and how many people click on links inside your messages. You'll get powerful "mail merge" options so you can send "personal" messages, using the recipient's name, city, or other information you have collected, within any messages you send.

Several options for third-party mailing list services are available to you, depending on your needs. For more information, visit BigPodcast.com/ resources for my list of recommended providers.

Increase Email Response

You need to focus on two things to get maximum response from your emails:

The first is making sure the people who receive your email are the best match for it. Gone are the days when a "one-size-fits-all" newsletter works. Today, people expect specialized information.

Let's say you're doing a series of small meetups for your podcast. In the next month, you're doing these events in three different places — New York, Los Angeles, and Atlanta.

Three *different* places. That's important to consider.

People in Atlanta are unlikely to fly across the country to Los Angeles to attend a small meetup. But true fans of your podcast who are in Atlanta would definitely go to a local event.

If you're doing something in Los Angeles, yes, you could announce it to your entire mailing list and somebody who couldn't make it to LA would be able to easily delete that announcement, but sending a general message like this might create another problem for you — email blindness.

"Email blindness" happens when sending out irrelevant messages to people on your list. Do this too many times and it becomes permanent.

Here's what it would look like in this situation:

1. You send an email to your list letting people know you're in Los Angeles this month.
2. A woman in Atlanta gets your message and it doesn't apply to her, so she starts to ignore future messages from you.
3. You send an email to your list letting people know you'll be in Atlanta next month. The woman in Atlanta, one of the most likely people to come to an Atlanta event, never learns you're coming because she's ignoring your messages now.

Are you doing a lot of local or regional events? You can easily segment your list based on the location of where people sign up (if signing up in person), area code, or zip code.

That's the first rule of increasing email response — you want to send messages to people who are most likely to read and respond to them, not waste the time of people who aren't a likely match.

The second rule of increasing email response is that *every* marketing email you send needs to have a single purpose. DO NOT bombard recipients with a ton of options. For example, don't send a message talking about your upcoming episodes, your new book, a conference you just attended, and a new t-shirt design.

One email, one choice.

"Do you want to listen to this episode?" Yes or no?

"Do you have a question you want me to answer on an upcoming episode?" Yes or no?

"Do you want to buy my new book?" Yes or no?

One email = one choice ... ALWAYS!

MODULE 5
PODCAST MONETIZATION

CHAPTER 042

SMALL PODCAST, BIG MONEY

Having been involved with podcasting since 2005 and spending years writing and researching the contents of this book, I've met and talked with *thousands* of podcasters. I've worked on hundreds of podcast projects.

The independent podcasters I've worked with fall into two groups: loud and quiet.

The most successful independent podcasters I know are the quiet ones. They're the people who show up, do the work, and make the money.

The topics they talk about aren't always sexy. In fact, most of these topics would be considered boring to outsiders.

An example of this is *The Pest Control Marketing Podcast*. On it, hosts Hal Coleman and Mike Stewart discuss ways people in the pest control business can attract new customers, get more referrals, and grow their pest control businesses.

The production isn't slick. It's basically two guys having a chat about how to run a pest control business.

How many people listen? Not many; they get about 1000 episode downloads per month.

Yet because of this podcast, and the relationships they've developed with those who *are* listening, they've brought in clients paying as much as $20,000 each.

You don't need a massive audience to make money with your podcast, you just need the right audience.

Tight Niche + Deep Relationships = Right Audience

Much like specific topics help you come up with more powerful show and episode ideas, limiting the number of people you appeal to by creating tight and focused content will deepen the relationships you have with listeners and increase your impact.

There are two ways to do this.

1. Niche Niche
2. Local Local

Essentially, both are the same thing — highly-focused content that is designed for a *very* specific audience. One is based on interests, the other geography.

By doing this, you'll be more likely to get listeners that care – listeners who aren't lukewarm about the content you're providing. These people *really* want what you've got, since it's made "just for them."

Listening to podcasts isn't as easy as turning on a broadcast radio show. Broadcast radio listeners rely on program directors to filter out mediocre content. Podcast listeners may go through dozens of mediocre podcasts to find yours. Because of this, when they discover your podcast, their motivation to listen to what you have to say (and buy what you're selling) is higher.

CHAPTER 043

THE RIGHT PODCAST SPONSOR

When your podcast has focused content, listeners will find you. When your podcast has momentum and exposure, sponsors will approach you.

It sounds great to think that you can focus on the creative aspects of podcasting while people approach you with offers of money in exchange for reading ads. The reality is, more often than not, the offers you get aren't a good match for your podcast or the people who listen to it. You're in control of your podcast and, like a cop, it's your responsibility to serve and protect the people who are listening to you.

That means saying no. A lot.

This sounds easier than it is. An offer that might not sound very good on its own starts sounding a lot better when money is attached.

The Drug Dealer

I was once approached by a company about running ads on *RED Podcast* for a supplement designed to increase alertness and boost energy. The pitch was that it was "perfect for entrepreneurs."

Working with entertainers as long as I have, I've seen people get into *very* bad situations with drugs. Because of this, I've very sensitive to the negative effects of any drugs, even "supplements."

Still, it's easy to justify offers when money is attached.

"It's just a supplement."

"The money from this deal will allow me to grow the podcast and get better sponsors later."

"It meets all FDA regulations."

Money can cloud your judgment and cause you to neglect the people who listen to your podcast. Because of this, it's a good idea to have a basic game plan for determining the overall type of sponsor you're okay with before sponsorship offers start coming in.

Negotiating With Potential Podcast Sponsors

When companies approach you about sponsoring your podcast, the first thing you'll typically get is a "feeler" email (or some other form of contact) to start the conversation.

Here's an example of an inquiry email I received:

> *Hi David and team,*
>
> *I'm emailing to introduce myself and the business I work for called [[COMPANY NAME REMOVED]].*
>
> *I'm also emailing to see if you would consider accepting a sponsorship from [[COMPANY NAME REMOVED]] for your podcast?*
>
> *We thought it might be interesting to do something with RED Podcast, as it seems to get in front of exactly the people who use our product, namely entrepreneurs, small business owners, creative people, etc.*
>
> *Would love to have a chat and possibly explore some options.*
>
> *Let me know what you think.*
>
> *Best wishes,*
>
> *John*

Note that this email was sent via a form on the "contact me" page of the *RED Podcast* website.

While I'm always open to working with the *right* sponsor, I'm not actively looking for sponsors. Nowhere on this site is sponsorship mentioned beyond links to sponsors on the pages of sponsored episodes.

If you have a quality podcast with a quality audience, sponsors will find you.

Most "potential sponsors" who email you are looking for an affiliate relationship. This means they pay you only when somebody buys something via a special link.

The "drug dealer" fell into this category. The offer to have an affiliate relationship was the first thing he approached me with.

He wrote me, "This is a win-win for both of us and the ideal model. There are no bounds to how much you can make. Basically, you rep/promote the product and provide your audience with a coupon code for our product. Anytime that coupon code is used, we pay you a commission. A lot of podcasters use this model."

Ideal model for whom? The only part of what he wrote that has any truth to is the part about "a lot of podcasters" using an affiliate model for sponsorship. Unfortunately, that *is* true.

But just because "a lot of podcasters" are doing it, doesn't mean you should. You want a partner who believes in what you do and is willing to share the risk involved with running advertising on your show, not somebody simply looking for free traffic.

This "opportunity" to be a commission-only affiliate for somebody, while not always obvious from initial outreach emails, is always waiting for you. It's for this reason that you should always respond to an outreach email with something like …

> *Thanks for reaching out.*
>
> *Happy to talk to you about sponsoring [[PODCAST NAME]]. Tell me more about what you're looking to do, what your goals for the sponsorship are, etc.*
>
> *Also let me know what your budget is. Once I have that, I can get options to you.*

A response like this lets your potential "sponsor" know a couple of things:

- You take what you do seriously.
- Because you take what you do seriously, you expect to be properly compensated for it.

Unless you have a well-known podcast with major traction, expect a response similar to this:

> *Thanks for coming back to me.*
>
> *We've seen some great engagement from working with podcasts in recent months, and we're always looking at ways to extend our reach to our target audience.*
>
> *The main goal is to offer a genuine [[NICHE]] solution for entrepreneurs and businesses who need [[SERVICE]]. We feel we can work with shows like RED Podcast to help support the business audience and community.*
>
> *We often start with understanding the size of audience and therefore CPM for the show. The overall budget comes down to how we track the profitable yield from a test on the show. We are happy to look at pre/mid roll options, along with further marketing through website/social media channels. We currently sponsor shows from $50 an episode to $6k+, so it really is a case-by-case basis.*
>
> *Look forward to seeing what options you might have.*
>
> *Appreciate your help.*
>
> *Best wishes,*
>
> *John*

This is good information to have, and pretty standard. In layman's terms, it means:

- He wants to "test drive" sponsoring your podcast to see how well your audience responds to his offer.
- He wants to pay based on the number of downloads an episode gets.

Here are five reasons *not* to take an offer like this, as well as ways to educate potential sponsors who want to advertise on your podcast:

1. Podcast sponsorship is a long-term play with success for the advertiser happening over an extended period of time. It takes more than an episode or two to get results and those results don't happen instantly.

Much like an exercise program, you'll only get good results from podcast advertising if you do more than "kick the tires."

Podcasts are most often consumed by listeners who are focusing on other things — driving or otherwise commuting, exercising, cooking, etc. These people aren't going to immediately respond to an offer or write down a special link, because they're busy doing something else.

Encourage advertisers to look at the big picture of advertising on your podcast. Some episodes will be downloaded more than others, and sales are often seasonal, even if what's being sold isn't. In the end, this evens out; the reach an ad gets, as well as the results a sponsor wants, will be there.

2. Frequently changing podcast sponsors doesn't show stability. This affects the perception of both listeners and potential sponsors.

We've all had that friend who seems to be dating a different guy every week. She's had a series of off-and-on engagements, live-in boyfriends, and relationship chaos for years.

Don't be *that* podcast.

Like a "40-something playboy" who's afraid of commitment, there's a repellent quality to a podcast that switches up partners (in this case sponsors) too frequently.

Yes, your listeners are judging you. But even worse, at least as far as sponsorship is concerned, potential sponsors listening to your podcast won't even bother to reach out because they'll assume advertising with you doesn't get results. Why else would you switch sponsors so frequently?

To attract a stable sponsor relationship, your podcast should reflect your stability. You can do this by releasing quality episodes that are engaging to your listeners.

3. Setting up "test" deals is a pain in the ass.

You job is to create a great podcast. When you have that, sponsorship takes care of itself.

You're not a trained monkey who does tricks on command hoping to get a treat. If you're consistently releasing great podcast episodes, your value to sponsors is already there for the world to see, so let them come to you with a good offer that shows some level of respect for what you do – not a test.

Never neglect what made your podcast successful in an effort to chase potential sponsors.

4. You're not offering ads — you're offering a relationship with listeners who trust you.

If somebody wants to buy a certain number of ad impressions, he can go to Google Ads, Facebook, or any number of places who sell them 1000 at a time. He'll be able to use very specific keywords to get his ads in front of very specific people.

But he won't get the relationships you have with the people who listen to your podcast… What's that worth?

Those relationships are worth a lot, which is exactly why he's coming to you instead of going elsewhere. He wants an endorsement, not just an "ad impression."

5. You're in control.

Good podcasts are much more rare than good sponsors, so let good sponsors come to you. Plenty of quality companies have money to advertise their products and services, but very few podcasts can offer sponsors the triple-threat of consistent production, great content, and a loyal audience.

Now that you understand these things, here's an example of how to respond.

> *Thanks for letting me know the goals you want to accomplish by sponsoring RED Podcast.*
>
> *If you'd like to talk by phone, let me know and we can set something up. Until then, here's more information about working with me.*
>
> *I charge a flat rate for advertising and do long-term commitments. There are several reasons for this, including:*
>
> 1. *I have a relationship with my audience that goes beyond CPM. You can get "ad impressions" by the thousand anywhere and target the same people who listen to RED Podcast (authors, bloggers, podcasters, etc.) anywhere, but actually advertising on RED Podcast is the only place to get the connection/endorsement that I offer.*
> 2. *Like any relationship, rapport between sponsors and listeners takes a while to develop. A sponsor who sticks around shows stability, and that's part of how I have the relationships that I do with listeners.*
> 3. *I'm looking for companies who believe in RED Podcast and want to develop a long-term relationship with me and RED Podcast listeners, not simply "hit it and quit it."*
>
> *Here's what I can offer you.*

A fixed-term sponsorship with a 30-second mid-roll read (usually longer) after the episode introduction. I work from talking points you provide, and each read will focus on the aspects of your product/service that best match that episode's topic. By doing this, listeners will be less likely to skip over your ads and more likely to take action on them.

You are guaranteed a MINIMUM of four episodes per month. The minimum term is three months. The maximum term is one year.

As of today, the minimum number of downloads an episode of RED Podcast gets is 10,000. The longer your term, the longer you're locked into this rate, even though the show is growing.

Your company will be linked on every episode page.

Here's the investment:

3-Month Term (12 Episodes Minimum) - $5000

6-Month Term (24 Episodes Minimum) - $7500

12-Month Term (48 Episodes Minimum) - $10,000

If you're interested in proceeding, please let me know.

David Hooper
RED Podcast

Note that the numbers mentioned above are for example only. How much you charge sponsors is up to you. But do …

1. Charge enough to make it worth your time.

You want to feel good about putting ads in your podcast, not be resentful because you agreed to a price that's too low.

2. Get paid upfront.

Remember, you are in control. Sponsors are a nickel a dozen, but good podcasts with engaged listeners are rare.

There Are Exceptions To Every Sponsorship Rule

Not all affiliate opportunities are bad, and there may be times when taking a commission-only or affiliate offer works for you. Pat Flynn of *Smart Passive Income* has built great trust with the people reading his blog and listening to his podcast, and it's not uncommon for him to make $100,000 (or more) *per month* via affiliate recommendations.

When reviewing affiliate opportunities or any other kind of podcast sponsorship, Pat's "affiliate rule" is good to remember.

My most important rule for affiliate marketing is: I only recommend products as an affiliate that I'm extremely familiar with – preferably products that I've used and have helped me achieve something. If I'm not confident in the product and I don't feel it will positively help people, I will not promote it.

Although affiliate products are created by others, the moment you promote something you become a representative of that product it reflects on you and your brand.

My second most important rule for affiliate marketing is: I never directly tell anyone to buy a product. I always recommend products based on my experience and in the context of what I've done or what I'm doing.

There's a huge difference (on several levels) between:

"Buy [product] now because you need it to grow your online business." and "This is how I used [Product] to help me achieve …"

CHAPTER 044

PODCAST SPONSORSHIP VS. PODCAST ADVERTISING

Sponsorship and advertising are very similar. More or less, with either one, you take money (or another form of payment, such in-kind products or services) for letting somebody have access to your audience.

Mentally, though, sponsorship and advertising are completely different things. And if you've got a new podcast or are just now looking at getting into the world of sponsorship and advertising, this difference will be very important to you.

Advertising is pretty cut-and-dried in the world of podcasting. The amount you get paid is based on the number of times you get an ad played. For example, if you get 1500 downloads (which we're going to assume have people on the other end actually listening to them), you get paid for 1500 ad impressions.

Advertisers come and go. If an advertiser gets results (usually in the form of increased sales), he'll stay. If not, he'll go.

This is the extent of your relationship with an advertiser.

Your relationship with a sponsor is different. A sponsor, like an advertiser, has the same goal of increasing sales or awareness, but approaches it in a totally different way.

A sponsor knows that his ad being listened to 10,000 times isn't necessarily twice as good as his ad being listened to 5000 times. He realizes that success with podcasts is as much (or more) about *who* is delivering the ad as it is the numbers game that straight advertising clients play.

A sponsor grows his business through his association with you. As you develop the relationship with your audience and develop more clout with them, his message within your podcast develops more clout as well.

Two Sponsorship Options

There are two main types of podcast sponsorships, and both are essentially the same in terms of how you approach potential sponsors. I'm segmenting them to encourage you to think long-term about both sponsors and the potential for the message you want to spread via your podcast.

Product (Or Brand) Sponsorship

This is the most common type of sponsorship. In this type of sponsorship, your podcast is affiliated with a single product or brand.

An example of what you're trying to do, but from the television world, was *American Idol*'s sponsorship with Coca-Cola. This story is also an example you can use in your pitch of potential sponsors for your podcast, as it perfectly demonstrates how getting in on the ground floor of something can pay off big in the long run.

When *American Idol* first appeared in 2002, it was basically an updated version of *Star Search*. The latter show's "talent contest" formula had worked well in 1983 and for several years afterward, but by the time *American Idol* hit the airwaves, *Star Search* was running on fumes.

Would *American Idol's* claim to "Search For A Superstar" be interesting enough to get people to watch something very similar to what they'd already seen every year for almost 20 years?

Executives at Pepsi didn't think so, and declined the opportunity. Coca-Cola took the chance though, signing an exclusive sponsorship for just $10,000,000. This not only included advertising during the show, but prominent placement within the show, such as multiple red and white cups with the Coca-Cola logo on the judges' table and branding of the show's green room into a "red room."

It paid off. The show was a surprise hit, with 38,000,000 people tuning in for the Season 1 finale. At its peak in 2006, *American Idol* averaged 31,200,000 viewers per episode – and Coca-Cola, not Pepsi, was there.

The moral of the story for sponsors? Get in early, get a bargain price for doing so, and ride the wave when things start happening.

Success for *American Idol* didn't last forever. Coca-Cola dropped its sponsorship after Season 13 as the show stopped connecting with people and its viewers started getting their entertainment elsewhere, via online outlets such as YouTube and podcasts.

This move by consumers from broadcast to online media is good news for you. As more people discover niche entertainment options such as podcasting, more companies are taking a chance on sponsoring these outlets.

Small Podcasts Can Become Big Podcasts

Ground-floor sponsorship and growth opportunities still exist for companies that are willing to take the chance on upcoming podcasts. Look up "top brands advertising on podcasts" in Google and you'll see a list of companies you know now, but had never heard of just a couple of years ago.

Companies like ZipRecruiter, Squarespace, Rocket Mortgage, Blue Apron, and Stamps.com all owe *a lot* to podcasting. More specifically, they owe a lot to the relationships and trust podcasters like you are building with listeners.

To really take advantage of this listener/host relationship, it's best for sponsors to come in early.

"When we launched, we hoped for 300,000 downloads." This is what Julie Snyder, co-producer of *Serial,* said when asked about her goals for the show.

The actual download numbers were over 175,000,000. Serial became a cultural phenomenon.

Its host, Sarah Koenig, went from obscurity to celebrity. Steven Colbert said she was his favorite guest of all time. *Saturday Night Live* spoofed the podcast in a skit.

Along for the ride was *Serial*'s sponsor, email marketing platform MailChimp. The ad, which featured a 14-year-old Norwegian girl mispronouncing the company's name, was so popular, it was mentioned in both the Colbert interview and the *Saturday Night Live* spoof.

MailChimp became so closely associated with *Serial* that the company had an 81 percent spike in Twitter mentions the day before and day of the podcast's second season debut. Additional *Serial* sponsors, who missed the ground-floor opportunity of being involved with the first season and didn't have established relationships with listeners, didn't get nearly the same results — Audible had a 19 percent boost during this time, and Squarespace mentions actually decreased.

Advertisers benefit from associating with a good podcast early, not only because of a lower rate, but because they go along on the journey with listeners.

New Media Vs. Old Media - A Sponsor's Thought Process

People know about broadcast media. Every business owner has considered advertising in traditional print formats, such as magazines and newspapers. And every business owner knows about traditional broadcast outlets such as radio and television.

Few business owners know about advertising options via podcasting.

The problem with traditional print and broadcast media is it's made for the general public. The goal is to reach as many people as possible, and this is done by providing general content.

Traditional mass and broadcast media is a "jack-of-all-trades, master of none" situation. It reaches a ton of people, but never with content that is specifically for any one of them. Because of this, when businesses advertise through traditional mass and broadcast media with a specific and targeted offer, the majority of people who hear that offer couldn't care less.

Podcasting is different. The audiences are smaller, but focused. And they're the exact people businesses in related niches are trying to reach.

For example, my radio show, *Music Business Radio*, has a highly concentrated audience of musicians and music business professionals. A general radio campaign would reach more people than advertising on *Music Business Radio*, but our advertisers don't want "more people" — they want people are who going to respond to their ads.

A guitar company doesn't care about people hearing their ads if those people don't play (and buy) guitars.

A microphone company doesn't care about people hearing their ads if those people have no need for microphones.

A distribution company doesn't care about people hearing their ads if those people have no music to distribute.

This is why so many companies never consider traditional media. It's not that traditional media doesn't work; it's that it's way too broad for most products and services.

Traditional media is like going into a crowded room and shouting your message. This works great for a general product like Coca-Cola, but if the offer is for something specialized, it won't apply to most people in the room, and there's zero chance of them taking advantage of it.

That's where "new media" outlets like podcasts differ. If somebody hears an ad for a specialized product on a similarly specialized podcast, he's going to perk up and listen.

We love to be sold. We love to consume. We love it when we find products and services that will make our lives easier, more fun, and more comfortable.

Specialized podcasts are the perfect medium for letting us know about specialized products and services, those things made just for us, that can add value to our lives.

Unfortunately, most companies have no idea how to use podcasting to its full potential. This is why you have to educate companies on the value of working with you and your podcast.

Podcasting flips traditional media on its head, because advertising on it isn't just about numbers. It's more like a game of skill than a random game of chance.

For example, you'd think that it's better to place an advertisement at the beginning of a podcast rather than the middle or end of one, because statistically, there are more people listening. And more people listening means better response, right?

No.

More *qualified* people listening is what increases ad response.

And who is most qualified to buy what's being advertised on your podcast? The people who are highly engaged in the content you're delivering and are listening to entire episodes, not casual listeners who lose interest and press stop before episodes are over, or those who are just testing the waters of what you have to offer, and only listen to the very beginning of an episode.

Businesses want qualified prospects for their offers; access to these qualified prospects is what your podcast can deliver.

CHAPTER 045

HOW TO PITCH YOUR PODCAST

Potential sponsors will approach you if you have a quality podcast. To get more opportunities from sponsors you really want to work with, though, you'll find it advantageous to approach them.

Start with the people you know.

The first podcast sponsorship I sold was to a guy I had an existing relationship with. Because he knew me, was aware of my previous work, and saw my vision for the podcast, he was willing to take a chance on me.

The price was $5000. For a show with zero audience.

This is the value of having relationships with people in your industry. And the value of *you* having an audience and good reputation, even though your show isn't yet proven.

I've done the same thing several times since then. And even if you're not established in your industry and have zero reputation, the rule still applies — people (and companies) who sponsor your podcast are sponsoring *you*.

The Time-Released Sponsorship Pitch – How-To Guide

The "Time-Released Podcast Promotion" can easily be retooled to help you to reach potential sponsors as well as build relationships with them.

Step 1 – Create Your Sponsor List

Who are the people and companies who would benefit from having access to your audience?

Create a list of *at least* 50 potential sponsors who have the following attributes:

- Have a quality product/service related to the topic of your podcast
- Have a marketing budget and will be able to pay you
- Have a good reputation within your market

Step 2 - Prime The Pump

There are two kinds of sponsors in podcasting — those who buy "by the numbers" and those who buy because of relationships.

If you want to sell advertising on your podcast based on download numbers, the easiest way to do that is via an advertising agency. Search "podcast advertising agency" and you'll find plenty of companies willing to place ads on your podcast based solely on how many downloads you get.

It's a race to the bottom.

You're better than that. And the people listening to your podcast deserve better than that.

If you've followed the strategies in this book, you're developing real relationships and connection with the real people who are listening to your podcast. That's worth more than a "cost-per-thousand" ad rate.

To get the premium pricing for your podcast sponsorships that the real relationships with real people are worth, you need to focus on the ad buyers who get what you do.

You also need to get what they do.

Like the real relationships you've built with listeners to your podcast, you also need to develop real relationships with podcast sponsors. But how do you start?

You're a journalist. That's your "in," and how you start relationships with people you want to meet.

Because you've got a podcast, you can call *anybody* and get your foot in the door by simply asking for an opinion. People *love* to be recognized, and this is the ultimate in recognition. Not only are you acknowledging their expertise, you're also making it known to the world.

Here's an example of how to do it:

To get connected with the decision-maker of a company, your best bet is via an introduction from somebody you both know.

Your best bet to convince that decision maker to work with you is to have that mutual acquaintance give you an endorsement.

Because you want to work with sponsors who are related to your podcast topic – and because you're technically a journalist and your podcast is technically a media outlet – one option to get to know potential sponsors is to reach out to them as sources, with questions related to both their company and your podcast topic.

Note that "topic-related" is relative; you have a lot of wiggle room here. As with podcast advertising in general, getting sponsors to see that *your* specific audience is one they want to reach may require you to educate them. That can be done using this method, and is one of the reasons it's so effective.

As an example, let's say you have a business podcast. Or a homeschooling podcast. Or a podcast for marathon runners.

And you know a certain mattress company has an advertising budget.

You could easily look the latest sleep research and call that mattress company (or its competitors) and ask for a quick comment on how businesspeople, students, or runners could improve their quality of sleep.

Don't make this too complicated. Your only job here is to "prime the pump." In other words, to get the recipient to be more receptive to future contact.

Get the answers you need. Follow up with postcards. Let them know when the content goes live.

And when you have another episode these "sources" would work for, repeat the process.

Step 3 - This Is Your Second Notice

Like multiple letters from a collection agency, you want the contacts you have with people in your industry to be a bit bolder each time, not in an aggressive sense, but one that lets you get to know them better. You want to move from "small talk" to meaningful discussion that will be beneficial for both of you.

Maybe this is a full-blown interview for your podcast. Maybe it's an in-person meeting at an industry event. *Maybe* it's getting somebody (or her company) involved with a giveaway, or a live event, or any number of other things you're involved with that would be beneficial for her.

You want the person (or people) in question to see your work, experience it, and know that it's something good to be involved with.

Step 4 - This Is Your Third (And Final) Notice

This is the ask. What do you want somebody to be involved with?

Get specific. What exactly are the deliverables and the benefits? You must have this, even if you have a relationship with a potential sponsor — he's not going to give you money just because he likes you.

This is how I was able to get $5000 for my first sponsorship. It wasn't just offering "awareness' or something general that could be purchased elsewhere, I was giving the sponsor something very specific. In this case, 10 five-minute segments, each featuring a client success story as well as a call-to-action to get listeners to call.

Anybody can sell 30-second ads. Or 60-second ads. And everybody does...

You want to offer something that can't be had except through you. This is how you get premium prices. Sell custom segments, sell endorsements, and sell giveaways.

For best results, sell a package of ten episodes or more. You want a sponsor who sees the vision of your podcast and is willing to partner with you, not somebody who is skeptical or wants to "test the waters."

CHAPTER 046

CUSTOM PODCASTS

When a songwriter in Nashville wants to get a specific artist to record one of his songs, he has two options — pitch a song that he's already written, or write a new song specifically for that artist.

Smart songwriters will often work *with* an artist to "co-write" a song together. This can dramatically increase the chance of a song getting recorded by that artist because, having been part of the song's creation, the artist is more attached to it, and also because the artist has financial incentives to record songs on which he's a writer.

As a podcast producer, you have similar options. You can pitch relevant sponsors about getting involved with the podcast you're already doing or you can work with them on creating a made-from-scratch, custom podcast (or custom segments within your existing podcast).

Branded Content

As a podcaster, it's nice to be able to create something where you have complete control. You choose the topic, you choose the branding, and you choose the name. You set the pace and let sponsors come to you.

A podcast like this isn't so much a partnership, where both people are driving, as it is you in control with your sponsor riding in the sidecar. It's not bad to have somebody along for the journey with you, but beyond money and (for some) a little credibility, the sponsor isn't adding a lot.

One sponsorship option for experienced podcasters who are willing to be flexible is working with sponsors to create a custom podcast or custom episodes within existing podcasts. Slate has done this with a podcast called *Placemakers*.

When you go to the "about" page for *Placemakers*, you'll see this:

All communities face certain challenges. But some people see challenges as opportunities. On *Placemakers*, we bring you stories about the spaces we inhabit and the people who shape them. Join us as we crisscross the country, introducing you to real people in real communities — people who make a difference in how we travel, work, and live. You'll never look at your community the same way again.

On the episode called "Mapping Urban Renewal," host Brian Babylon talks about "game-changing revitalization projects" spearheaded by JPMorgan Chase.

JPMorgan Chase is a multinational banking and financial services company headquartered in New York City. It is the largest bank in the United States, and the world's sixth-largest bank by total assets (about $2.35 trillion).

JPMorgan Chase paid for the "Mapping Urban Renewal" episode of *Placemakers* as well as two other episodes, all designated as "Paid Podcast" in their titles. Before each episode, the listeners hear "The following is a paid podcast from JPMorgan Chase. This special message from JPMorgan Chase highlights its work in communities around the country."

There's another notice when the episode is introduced. On the "Elevating The Neighborhood" episode, for examples, listeners hear, "Hey, it's Brian Babylon again, back for another paid episode of *Placemakers* from JPMorgan Chase. In these episodes, I'm digging into incredible urban revitalization projects spearheaded by JPMorgan Chase."

This episode ends with a similar announcement, "I'm Brian Babylon, and this has been a paid episode of *Placemakers* from JPMorgan Chase. Subscribe to *Placemakers* wherever you get your podcasts, and head to jpmorganchase.com to learn more about JPMorgan Chase's corporate responsibility program."

This is one way to do a "sponsorship" — instead of reading a traditional advertisement that lasts 30 or 60 seconds between editorial content, the entire episode is one long ad.

Gimlet Media, the podcast company founded by award-winning radio journalist Alex Blumberg, creates "branded content" via its Gimlet Creative branch. Its podcast, *Open For Business*, is sponsored by eBay.

Panoply, a podcast network owned by Slate, has produced multiple sponsored podcasts, including *Dogsmarts* for Purina, *Points Of Courage* for Hixcox, and the sci-fi audio drama, *The Message*, for General Electric.

Pacific Content, a Vancouver-based media company, has produced branded podcasts for companies like Slack, Shopify, and Envoy.

Here's their pitch.

Content Consumers Have Choices

- *Consumers choose what they want to consume and when they want to consume it*
- *81% of podcast listeners skip commercials*
- *86% of television viewers skip advertising*
- *94% of online video viewers skip pre-roll ads*

Build An Audience (Don't Rent One)

- *Audiences are built by creating value*
- *Value = content people love (not ads they hate)*
- *Great stories create positive emotion (which is transferred to the sponsoring brand)*

This space is wide open and may be an opportunity for you.

As the podcasting space gets more and more crowded, companies who want to get involved in podcasting are looking for different ways to stand out. Sponsored content allows them to do this while showing different, often more personal, aspects of their businesses.

Sponsored Mini-Series And Segments

"Branded content" isn't limited to entire podcasts created from the ground up. There's plenty of room to make money using this concept within your current podcast.

Pacific Content's view of what audiences love in a podcast is correct — people find (and respond to) good stories and helpful content, not "ads."

How can you combine the two using your already established podcast? Here are two options:

1. Sponsored Mini-Series

Think of a sponsored mini-series like renting part of your house for the weekend. You still own the house and you're there while your guest gets the benefit of a place to stay for a few days, electricity, and a parking space.

Like a temporary house guest, a sponsored mini-series can agitate the people you normally share your house with. He'll likely disrupt their routines and, because of this, may strain the relationship you have with them.

But maybe, he's really cool, helpful, and interesting. In that case, they might not mind.

A sponsored mini-series is typically two or three full episodes of content *related* to that of your normal podcast, but a bit biased and possibly "salesy." In other words, it fits the basic feel and format of your normal podcast, but the content guidelines are a bit more lax.

Maybe you loosen your standards on who you interview or what you let that person pitch. Or maybe you pitch a sponsored product for the interviewee, giving an endorsement or otherwise going way beyond what you would do on a normal podcast episode.

How you do this is up to you.

Is it a good idea? Maybe.

Consider the pros and cons before agreeing to any sponsorship, especially something like a sponsored mini-series. Running this kind of content can be a great opportunity and helpful to listeners, but it isn't worth losing the trust of your audience.

2. *Sponsored Segments*

Think of sponsored segments as "mini-episodes within full-length episodes" that also function as advertising. For example, a "_____ Of The Week" segment where you highlight or acknowledge a certain person, place, or situation.

The same rules that apply to a sponsored mini-series apply to sponsored segments. Although sponsored segments are shorter than sponsored mini-series, because they are within standard, full-length episodes, they are not necessarily less intrusive to listeners.

As with any podcast sponsorship you do, use your best judgment with sponsored segments. Don't put short-term money ahead of long-term trust and relationships.

If done right, sponsored segments are the best of both worlds; they will provide both great content for your audience and great value for sponsors.

If you have a nonfiction podcast, such as a self-publishing or public speaking podcast, it's likely that you're already featuring listener success stories in some way. These stories are valuable to your audience as they show that success is possible and, more specifically, link the advice given on your podcast to that success.

Brands can benefit in the same way. Formalized "client success segments" associates sponsors with featured success stories. Even if a story doesn't directly involve a sponsor, acknowledging a success will often associate the two in the minds of listeners, which many sponsors will find worth paying for.

An example:

A "weight loss success story" featured on a fitness podcast may not have anything to do with the gym sponsoring the segment, but because the story shows weight loss is possible, the gym will benefit.

The Downside Of Custom Podcasts

Sponsors come and go. This won't keep you from pressing forward with a podcast you own, but when a company decides it no longer wants to sponsor the custom podcast you've created for it and which it owns the rights to, that's the end — game over.

Obviously, when you work with a company on a creative project, you can come up with whatever deal you want as far as creative control, ownership of content, ownership of ideas, ownership of intellectual property (the name of the podcast, for example), and what happens in the event you and the company decide to part ways. Know that most companies you work with, if they're giving you the money and other resources to develop a podcast for the purpose of marketing, are going to want to control *everything* about the work you do in that capacity.

What this looks like:

Spencer Silver was given the task to create a super-strong adhesive for use in the aerospace industry. In 1968, he did the opposite — an invention that would stick to things, but only lightly.

Arthur Fry was Product Development Engineer at the same company. He sang in a church choir and was always losing his place in his hymnal.

Fry's idea for the adhesive product was to "put it on a piece of paper and then we can stick it to anything."

This invention, known today as the Post-It note, has made billions of dollars for 3M Corporation. Silver and Fry, because they were employees of 3M, have no ownership of Post-It products and never received any royalties.

When you take money on the front-end to create something, if it takes off, you'll lose out on backend opportunities because you have no control or ownership of the work you do. Can you live with this?

For Silver and Fry, there was something bigger — something beyond money.

"An inventor has a chance to intercede in people's lives with their ideas," Fry said in an interview with NPR. Silver added, "Part of you is out there in the world. Now, my adhesive, which previously didn't exist, is out there forever."

The same could be said for any content you create and release through a podcast. Like anything you release online, once a podcast has been published, it's out in the world forever.

The deep pockets and other resources of a big company will likely make getting a message out to the world easier than you could do on your own. The potential downside is that you may have to make compromises about everything from the content itself to how it's delivered.

Are you ok with being the identifiable front man for someone else's ideas? Can you live with a watered-down version of your original ideas? Perhaps more importantly, can you live with a watered-down version of yourself?

"Edgy" scares people. The majority of big companies play things safe rather than do anything risky that could that could upset listeners.

If you take money from a company to create a podcast from scratch, this is what you'll have to work with. If you want to have a big personality and take chances, you're much better off creating a podcast yourself, without any outside money, and approaching sponsors later, once you've proven that your idea works.

CHAPTER 047

PODCAST ARBITRAGE

Most companies you'll work with when it comes to sponsorship don't understand the intricacies of a great podcast. They don't get all the work that goes behind the scenes, such as outlining great episodes, quality editing, and what it takes to get people to listen.

They do understand numbers, though – specifically, the number of people who listen to a podcast. And as sad as it is, this may be the deciding factor when it comes to companies working with you.

You can have the most technically perfect podcast in the world, but if nobody hears it, you're going to have a hard time getting sponsors to take interest. Arbitrage can help you increase your audience quickly.

In economics and finance, arbitrage is the practice of taking advantage of a price difference between two or more markets, creating deals that take advantage of the imbalance. For the example below, you can think of arbitrage as "buy low and sell high."

This is how you should think about not only paid traffic to your podcast, but also any advertising/audience trade or "lead magnet" promotions.

You've probably been to various "news" sites, often linked from Facebook and other social media posts, which are full of sensational clickbait-style stories, lists, and images.

Things like:

"The Trick-Or-Treat Murderer — Every Parent's Worst Nightmare!"

"This Is How Much Coffee It Would Take To Actually Kill You"

"What To Do If A Cop Pulls You Over (And You've Got Weed In Your Car)"

"9 Celebrities Who Are Secretly Gay"

"Doctors Say It's Worse Than AIDS"

These headlines are usually paid ads designed to look like news and likely link to a page that makes money via arbitrage — the cost of getting traffic to the page is less than the money being made from traffic *on* the page.

Because arbitrage is often seen via sensational links like the ones above and focuses on low-quality traffic that can be purchased cheaply, it has a bad reputation. The underlying concept is solid, though, and arbitrage is something that may work for you and help grow your audience.

To make arbitrage work and build a quality audience for your podcast, you're going to have to put in some effort. Stay away from the "buy website traffic" companies and people on freelancer sites who promise something for nothing. This isn't what you're looking for, because most of the traffic you'll get is from bots.

You want to focus on quality — listeners who love what you do and will respond to your offers. If you can find these quality listeners via advertising, here's how to make the numbers work.

Let's say you're a life coach, a chiropractor, or a consultant, and you make an average of $1000 on every client you get. Your podcast is designed to get you more of these $1000 clients.

To get more clients, you need more people listening.

For every 100 people who subscribe to your podcast, you know that one will become a client within the year. This means every additional 100 people who subscribe to your podcast will be worth an average of $1000.

How much would you be willing to pay for a $1000 client? That's the number you should also be willing to pay for 100 additional subscribers.

Buy listeners at a low price, then sell them things at higher prices, so you're able to make a profit. If you can find a way to make the numbers work, you can do this day in and day out, increasing your audience (and your income).

Note that you don't have to always pay money for new listeners. If you're on a budget or can't find a way to make paid traffic profitable, you also have options to make arbitrage work for you. You can "buy" traffic using a commission-only affiliate model, a straight trade, or by giving away content that costs you nothing to replicate or distribute, such as downloadable reports, checklists, and online videos.

If you can make the numbers work, the amount you grow your audience is limited only by the amount of money you're willing to invest.

CHAPTER 048

DON'T CHASE THE MONEY

Don't chase the money. That's my "big advice" when it comes to your podcast's sponsorship.

Imagine you're living in a great community. You and your neighbors take a lot of pride in it, maintain your homes, and participate in issues which affect residents, such as making sure neighborhood schools have quality teachers, roads and sidewalks are kept in good condition, and needed services, such as medical care, are easily accessible.

Plenty of companies that would love access to a neighborhood like this. McDonald's would love to sell Big Macs in the school cafeteria. Waste management companies would love to bury trash under the fields in your park. There are casinos, payday loan stores, and tobacco companies that would love to advertise in your community newsletter.

Do these things seem like a good match for the community you and your neighbors have invested so much in?

Most people would say no. Yet, as podcasters, we let similar situations happen to us and our podcasts all the time.

You've put a lot of time and effort into building your podcast and attracting the people who listen to it. Don't let them down by taking a few bucks from a sponsor who doesn't have their best interests in mind.

A Different Kind Of Podcast Sponsorship

Listener funding is an option for *some* podcasters.

Look at the Top 20 podcast list on crowd-funding platform Patreon and you'll notice two things:

1. Celebrity hosts who came into podcasting with already established fanbases
2. Niche content

People value content that is made specifically for them and not available elsewhere. They value hosts they have a relationship with.

Are you your audience? Do you make the podcast that you'd want to hear? If so, a listener-funded option may be for you.

Jen Briney of *Congressional Dish* did this. She started paying attention to world events while studying in Germany in the spring of 2003, when the United States overthrew the government of Iraq.

After experiencing the war from outside the United States, she started asking questions. Every answer led to fifty more questions.

She started watching C-SPAN in order to get raw, unfiltered information about how Congress was changing our laws. After watching a congressman slip a provision protecting secret campaign contributions into an Energy and Water funding law (and bragging about it on the floor of the House of Representatives), Jen was stunned to discover that not a single television station, newspaper, or even blog covered the scandal.

She started reading the Congressional Record. She found more things she was frustrated with.

In 2012, she launched *Congressional Dish* in order to share the information she was finding, to have an emotional outlet for dealing with her discoveries, and to create a community of people who were interested in Congress's effect on our lives.

Today, *Congressional Dish* is her full-time career, thanks entirely to the support from listeners.

Here's how she explains her funding model:

"Corporate advertising is the funding model of most sources of information, which makes large corporations – not you – the mainstream media's main customer. They aim to keep their advertisers happy; Congressional Dish aims to keep you informed and entertained. By supporting Congressional Dish and its value-for-value funding model, you are allowing the podcast to remain free of corporate sponsorship, which not only leads to a better listening experience but keeps the podcast accountable only to you, the voter/listener."

This is the kind of dedication it takes to have a listener-supported podcast.

Nobody Wants Your Tote Bag

For years, when you'd give money to NPR, when you gave at a certain level, you'd get a free tote bag.

Have you ever seen somebody using one?

Neither have I.

That's because people don't give money to NPR to get a tote bag; they give money to NPR because they want more of NPR.

The same is true for your listener-funded podcast. Sending people branded goods (or other physical bonuses) won't hurt your ability to raise money via donations, but it's not going to help you nearly as much as giving people more of the content they love.

Jen Briney has one "gift" for you when you support *Congressional Dish.* You get an on-air thank you.

People don't want a tote bag; people want you.

Mom vs. Baker

Imagine your drop by your mother's house. She's baking homemade chocolate chip cookies.

They smell delicious, so you happily say yes when she asks, "Would you like a couple?"

Then she offers a glass of milk. "I'd love some," you say.

You eat the cookies. They're delicious.

Then your mother says, "That will be $7."

You'd expect that from a baker, but not your mom. And by the same token, your listeners expect certain behavior from you, especially when it comes to the monetizing of your podcast.

Don't muddy your message. You can have sponsors or you can have a listener-supported podcast. You can't have both.

CHAPTER 049

FINAL THOUGHTS

Most successful podcasts come after several failed attempts. The hosts who sound great developed that skill through deliberate work over a period of years.

Success in podcasting, like anything, takes time. There are "best practices" you can follow, but no shortcuts. To be great, you must do the necessary work.

That work starts now.

You don't need the best equipment to start developing your persona and broadcasting skill set. You can do this with anything that will record your voice, including your mobile phone.

When I was a kid, I picked up a "wireless intercom" system made by Radio Shack at a neighborhood yard sale. It had two parts, both of which could talk to each other via FM radio.

I set one to "receive" and put it in the living room. I took the other to my room and started broadcasting via the "talk" function. I tried to emulate Dick Clark announcing acts on *American Bandstand* and hosts I'd heard on the radio.

Was anybody listening? No. But I didn't care, because it was fun.

Podcasting *should* be fun. Even if the main purpose of your podcast is to market something, it should be enjoyable.

Like a kid broadcasting through a glorified baby monitor, you may have zero people listening on the other end when you get started. Fortunately, with podcasting, reaching people is a real possibility. If you stick with it, you'll find your audience. And the skills you developed while doing so will give them something worth listening to.

Keep Moving Forward

The saying "if you keep doing what you're doing, you'll keep getting what you're getting" doesn't apply to podcasting.

Podcasting is constantly changing. If you "keep doing what you're doing," you'll be left behind.

To keep moving forward with your podcast, you must evolve.

Podcasting is constantly changing, especially when it comes to how podcasts are distributed and money is made. The way we consume podcasts today is completely different from how we consumed them even just a few years ago.

I challenge you to be an innovator. Like Kenneth Cole successfully launching his shoe company from a 40-foot "movie" trailer, a little creative thinking is all it takes to get attention for yourself and your message.

THE MOST IMPORTANT PART OF THIS BOOK

Your message matters, and there are people waiting to hear it. Maybe not everybody, but *some* people, who will really be helped by what you have to share.

Focus on those people, not the ones who aren't a match for what you do, or are too busy with other things to care. Your job as a podcaster is to plant a flag, not to convince people to salute it.

Lee Silverstein's *We Have Cancer* podcast has a small, niche audience, and what he talks about isn't pretty. In fact, he's never had a single episode get more than 1000 downloads.

But Lee's podcast makes impact. Those who are interested in what he has to talk about are *really* interested.

Which is why he gets feedback like this ...

> *"While I lay there after my first infusion of this very strong medicine, sad, depressed, scared, I began searching for ... hope online, and I came across something I had never tried before, a podcast called We Have Cancer. So I listened to my first podcast ever, and hope really was activated inside. Stories of Hope and Survival! Exactly what I needed to hear. Around this time I was also learning about the benefits of exercise, how it can possibly slow recurrence. I felt I needed to get up and move all of a sudden, maybe this was my ticket!! My second infusion of (chemo) came, and when the pump came off 46 hours later, I loaded up some episodes of We Have Cancer and began my new favorite hobby ... walking. I walked. Slow, very slow. And I sent a message on Facebook to the guy running it to say thanks. His name is Lee, and he helped to save my life, and I'll always love him for that. Lee, I love you man, you helped save me, and I will*

never forget. I hope to do like you, and inspire others to help keep them alive, and in turn they will do the same. Thank you for all you've done."

What's your version of this story? Who are you, and how can you use podcasting to connect with others in a powerful way?

Success with your podcast is whatever you want it to be, and it's attainable. Define what you want and work your way backwards to make it happen.

Good luck!

Acknowledgements

This book wouldn't have been possible without some truly amazing people who not only believed in it, but believed in me personally.

Thanks to my wife, Laurel, for your support during every aspect of getting this book done. Most people would have given up on a "90-day project" after the first year, but here we are at almost 1600 days and you're still with it (and also me).

Thanks to Wendy Wallace for being part of yet another publishing adventure and helping to turn a "big jumbled mess" into something great. None of this would have happened without your help.

Thanks to Paula Felps and Cindy Baldhoff for going way beyond the call of duty with editing and organization. You appeared just when I needed a fresh perspective and were exactly what I needed to get unstuck and move forward.

Chester Goad and Sandy DeWald, thanks for reading the (very) rough draft and helping to make it better with your comments and suggestions. Beyond that, thanks for supporting the other work I've done during the process of getting this book out.

Jodi Compton, thank you for seeing the vision and stepping in to clean up all the loose ends. I'm looking forward to doing more projects together in the future.

Thanks to Dave Jackson for your inspiration with Musicians' Cooler, then sharing your how you did it with me and everybody else. You've helped thousands to make their voices heard and started a ripple that's still being felt.

Thank you Rik Roberts for jumping in with me for the first Big Podcast live event. It's scary as hell to book an empty room and try to fill it, but it was less scary with you there.

Clark Buckner and Angus Nelson, thanks for establishing Nashville Podcasters and giving me a place to share new marketing ideas. And thanks to the wonderful podcasters who show up every month, make podcasts that matter, and because of those podcasts, let the world know our city's audio production isn't limited to songs about attractive young women, partying, and pickup trucks.

Thanks to Lester Turner and everybody at WRLT, Lightning 100, especially Gary Kraen, Dan Buckley, Ryan McFadden, and Stephanie Lesher, for taking a chance on Music Business Radio and continuing to believe it in since 2005.

Made in the USA
Columbia, SC
18 August 2019